ARCHIVAL ENTANGLEMENTS

ON POSSIBILITY: SOCIAL CHANGE AND THE ARTS + HUMANITIES

Wendy S. Hesford, Puja Batra-Wells, and
Dionne Custer Edwards, Series Editors

ARCHIVAL ENTANGLEMENTS

Edited by Puja Batra-Wells
and Harmony Bench

THE OHIO STATE UNIVERSITY PRESS
COLUMBUS

Library of Congress Cataloging-in-Publication Data
Names: Batra-Wells, Puja, editor | Bench, Harmony, editor
Title: Archival entanglements / edited by Puja Batra-Wells and Harmony Bench.
Description: Columbus : The Ohio State University Press, [2026] | Series: On possibility: social change and the arts + humanities | Includes bibliographical references and index. | Summary: "An interdisciplinary collection that probes the possibilities and limitations of the archive, arguing for the importance of considering its many complexities. Contains perspectives from digital humanities, performance studies, race and ethnic studies, and more"—Provided by publisher.
Identifiers: LCCN 2026023676 | ISBN 9780814216224 hardback | ISBN 0814216226 hardback | ISBN 9780814259955 paperback | ISBN 0814259952 paperback | ISBN 9780814285145 ebook | ISBN 0814285147 ebook
Subjects: LCSH: Archives—Social aspects | Archives—Philosophy | Archives—Methodology | Collective memory | Material culture Classification: LCC CD971 .A696 2026
LC record available at https://lccn.loc.gov/2026023676

Cover design by adam bohannon
Text design by Juliet Williams
Type set in Minion Pro

♾ The paper used in this publication meets the minimum requirements of the American National Standard for Information Sciences—Permanence of Paper for Printed Library Materials. ANSI Z39.48-1992.

CONTENTS

ILLUSTRATIONS

INTRODUCTION

Entangled with the Archive

PUJA BATRA-WELLS AND HARMONY BENCH

To be entangled is to be caught up in something. It might be a little messy, as tangles imply the inability to extract one element from another. Entanglements tie things together, but not in the intentional way that braiding or weaving can create strength from interdependence. Instead, entanglements are unruly and complex systems. They often contain any number of elements whose operations are unintentional, circumstantial, or covert. Disentanglement is therefore a cherished analytical practice, a way to find some order or reason that can explain the enabling and disabling functions of various interconnections. But even in a conceptual domain, pulling at one thread in search of clarity deforms the whole. Children with tangled hair, wildlife tangled in nets—sometimes the only solution is to pull out the scissors. But what if we commit to "staying with the trouble," as Donna Haraway suggests? What if instead of rushing to cut out the unruly bits, we recognize them as constitutive? What can be accomplished through continued rumination on the many knots in which the histories, uses, and misuses of the archive continue to entangle humanistic thought?

At the heart of the archive are questions of memory and memorialization, and therefore, how a society organizes itself with regard to the past and the future. What is remembered and what is forgotten, and how is each entangled in the other? Are specific individuals charged with safeguarding memory? Or are institutions preferred, with their collections of documents and artifacts? Is memory something that is alive and active, or is it located in the past as relatively inert history (Nora)? Is what is forgotten considered lost? Are erasures from memory forms of epistemic violence (Spivak), or can they also be modes of healing—even of fugitive possibility? What kinds of relationality are displayed through what is remembered and what is forgotten?

Archival traditions once upheld the archive as a natural, authoritative container and understood the archivist as an impartial custodian of records accumulated and preserved under principles like provenance, *respect des fonds,* and appraisal of value (Jenkinson; Schellenberg). But archival studies has since pivoted away from a modernist approach to artifacts as static records toward a more dynamic and fluid postmodernist understanding of the archival (Lee 31–38; see also Caswell, *Urgent* 35–36). Archivist-scholars such as Schwartz and Cook criticize the presumed neutrality of the archive and underscore its active role in shaping memory through selection, interpretation, and power, revealing how archival work is deeply embedded in social, political, and epistemic contexts. In other words, archiving produces history as much as it records it.

In "Theories of the Archive from Across the Disciplines," Marlene Manoff highlights the growth of archival discourse, noting that this surge in interest is driven not only by digital technologies but also by broader intellectual, political, and disciplinary shifts (10). She identifies two central trends shaping this complexity: conflation, where libraries, archives, and museums are increasingly treated as analogous, and inflation, where the term *archive* has expanded far beyond its traditional meaning to encompass a wide range of metaphors and disciplinary uses (10–14). Scholars from fields such as history, anthropology, and literary theory now turn to the archive as a key site for exploring national identity, political power, memory, and resistance, making it both a literal institution and a symbolic framework for understanding how knowledge and authority are constructed (10). Manoff observes that the proliferation of terms such as the *social archive, imperial archive, postcolonial archive,* and *archival consciousness* reflects the archive's expanded conceptual reach as scholars interrogate the construction of knowledge, disciplinary boundaries, and the politics of representation.

In her pointed essay "'The Archive' Is Not an Archives," critical archival studies scholar Michelle Caswell rightly critiques the humanities for not adequately acknowledging the field of archival studies, and therefore failing at the very interdisciplinarity to which many such scholars subscribe. Yet her claim that "for humanities scholars, 'the archive' denotes a hypothetical wonderland" (para. 3) disconnected from archival praxis is precisely what has motivated the richness and explosion of archival discourse. As an example of what Edward Said calls "traveling theory,"[1] which can lose or gain strength by virtue of its

1. Said writes, "Notice, for example, that when professional students of literature now use words like 'theory' and 'criticism' it is not assumed that they must or should confine their

circulation across contexts (226), the archive is a means through which to pose fundamental questions. Archival research methods may belong to historians and preservation of collections to the archival sciences, but memory, knowledge, power, and futurity are concerns that are fully entangled with the archive while also being shared across the disciplines. The malleability of archival discourse has thus facilitated interdisciplinary engagement and critical reflection on disciplinary frameworks of knowledge production across the arts and humanities.

The archive is only one technology of memory, but it is the one around which the contributions in this volume are gathered as they consider multiple and entangled archives of objects, environments, land formations, bodily practices, and even genetic sequences. *Archival Entanglements* arrives in the wake of the archival turn across the arts and humanities to consider the archive anew. "Is it too bold to say that the time of the archive has passed?" Julietta Singh asks in her book *No Archive Will Restore You* (25). Indeed, perhaps the archive is over. Certainly, archival authority has been shaken as both scholars and political figures have chipped away at the monumentality of THE ARCHIVE to reveal the fragility of actual archives and the care and labor required to sustain any site or practice of memory. But perhaps this is precisely why it is time now, again, to return to the archive—to activate its possibilities in alternate directions by beginning rather than ending with multidisciplinary and cross-disciplinary entanglements.

To that end, this volume reaches across fields of study and methodological orientations within the humanities without reducing the unique perspectives of each modality in the process. Contributors come from performance, labor studies, digital humanities, area studies, history, literature, and visual arts, with perspectives on race and ethnicity, gender and sexuality, trauma, de/colonization, and more. Some contributors are engaged with what feminist scholar Ann Cvetkovich calls "actually existing archives" (*Archive* 268). Others are engaged with the archive as a structure of power and as a concept that is itself laden with history, evidencing the ongoing influence of philosopher Michel Foucault's *Archaeology of Knowledge*, in which he conceptualizes the archive not as a repository of records but as the set of discourses that regulate what can be said and therefore what can be known. By now, the archive has been thoroughly challenged, deconstructed, multiplied, and reinvented, so with what new questions do scholars and artists return to the archive?

---

interests to literary theory or literary criticism. The distinction between one discipline and another has been blurred precisely because fields like literature and literary study are no longer considered to be as all-compassing or as synoptic as, until recently, they once were" (227).

Reflecting the diversity of contributions, *Archival Entanglements* posits the archive as simultaneously a generative mode of inquiry, an invention, a form of memory-holding, and a site of knowledge production, even as it is also a conservative force of institutional consolidation around dominant narratives. We find that the connection between archives and official histories remains an important one, as demonstrated by the consequential tussles between the US National Archives and the White House regarding presidential records during Trump's first administration, and disappearing federal data in his second. However, this volume focuses more on unofficial archives, incompleteness in the record, and archiving from the margins. With these emphases, *Archival Entanglements* is situated within a vibrant literature that addresses the limitations and harms of archival thought, as well as how bodily, nonmaterial, and digital practices of memory-keeping offer archival alternatives. In the remainder of this introduction, we focus on texts and approaches that have informed this specific collection, and then lay out central themes that guide the organization of this book. We conclude by framing our own stakes in these conversations as editors.

More Than One Archive

Demonstrating its power as a structuring concept, the archive has fueled rich debates across the arts and humanities. Especially provocative have been engagements with the archive from the perspectives of those who have not seen their voices and experiences reflected in the artifacts deemed valuable enough to save. There is the recognition that what is preserved shapes the histories we can tell and the futures we can imagine, but also that the importance of the archive has come to overshadow the many and varied approaches to historical, intergenerational, and ancestral memory. Contending with the archive has meant grappling with whose histories are legitimated and whose are obliterated, reading the archive against the grain for that which was not intended to be saved or shared, and holding the traces of human lives that are either presented there or that have gone missing. This volume lingers with the complexities of the archive, and it is deeply informed by scholarship on how archives are entangled with identity, memory, and access.

Scholars have recognized archives as sites of exceptional trauma and violence. In *Along the Archival Grain,* for example, anthropologist Ann Laura Stoler argues that archives are deeply entangled with colonial projects of knowledge and power, producing epistemic violence through selective preservation. Critical archive scholar Tonia Sutherland notes how this selectivity, which is core to archival collection, can be a form of what she calls "archival amnesty," describing how refusing to collect evidence of violence against marginalized populations benefits the perpetrators and perpetuates harm (1–2). For such reasons, Verne Harris, the archivist for the Nelson Mandela papers, observes the relationship between oppression and recordkeeping in *Archives and Justice,* arguing "that the political is archival; that the archive is the very possibility of politics" (248). To engage with the archive is to confront this violence and to recover knowledges that have been silenced.

But violence is not the totality of archival possibility. As Ann Cvetkovich contends in her analysis of queer archives in *An Archive of Feelings,* trauma is entangled with "a vast archive of feelings, the many forms of love, rage, intimacy, grief, shame, and more that are part of the vibrancy of queer cultures" (7). These records, perhaps unconventional in themselves, shine a light on both the "ordinary" and unconventional in the lives they index, "providing a sense of a life that lies beyond the folders" and which necessarily escapes the archive (Cvetkovich, "Ordinary" 115). "The archival record," Verne Harris cautions, "is but a sliver of social memory" ("Archival Sliver," 135). And Jenny Sharpe, a scholar of Caribbean literatures and the Black Atlantic, likewise recognizes that documentary evidence favors dominant populations, and therefore argues instead for the immaterial or intangible archives of "affects, dreams, spirits, and visions" as a way to bring forward stories that have been silenced (3). Memory is visceral. The absence of documentation should not be confused with absence of evidence, but it does require an expanded understanding of what archival evidence can be and where it can be found.

Theorists of performance have long acknowledged the human body as itself a repository for histories and practices shared across generations, which they have sometimes positioned as an alternative to the archive and sometimes as an alternate form of the archive. Performance scholar and Latin Americanist Diana Taylor argues in *The Archive and the Repertoire* that "embodied performances have always played a central role in conserving memory," but she cleaves the repertoire from the archive as a mode of memory-keeping even as she underscores their interrelationship (xvii–xviii). Scholar of transnational Indian performance Priya Srinivasan brings these terms back together in what she terms the "bodily archive," which "leaves its traces in live bodily interactions, whose history remains captured in muscle memory and through bodily labor and kinesthetic contact" (17). Srinivasan situates the archive in the body and the body in the archive such that, when encountering the written record, researchers find bodily traces therein. Archivist and documentary filmmaker Jamie A. Lee echoes this formulation in articulating "bodies as archives and archives as bodies," arguing that "individual embodiment *can be* considered both an archival *practice* and *location*" (115, original emphasis). Jeannette Bastian and Andrew Flinn similarly expand the concept of the archive beyond institutional frameworks to include memory, performance, and artistic practice in their exploration of community archives. And Liz Moor and Emma Uprichard also draw attention to the physical and aesthetic qualities of archival materials, such as handwriting, paper texture, and document layout, as elements that invite sensory engagement and shape affective responses and meaning. Together, these orientations exemplify increasing attunement to the archive as a site not only of preservation but of physical contact and embodiment. The inclusion of material and social dimensions within archival practice has redefined what constitutes evidence and raised critical questions about archival authority and the criteria for assessing an object or collection's value.

Digital media has also disrupted traditional understandings of what an archive is and who can be an archivist. Media theorist Abigail De Kosnik argues that archiving no longer belongs to the institutions charged with conserving cultural and national memory. Instead, she contends that "rogue archivists," including hackers, fans, and online enthusiasts of various stripes, now "explore the potential of digital technologies to democratize cultural memory" (3). Memory work has been amateurized through the participation of nonprofessionals—part of a postcustodial turn that reimagines archival responsibility as active engagement that breaks down traditional hierarchies between professional archivists and communities (Becerra-Licha). Participatory archives employ the affordances of digital media such as social tagging, crowdsourcing document transcription, and commenting functions that can bring together multiple stakeholder viewpoints without resolving into a single "truth" (Benoit and Eveleigh; Theimer). Furthermore, without discounting digital media's very real but largely hidden physical footprint, digital storage far exceeds the capacities of climate-controlled brick-and-mortar buildings required for preserving physical artifacts. Due to the proliferation of digital communication networks and the surge of investment in machine learning and artificial intelligence, big data archives are becoming of paramount importance, laying bare how "both capture and exclusion have important ethical consequences" that are accelerating in reach, scale, and impact (Thylstrup et al., 10), which further requires guidelines for stewarding and utilizing collections as data (Padilla et al.).

Some of the most salient critiques of archives have come from those who have experienced harm, especially Indigenous communities whose histories have been negated under settler colonialism and racialized capitalism (Tuck and Yang). In light of these critiques, emerging directions in contemporary archival practice prioritize communally held expertise and validate non-Western approaches to recordkeeping as part of a larger decolonial agenda. Repatriation efforts actively contest historical erasure and reclaim Indigenous voices (Withey), inviting communities from whom materials were taken into new relations organized around care. Reparative description in finding aids and catalogs replaces inaccurate or insensitive terminology with terms communities use to describe themselves. And community archives charge archivists with activating their collections toward a liberatory paradigm, proactively facilitating access to records by community members and thereby transforming archives into spaces that elevate community, care, social justice, and belonging (Caswell, *Urgent*). Archivists have developed such practices to explicitly confront and ameliorate histories of bias and erasure in the archive.

Chapter Overview and Themes

The perspectives gathered in *Archival Entanglements* are intentionally diverse. As editors, we did not wish for agreement among the contributions, even on how to define an archive. The book thus advances multidisciplinary understandings of how archives exist today as networked, multimodal, and relational assemblages, as contributors grapple with the persistence of archival inheritances amid changing archival practices. We have prioritized the dynamic conversations that emerge from considerations of embodiment, materiality, digitality, and social practice, without privileging any single way of knowing. There is consensus on one point, however: Contributors agree that archives produce knowledge. This backdrop assumption informs both critiques of the archive as a hegemonic site of colonial investments and affirmations of archives' liberatory potential.

Archival Entanglements retains the archive as a site of possibility. Not limited to the study of historical records, the volume considers social and expressive practices such as spoken language, performance, gesture, and rituals as dynamic parts of cultural and historical memory. In this way, we aim to engage modes that expand existing archives, and compel the creation and analysis of new entanglements. This is not to perpetuate an inflationary approach to the archive that extends to all forms of memory-keeping until the archive is no longer a useful concept, but as editors we also do not find archival thought to be so culturally narrow that it must be abandoned. Being entangled with the archive also means unsettling it. There is much more to consider when one refuses to take the archive as given, and we are excited by how this volume returns to the archive as a problem, which is to say, as a set of unresolved questions and imagined possibilities. Each of the contributions in *Archival Entanglements* demonstrates the epistemic humility required to study in, with, and alongside the archive, and a willingness to grapple with dissonance, partial truths, privilege, and uneven access.

Gaps, Erasures, and an Ethics of Recognition

Our first section gathers together a series of meditations on absence in the archive, and what can be made of these absences. Fragments, fissures, gaps, silences, and erasures emerge as prominent themes, along with vulnerability, care, relationality, and recognition. Contributors feel their way toward an ethics grounded in the materiality of the archive and the human beings represented there. They read and construct archives against the grain, and even expand our collective understanding of what constitutes an archive. This section orients around what can be gleaned from spaces of archival enclosure and new relationships that may be forged in the process of approaching archives and memories as vibrant and living—and therefore deserving of care in the present. In this way, recognition is offered across distances of time, geography, and culture, ultimately proposing that the entanglement of researchers, artists, and memory practitioners with the archive shifts the ethical arrangements that the archive as a structure of power has implied.

Mimi Ọnụọha's "The End of a World / As We Knew It" opens the collection with just this emphasis on gaps and fissures in the archive that imbue the historical record with partiality and unknowability. Anchored by the discovery of a mass grave near her childhood home, this haunting contribution is also a deeply personal testimony to the writer's own disorientation in response to an unsettling revelation. A relic of historical trauma, the grave evidences not only the brutality of forced labor and racialized violence; it also exposes the psychological and cultural processes that obscured this site from the historical record. The archive in this context is not just a technology that apprehends the past; it actively participates in constructing what a community knows about itself. Inside the archive, things that resist comprehension, documentation, and recognition are designated as unknowable. Ọnụọha argues that the existence of the unknowable challenges the foundational paradigms upon which histories are written—these are not gaps waiting to be filled, but absences that call into question the very epistemic frameworks through which we seek to know the past. Ọnụọha's essay serves as a reminder that "what is missing is still there," and she asks us to take responsibility for reshaping the structures that perpetuate erasures. Accountability and even academic "rigor" take on different meanings when one confronts the fact that much of what is "known" is built on the pain and imposed silence of those deemed unknowable.

As a phenomenological event, pain resists articulation (Scarry). Yet a political demand for recognition requires that trauma be made intelligible—it must be narrated. The tension between the demand to be seen and the inability to be understood is the paradox at the heart of Martin Joseph Ponce's analysis in "Emily Jungmin Yoon's Archival Poetics: 'Comfort Women' Testimonies and Literary Justice in *A Cruelty Special to Our Species.*" Yoon's 2018 collection of poetry draws on an archive of narratives from Korean "comfort women" who were subjected to sexual slavery under Japanese occupation during World War II. Inverting the procedures of redaction, which hides government intelligence under impenetrable black marks, Yoon employs erasure to amplify the women's voices, absenting words from the record to distill their reflections in service to recovery. The convergence of wartime dynamics, colonial legacies, and cultural attitudes toward gender and sexuality complicate "comfort women's" narratives, often occluding the full scope of their suffering. Ponce shows how Yoon's use of fragmentation, omission, and recursion brings attention to the enduring impact of the women's trauma. Like Ọnụọha, Ponce is interested in making space for the unknowable. What possibilities might the poetic form offer in representing the incomprehensible events embedded in these testimonies? Can literary justice offer reparative healing? As Ponce reveals, Yoon refuses the spectacle of suffering (Hartman) and does not reduce the women's lives to their experiences of sexual violence. For Ponce, Yoon's work advances a true ethics of recognition—one that centers survivors' voices and subjectivity in the archive.

Iñaki Bonillas takes an altogether different approach to fractured patterns in "Marginalia." Images sourced from books in the artist's own library are situated against a black backdrop, which provides a structuring absence. A white path connects these scenes of "people on the move," drawing them into a relation they do not otherwise possess. The patchwork of images connected edge-to-edge or corner-to-corner is a shuffle of scenes that include crosswalks and train tracks, depictions of sun and snow and rain, beaches and boats, buildings and the pyramids. Bonillas advises us to observe the collaged images obliquely. The visual path guides us from one image to the next as it zigs and zags across these cuts of time, calling upon us to fill in the blanks by physically and mentally connecting these moments threaded together into a new geography of place and intimate distance (Dillon). Whose memories do these snapshots index? Who is the collective behind the collection?

Of course, memory is fluid, mutable, and continually modified by the needs of those who remember. Techniques of preservation affiliated with the archive are often criticized for transforming the dynamic nature of memory into fossils to be stored, cataloged, and held inert by the historic record at a distance from lived and embodied entanglements. Melissa Anne-Marie Curley's chapter, "Caring, Keeping, and Kinship-Making: Unaffiliated Ancestors in the Space of the Archive," offers an alternative model for intergenerational and intercultural stewardship. Her analysis of how human remains intersect with modern memory institutions centers around two cases: the treatment of Buddha statues containing cremated human remains at the Pure Land Buddhist temple Isshinji, and the treatment of corpses preserved in Northern European peat bogs displayed at the Canadian Museum of Civilization. The history of human remains in memory institutions is marred by colonial violence and scientific racism, and, as Curley argues, ongoing indifference. Such "captive bodies" have been severed from their personhood, their ongoing social and cultural contexts, as well as from their kin and descendants. What kinds of ethical responses might memory institutions develop to recognize deceased ancestors as deserving of care and hospitality? Can they become enlivened through such kin-work, and even foster healing?

The sculptural form carries a different weight for Amy Shuman, who considers the disposability and ephemerality of taken-for-granted objects in "Archival Instabilities: From Ephemerality to Newfound Significance." Shuman is interested in the plaster models that artisans in Pietrasanta, Italy, use to carve reproductions of marble sculptures, from the statue of David to Catholic saints to contemporary art. These plasters are sometimes displayed as evidence of artisanal craft, but they are more frequently stored out of sight, hidden away within a hierarchy that cares more for the finished marble forms than for their means of reproduction. Replaced by their copies, the models are both highly valued and without value, forming a fragmented archive of embodied knowledge that both reveals and conceals itself when enacted into marble. As with Curley, Shuman asks us to reconsider how we relate to such objects, and to artistic processes that expose a multiplicity of timelines embedded within what are marketed as completed works.

Temporality takes on a new dimension in Brian Eugenio Herrera's contribution "Archival Forethought." A theater scholar, Herrera is accustomed to artists delaying preservation of their own materials to some other time and hopefully some other person who will take up the charge of writing them into history. The incursion of digital programs and QR codes into performance spaces responds to real problems regarding environmental sustainability, but replacing printed playbills with digital files creates challenges for scholars: How shall histories of performance be written when the documents tethering this ephemeral art form to the archive disappear just as quickly as the performances themselves, or are continuously modified so that the record becomes wholly unreliable? Erasures in the archive here are not due to violent suppression but to a lack of forethought entangled with a contemporary medial condition. Situated at the end of the section, Herrera's critique of digital fallibility pivots the conversation in *Archival Entanglements* toward distributed networks of support, digital spaces of recollection, and the work of presencing forgotten histories taken up in the volume's second section.

Networked Memories and Minor Histories

This section builds on the ethical questions of memory and forgetting posed in the first section with attention to the profound consequences that the ascent of digital archives has had for memory-keeping and knowledge production. With their capacity for access, storage, participation, and collaboration, digital archives are important vectors for democratizing information. In addition to broadening access beyond institutions to recognize diverse constituencies, however, digital archives present complementary challenges to their physical counterparts, for which they are often a stand-in. Such challenges include ever-expanding storage needs, take-down notices for materials under copyright, platform obsolescence, cyberattacks, and more. Whereas traditional collections preserve the materiality of artifacts and ephemera in their holdings, digital archives reformat such objects in light of what can be rendered computationally—generally favoring their visual, textual, and sonic attributes. Preserving the feeling of physical objects and experiences is difficult within the medium-specificity of digital collections, whose materiality is expressed in the infrastructure of networks, metadata, and servers upon which they rely (Parks and Starosielski; Pink et al.). But archives are rich troves of data in their own right as well, and can be activated for new experiences and new engagement beyond the histories they document. Each of the contributions in this section brings forward lived experience and sensory engagement to acknowledge how memory work is a physical practice in which activation is the mode of preservation.

As the creator of a digital collection encompassing over five thousand T-shirt images, Eric Gonzaba elasticizes the notion of what an archive can be in his chapter "The American Gay Bar T-Shirt: Understanding Queer Nightlife Histories with the *Wearing Gay History Archive*." This collection aims to preserve the rich legacy of queer life in the American Midwest and South—places that have long been neglected because of what Gonzaba describes as a "bicoastal bias" in LGBTQ+ history. A potent cultural artifact of the post-Stonewall era, the gay T-shirt became a tangible signifier of self-expression, resistance, and pride. As sanctuaries for queer communities, bars and nightclubs have played an important role in the distribution and visibility of such clothing. Gonzaba offers a semiotic reading of gay bar T-shirts as a material record of LGBTQ+ activism, performativity, representation, and commodification. His reading reveals how T-shirts carry histories of resistance and vulnerability, and encode political resistance within the everyday act of dressing. Furthermore, attending to material dimensions of LGBTQ+ culture highlights how the ordinary is central to human experience and brings the embodied and sensorial into view. These T-shirts literally hold the bodily histories of their wearers. Although the digital archive cannot make that level of physicality accessible to viewers through the screen, it does expand the space for queer recognition and coalition-building in the face of erasures due to heteronormative historiography.

Like Gonzaba, Mariah Marsden is interested in how the archive chronicles covert histories—in this case, of lesbians in the Ozark region of rural Missouri. In "Archival Encounters: Lesbian Newsletters and Rural Visibility," Marsden traces the history of a women's potluck and social group, called "Blossom," an acronym for "Brave Lesbians Organizing Some Saturdays of the Month." Marsden draws on a collection of Blossom's newsletters to show how this community of women navigated queer visibility, erasure, belonging, and place-making. For Marsden, the role of print technology is particularly significant given its predisposition toward "collaboration, multiplicity, gathering, and negotiation." Especially compelling here is what the archive conveys about the role of cultural geography in the constitution of genders and sexualities. While the perceived insularity of rural spaces creates a sense of constraint, they are also spaces rife with imagination and possibility, where queer individuals might seek refuge and safety through the creation of intentional communities. Marsden maps out this minor geography that provided both community and cover. Before the chat rooms where queer folks would later gather online, the newsletter format afforded a safe space for lesbian women to self-represent, to build an "imagined community" (Anderson) and to "translate embodied experiences into textual and archival memory" as Marsden says. In so doing, they constituted a networked counterpublic (Warner) across a politically hostile landscape.

Brian Harnetty's contribution, "*Forest Listening Rooms*: Sound, Archives, and Social Engagement in Appalachian Ohio" extends this emphasis on regional and rural histories as he explores the role of community and embodied archives in fostering social change. Anchored by his socially engaged sound art project, Harnetty asks, "What does social change sound like?" He prompts the reader to consider listening together as a modality for healing, for engaging the archive, and as a radical act of resistance. As part of the project, residents of Wayne National Forest in Appalachian Ohio were invited to contemplatively listen to the sounds of the forest in conjunction with archival recordings of regional oral histories, field recordings, and music. Harnetty's "archival performances" provide a historical backdrop for environmental changes and ecological crises that have unfolded over time, and which are evidenced not only in the human presence that has violently carved itself into Appalachia's landscape but also in nature's generations-long recovery from these scars as trees, birds, water, and all the living things that call the forest home (re)sound. Attendees are invited to be in community with each other and with their nonhuman surroundings. How might these novel sonic convergences open opportunities to rethink the legacy of shared lands, bridge geographic and temporal divides, and challenge dominant extractive compulsions? For Harnetty, archival listening is a radical act. It is not only a way to refuse the commodification of time and space—it becomes an ethical demand to recognize the fragility of our shared existence. Another world is possible, if we will listen.

Nicole Wood is also engaged in sourcing lived experience from archival documents and returns to the digital realm via the nineteenth- and twentieth-century environmental data she finds in diaries and other records kept by farmers, homemakers, migrants, and miners. Connecting with Harnetty's insistence that forests also have histories, in "Countering Environmental Narratives with Archival Latencies," Wood shows how archives are filled with "latent data" (Veel), including climate and ecological data. She searches the archive for such data in two case studies—one on the devastating American chestnut blight in Tennessee, the spread of which she reconstructs geospatially, and the other on historical rainfall in California. Her analysis not only shows how climate data resides in archival documents prior to the standardization of quantitative measures, it also points to historical manipulation and falsification of data for personal and political gain. "Archivists can only preserve data that exists," Wood cautions, tying the creation of her historical datasets to the destruction of contemporary federal climate data as part of a politically motivated purge. Yet her methodology is a strong reminder that official archives are not—and must not be—the only records, and that communities have always been creators and stewards of archival data.

Leigh Bonds's contribution, "Imagining Digital Bibliography as Archival Intervention," approaches archival data from the other side, as metadata collected about historical subjects. She shows how digital bibliography plays an important role in streamlining how researchers of textual studies identify, structure, and engage with scholarly materials. Using her work on the *Mary Robinson Project* as an exemplar, Bonds assesses the strengths and weaknesses of the format with consideration to "data structure, platform affordances and limitations, and sustainability" as priorities. Here, digital infrastructure is not taken for granted but is actively created, with each resource added in a larger effort to recover Robinson's work after she disappeared from the scholarly record. In traditional print bibliography, researchers engage existing catalogs or finding aids while relying on sequential exploration, and they often face limitations imposed by the spatial confines of the archive. By contrast, Bonds contends that digital bibliography is more expansive and fluid. Consolidating interconnected citations, hyperlinks, and metadata, digital bibliographies "serve as portals" to a broader ecosystem of relations from which discoveries can emerge.

The contributions in this section emphasize the liberatory potentials of archival work in recovering muted voices and marginalized histories, and the usefulness of digital means for doing so. And yet. What if the archive is an irredeemable Western modality, one that cannot be reimagined or recovered no matter how far one expands the notion of the archival? The final section of *Archival Entanglements* preserves the space of hesitation, of sitting with the difficulties of the archive.

Ancestral Practices and Otherwise Archives

What if no amount of reading against the grain or recovering historical fragments can offset the epistemic and other violences implicit in archival inheritances? The final section of this book tackles the archive head-on, examining its limits and misdirections. If it cannot be recuperated, what can be imagined in the aftermath of the archive? What other logics of memory—visceral, material, affective, communal—unfold alongside archives while offering contrapuntal or contradictory registers? Contributions in this section particularly explore the otherwise that opens up when the hegemony of archival thought loosens its grip as a regulator of historical memory. Nowhere in this book is the archive taken as given, but contributors in the final section take up refusal and redirection to articulate a beyond-archive. Coming full circle to where *Archival Entanglements* opens, this necessitates rethinking the epistemic foundations of the archive, including which knowledges are amplified, erased, or silenced.

To reach beyond the limits of the archive, perhaps we must forge new spaces of remembrance, narration, and engagement. This is the mandate that

Michelle Wibbelsman takes up in a powerful interrogation of twin dilemmas that impact Indigenous representation in the archive in "Indigenous Meaning-Making, the Limits of Archives, and the Promise of Practice." The first dilemma she identifies is that Western archives are built upon impulses to taxonomize and preserve that fail to account for Indigenous epistemologies, which are often fluid, relational, and transient. Wibbelsman's work with the Kawsay Ukhunchay Andean and Amazonian Indigenous Art and Cultural Artifacts Research Collection offers strategies for decentering archival tendencies toward objectivity, linearity, and permanence, and for redressing some of the biases and exclusions that result from this epistemic mismatch. Yet, while navigating these decolonial interventions, Wibbelsman found herself coming up against a second, more unsettling dilemma—that perhaps the archive is not a meaningful or ethical framework to understand non-Western cultures at all. Wibbelsman's contribution challenges us to consider what it might mean to abandon the violence of archival thinking. How might we engage cultural forms that refuse possession—that are perhaps not meant for outsiders to access or interpret? What might a new ethics of interaction and obligation look like?

Obligation can have both positive and negative valences, and Anurima Banerji questions how archives can impose processes to which, in her analysis, dance specialists may become bound. "The Laws of Movement: The *Natyashastra*, Caste, and Archives of Indian Classical Dance" plumbs the history of this ancient text of aesthetic theory that Banerji contends maintains a "formidable hold on Indian/diasporic artistic imaginaries and scholarship." Specifically, she considers how the *Natyashastra* both constructs and reproduces the caste system, aligning social norms and aesthetic practices under a single regulating force. As a repository of tradition that continues to hold sway, the text's aesthetic principles function as ideological principles that uphold caste divisions and restrict artists' possibilities for interpretation. For Banerji, the archive and the law bleed into one another such that the archive becomes a kind of law, invested with the authority to regulate the identities and representations of caste-oppressed peoples.

In "Labor History, Social Death, and the Birth of the Black Worker," Franco Barchiesi examines how labor is represented in archival holdings and presents a particularly withering analysis of racial erasure in service of extractive capitalism. To look at labor's history is to confront a distortion—one where Black workers appear not as subjects of history but as abstractions—reduced to and obscured by semantic deception, economic outputs, or legal categories. Forged at the intersections of empire and enslavement, Barchiesi shows, the colonial underpinnings of the archive actively foreclosed the possibility of Black subjectivity within the historic record. His case studies of Barbados and South Africa also illuminate how liberalism's preoccupations with progress, universal rights, and equality offered the archive a veneer of neutrality. By framing slavery and racialized labor as regrettable deviations from liberal progress, the archive—under liberalism's influence—did not need to engage with the continuing structural dimensions of its antiblackness. Barchiesi prompts us to consider whether ongoing engagement with the archive runs the risk of reinscribing the same modes of racial violence that are foundational to its constitution.

Rebecca Schneider's contribution, "What Else: Gesture and Glitch in 'What Is a Better Life,'" does not resolve this impasse, but Schneider does make space for irresolvability in her account of viewing Alberta Whittle's film "What is a better life (exorcised in the middle)," while acknowledging the neocolonial consumption of Black and Indigenous thought by white scholars. Focused on a glitch that occurred during a webinar screening of the film, which shaped her experience and understanding of the work, Schneider plumbs the possibility of what should not be there, but which, by being there, offers something meaningful. The glitch jars Schneider as a viewer and disrupts the continuity of her experience. It cuts through an image that both alludes to Black suffering through a "scene of subjection" (Hartman) and undercuts that very image by disappearing, leaving only the sonic reverberation of an iron ring hitting stone. This absent-presence or present-absence is a form of refusal, but it is embedded in a form of repetition. The image recurs as a reminder, but it also refuses the space of violence to which it refers. Interruption breaks through totality and makes way for the "what else" (McKittrick).

Archival Entanglements comes to a close with a gathering around the work of Tanya Lukin Linklater, an artist whose work spans choreography, writing, and other forms. Lukin Linklater's "*Slow Scrape* Event Scores" are introduced by curator Kelly Kivland, who organized her 2024 residencies and exhibition at the Wexner Center for the Arts: *Inner blades of grass (soft) inner blades of grass (cured) inner blades of grass (bruised by the weather).* The scores are followed by Johannah Bird's poetic response in relation to open rehearsals with Lukin Linklater and dance artists Sam Aros-Mitchell, Ivanie Aubin-Malo, Talia Dixon, and lisa nevada, which accompanied the exhibition. Scores and poems are deliberately open forms. They offer a vehicle for imagining alternate spaces and times of relation (including relations invited and relations refused) but which nevertheless structure what we experience as well as what and how we remember. Working within a settler colonial situation but not defined by it, these contributions point to multivalent lineages of practice and modes of activating memory as a bulwark against Indigenous erasure and as sustenance for Indigenous futures. If Lukin Linklater's written scores forge (or reveal?) adjacencies with historical and contemporary protagonists from ballerina Maria Tallchief to critical Indigenous theorist Eve Tuck, among others, Bird's process of "writing adjacently" demonstrates the practice of being-alongside as a way to engage critically and creatively while honoring difference and unknowability.

Editorial Entanglements

As editors, our own relationships to the archive and practices of memory-keeping are complex. Harmony is a dance and digital media scholar, and Puja is a folklorist; our fields have both been marginalized by archival thinking and have been deeply impacted by the archival turn. Which is to say, we find ourselves entangled in the archive—caught up in what it enables but never fully at home with it. Importantly, we do not wish to free ourselves from our archival entanglements. The archive is a problem. We want to keep it that way.

As philosopher Jacques Derrida insists, the archive "is a question of the future, the question of the future itself" (36). Similarly, archivist Terry Cook reminds the scholarly community that "as archivists appraise records, they are doing nothing less than determining what the future will know about its past: who will have a continuing voice, and who will be silenced" (606). This view invites us to reconsider how memory, power, and meaning are organized in service to what lies ahead. *Archival Entanglements* explores archives as inchoate fields animated and held together by structuring tensions between material and nonmaterial, presence and absence, memory and speculation. It is our hope that by continuing to trouble the archive while remaining entangled within it, this volume affirms the archive as a vital locus of contestation that also makes space for counterimaginaries through which to realize other possible futures.

Works Cited

Anderson, Benedict. *Imagined Communities: Reflections on the Origin and Spread of Nationalism.* Verso, 1983.

Antebi, Susan. *Embodied Archive: Disability in Post-Revolutionary Mexican Cultural Production.* University of Michigan Press, 2021.

Bastian, Jeannette A., and Andrew Flinn. *Community Archives: Sustaining Memory.* Facet Publishing, 2019.

Becerra-Licha, Sofia. "Participatory and Post-Custodial Archives as Community Practice." *Educause Review*, vol. 22, no. 6, 2017, pp. 90–91.

Benoit, Edward, III, and Alexandra Eveleigh. "Defining and Framing Participatory Archives in Archival Science." *Participatory Archives: Theory and Practice*, edited by Alexandra Eveleigh and Edward Benoit III, Facet, 2019, pp. 1–12, https://doi.org/10.29085/9781783303588.001.

Caswell, Michelle. "'The Archive' Is Not an Archives: On Acknowledging the Intellectual Contributions of Archival Studies." *Reconstruction: Studies in Contemporary Culture*, vol. 16, no. 1, 2016, https://escholarship.org/content/qt7bn4v1fk/qt7bn4v1fk.pdf.

Caswell, Michelle. *Urgent Archives: Enacting Liberatory Memory Work*. Routledge, 2021.

Cook, Terry. "The Archive(s) Is a Foreign Country: Historians, Archivists, and the Changing Archival Landscape." *The American Archivist*, vol. 74, no. 2, 2011, pp. 600–632.

Cvetkovich, Ann. *An Archive of Feelings: Trauma, Sexuality, and Lesbian Public Cultures*. Duke University Press, 2003.

Cvetkovich, Ann. "Ordinary Lesbians and Special Collections: The June L. Mazer Lesbian Archives at UCLA." *Turning Archival: The Life of the Historical in Queer Studies*, edited by Daniel Marshall and Zeb Tortorici, Duke University Press, 2022, pp. 111–40. *JSTOR*, https://doi.org/10.2307/j.ctv2wbz11g.8.

De Kosnik, Abigail. *Rogue Archives: Digital Cultural Memory and Media Fandom*. MIT Press, 2021.

Derrida, Jacques. *Archive Fever: A Freudian Impression*. Translated by Eric Prenowitz, University of Chicago Press, 1996.

Dillon, Elizabeth Maddock. *New World Drama: The Performative Commons in the Atlantic World, 1649–1849*. Duke University Press, 2014.

Foucault, Michel. *The Archaeology of Knowledge and The Discourse on Language*. Translated by A. M. Sheridan Smith, Pantheon Books, 1972.

Foucault, Michel. *Power/Knowledge: Selected Interviews and Other Writings, 1972–1977*. Edited by Colin Gordon, Pantheon Books, 1980.

Haraway, Donna J. *Staying with the Trouble: Making Kin in the Chthulucene*. Duke University Press, 2016.

Harris, Verne S. "The Archival Sliver: A Perspective on the Construction of Social Memory in Archives and the Transition from Apartheid to Democracy." *Refiguring the Archive*, edited by Carolyn Hamilton et al., Springer, 2002, pp. 135–60, https://doi.org/10.1007/978-94-010-0570-8_9.

Harris, Verne S. *Archives and Justice: A South African Perspective*. Society of American Archivists, 2007.

Hartman, Saidiya. *Scenes of Subjection: Terror, Slavery, and Self-Making in Nineteenth-Century America*. Oxford University Press, 1997.

Jenkinson, Hilary. *A Manual of Archive Administration*. 2nd ed., Clarendon Press, 1937.

Lee, Jamie A. *Producing the Archival Body*. Routledge, 2020.

Manoff, Marlene. "Theories of the Archive from Across the Disciplines." *Portal: Libraries and the Academy*, vol. 4, no. 1, Jan. 2004, pp. 9–25.

McKittrick, Katherine. *Dear Science and Other Stories*. Duke University Press, 2021.

Moor, Liz, and Emma Uprichard. "Materializing the Archive: Writing Bodies, Mapping Affect." *Qualitative Research*, vol. 17, no. 4, 2017, pp. 419–36.

Nora, Pierre. "Between Memory and History: Les Lieux de Mémoire." *Representations*, no. 26, 1989, pp. 7–24. *JSTOR*, https://doi.org/10.2307/2928520.

Padilla, Thomas, et al. *Vancouver Statement on Collections as Data.* 13 Sept. 2023. *Zenodo,* https://doi.org/10.5281/zenodo.8342171.

Parks, Lisa, and Nicole Starosielski, editors. *Signal Traffic: Critical Studies of Media Infrastructures.* University of Illinois Press, 2015. *Silverchair,* https://doi.org/10.5406/illinois/9780252039362.001.0001.

Pink, Sarah, et al., editors. *Digital Materialities: Design and Anthropology.* Routledge, 2020.

Said, Edward W. "Traveling Theory." *The World, the Text, and the Critic,* Harvard University Press, 1983, pp. 226–47.

Scarry, Elaine. *The Body in Pain: The Making and Unmaking of the World.* Oxford University Press, 1987.

Schellenberg, Theodore R. "The Appraisal of Modern Public Records." *Bulletins of the National Archives,* vol. 8, October 1956, pp. 233–78.

Schwartz, Joan M., and Terry Cook. "Archives, Records, and Power: The Making of Modern Memory." *Archival Science,* vol. 2, no. 1–2, 2002, pp. 1–19.

Sharpe, Jenny. *Immaterial Archives: An African Diaspora Poetics of Loss.* Northwestern University Press, 2020.

Singh, Julietta. *No Archive Will Restore You.* punctum books, 2018.

Spivak, Gayatri. "Can the Subaltern Speak?" *Marxism and the Interpretation of Culture,* edited by Cary Nelson and Lawrence Grossberg, University of Illinois Press, 1988, pp. 271–313.

Srinivasan, Priya. *Sweating Saris: Indian Dance as Transnational Labor.* Temple University Press, 2012.

Stoler, Ann Laura. *Along the Archival Grain: Epistemic Anxieties and Colonial Common Sense.* Princeton University Press, 2009.

Sutherland, Tonia. "Archival Amnesty: In Search of Black American Transitional and Restorative Justice." *Journal of Critical Library and Information Studies,* vol. 1, no. 2, 2017, pp. 1–23, https://doi.org/10.24242/jclis.v1i2.42.

Taylor, Diana. *The Archive and the Repertoire: Performing Cultural Memory in the Americas.* Duke University Press, 2003.

Theimer, Kate. "The Future of Archives Is Participatory: Archives as Platform; or, A New Mission for Archives." *ArchivesNext,* 3 Apr. 2014, https://web.archive.org/web/20160306065255/http://www.archivesnext.com/?p=3700.

Thylstrup, Nanna Bonde, et al., editors. *Uncertain Archives: Critical Keywords for Big Data.* MIT Press, 2021.

Tuck, Eve, and K. Wayne Yang. "Decolonization Is Not a Metaphor." *Decolonization: Indigeneity, Education & Society,* vol. 1, no. 1, 2012, pp. 1–40.

Veel, Kristin. "Latency." *Uncertain Archives: Critical Keywords for Big Data,* edited by Nanna Bonde Thylstrup, et al., MIT Press, 2021, pp. 313–19.

Warner, Michael. *Publics and Counterpublics.* Zone Books, 2005.

Withey, Kimberly Christen. "Sovereignty, Repatriation, and the Archival Imagination." *Collections: A Journal for Museum and Archives Professionals,* 1 June 2015, pp. 115–38.

PART 1

GAPS, ERASURES, AND AN ETHICS OF RECOGNITION

PART 1 INTRODUCTION

PUJA BATRA-WELLS AND HARMONY BENCH

This first section, Gaps, Erasures, and an Ethics of Recognition, troubles the relationship between archives and knowledge, highlighting paradoxical and contradictory perspectives in relation to presence and absence, and what is known and unknown. We have grouped these six contributions together to highlight how scholars, artists, and memory practitioners are shifting ethical arrangements in the course of their work with archives and artifacts. Throughout this volume, the archive is an ambivalent space, holding both cherished memories and traces of violence. Erasure, forgetfulness, and disappearance take on primary roles in this section, without coming to a clear consensus as to what the results of these gaps in memorialization might be. For some, there is a desire to be embraced by the archive and its logics—or at least a feeling that the archive could be useful if its scope of stewardship shifted to accommodate that which prior generations deemed without value (Ọnụọha, Bonillas, Shuman, Herrera). This section thus expands the notion of the archive to include other spaces and practices of memory-keeping—most notably the museum—and broadens an understanding of what is preserved to include human remains, bodily practices, and trauma (Ponce, Curley, Shuman). Alongside this expansion, care and recognition emerge as strategies for deepening ethical entanglements with the past, which these contributors understand is very much a part of the present.

Mimi Ọnụọha distinguishes among the known, the unknown, and the unknowable, stating that "what's known can be managed," and whereas the unknown simply points to missing information, "the unknowable can only disrupt." The unknowable produces an experience of extreme disorientation that requires significant change. Ọnụọha reflects that her own confrontation with the unknowable—which in her case was learning about a mass grave in her hometown—"has rearranged [her]." Ọnụọha's emphasis on unknowability introduces a pause in the stereotypical progress narrative through which we move from the unknown to the known, confidently filling in gaps in knowledge. For Iñaki Bonillas, images drawn from his library form a fractured collage, through which there is no progress as such. Privileging adjacency and absence over continuity or linearity, the images create connection through disruption, requiring viewers to decenter themselves and move toward the edges, "away from the heart of the images to observe them obliquely." What connections can be made from this rearranged perspective, where fractured pathways create a bodily bridge to the viewer, who makes sense of the unknowable from the sidelines? And how might attending to this periphery inform how we reckon with unresolved or even unresolvable histories?

Martin Joseph Ponce also explores the rupture of the unknowable through Emily Jungmin Yoon's "poetics of erasure" as the latter reimagines testimonies of Korean "comfort women," weaving new poetic forms by introducing absences and erasures into verbatim texts documenting the violence they endured. Ponce shows how Yoon opens new interpretive possibilities by literally making space in the texts, disrupting the speakers' voices in order to amplify them. Yoon's erasures provoke new reflection by creating rather than eliminating gaps, and in the spaces opened up, Ponce proposes that Yoon achieves a kind of "interim mode of literary justice" that distinguishes itself from both Japanese state reparations, which have not yet materialized, and ongoing political activism. Yoon's erasures resonate with what Melissa Curley describes as a kind of remembering that "involves—indeed, requires—some ritualized forgetting." When ancestors are understood to retain their liveliness and agency, they can make claims on the living, including demanding to be cared for, to be allowed to rest, and to be "less than fully known." Affording strangers the same respect as one's kin and establishing affiliation across temporal and/or cultural distances to offer oneself in service to the dead requires an expanded understanding of self in relation not only to the past but also to the future.

Brian Eugenio Herrera frames this orientation to the future as "archival forethought," an anticipatory posture required lest "minoritarian performance histories" in particular be forgotten because of the dual challenge of their absence from the archives compounded by overrepresentation of already dominant histories. As digital artifacts supersede the physical artifacts on which historians so rely, and as those digital artifacts change, deprecate, and reveal vulnerabilities to corporate and political whims, a new habit of thought is required to "cultivate an ethical practice of archival forethought." This mandate also requires a reconsideration of hierarchies of value, as Amy Shuman shows. Historically rich materials are often dismissed as unimportant or "taken for granted." Collection and contextualization of sculptural models, which are activated primarily in the context of their use, retains the proximity of these objects to the embodied knowledge they evidence. The display of plaster models typically stored away from view elevates them from the ordinariness of their function and emphasizes their artisanal value while also serving to fix them in the past. The gap here between past and present is one of perception rather than the passage of time, as display itself serves a temporal function.

Across a range of contexts and perspectives, the contributions in Gaps, Erasures, and an Ethics of Recognition ask us to consider: How do we demonstrate ethical relationships to the past through our work? How does an embrace of proximity and intimacy change research and scholarship? How do personal memories and memory practices interact with or challenge institutional forms of remembering? To what extent do gaps in the record represent failures of representation versus preserving the peace of ancestors? How do erasures and intentional absences function as malicious or as benevolent? In what ways can fracturing open up new spaces of engagement? What hierarchies of value run through archival logics? What alternatives already exist, and what others could be created? What aims can an archival disposition serve for communities that have historically been left out of institutional forms of memory-keeping? What generative possibilities reside in the unknown or the unknowable?

CHAPTER 1

The End of a World / As We Knew It

MIMI ỌNỤỌHA

I learned about the mass grave in 2018.[1] It is located about five minutes by car from the Texas house I grew up in. I had driven past it every morning on my way to school, in the last dark hour before the sun took to stage.

When I heard about the grave, I felt a slick iciness in my chest. I was angry. As if I had been the last one to learn a family secret, and the secret was about me.

But the grave, though hidden, was no secret. It was created after the Civil War, at a time when Southern states were desperate to rebuild and Northern states were eager to invest. The result was a shared interest in cheap labor, and in the aftermath of slavery's dishonorable discharge, convicts—or Black Americans who were easy to recast as convicts—became the solution. The conditions were horrible. But they were documented, even if it was in that slippery way that the marginalized are often recorded, counted, and bemoaned, but never quite seen.

Once I learned about the grave, I saw hints of its existence all over. There they were, in the city streets and institutions named after the men who orchestrated forced labor agreements. There they were, spoken from the mouth of a former prison guard who had tried to tell local officials about the grave's existence. There they were, everywhere.

There they were, even though in truth, the evidence was also nowhere. The grave was conspicuously absent from my town's historiography. The same

1. This essay is republished from *e-flux Architecture* with the author's permission.

institutions whose names bore witness to it carried no direct mentions in their own histories. None of my friends or family knew about it. I, too, had driven by the grave multiple days a week for ten years without the barest hint of awareness. It was as though for a long time there was some quality of the grave that made it impossible to know about.

But what I knew then, even without being able to explain how, was that if the grave was unknowable, it wasn't because of the remains it held or any haunting from beneath the ground. It had something to do with the town itself. It was the world above that rendered the grave below not just unknown, but unknowable.

"When what we know changes," science historian James Burke once wrote, "the world changes and with it, everything" (7). The world changes when a new thing is able to become known. But Burke didn't mention that the prospect of the world changing can be staggering, even terrifying. Change carries uncertainty. One way to stave off upheaval is to—whether consciously or not—tightly draw the curtains on what is already established. What's known can be managed. The unknowable can only disrupt.

•

Thinking about the unknowable takes some prep work, mostly because the idea of unknowability seems so vague. When I say "the unknowable," you might picture a mass of nothingness, the blank white loading zone of the Matrix, or maybe outer space. With this, you are imagining an abstraction, the opposite of thing-ness. You're envisioning whatever you think absence looks like. But the idea of the unknowable can be pinned down. To do so merely requires some distinctions.

First of all, the unknowable is not the same as the unknown. You may not know how to juggle, or how to speak Hausa, or how to use a scanning tunneling microscope. You may not know the number of Lebanese people outside of Lebanon or the name of the Chinese mariner who sailed an impressive amount of the world in the fourteenth century. These are all practices and facts that may be unknown to you, but you *could* learn them. Even more importantly, you know how to figure out what it would take to learn each of them. I'm not saying it would be easy, just that it's possible.

Second, the unknowable is also bigger than what you don't know how to know. Scientists don't yet know how many exoplanets exist or are inhabited. This is missing information, not unknown information. That word "missing" implies an *ought,* for many scientists would surely like to know the details of exoplanet inhabitation. But a current lack of sufficiently sophisticated tools is what obscures the answers. In other words, scientists may not know how to know the answers, but they clearly know the questions.

Further, when I talk about the unknowable, I'm not alluding to Donald Rumsfeld's famous "unknown unknowns." That phrase has always irritated me, because it treats the unknown as individual pieces of information that you might uncover in the same way a botanist in the Amazon might discover a new species of plant.[2] "We didn't even know that we didn't know about this thing!" the imaginary intrepid explorer exclaims. Sure, there are some events that do exist like this—a fire, an earthquake, and a global pandemic are all events that can't be predicted. But they are unknown mostly in the sense of being unexpected and unanticipated. They are not unknowable.

All of these unknowns fit into a familiar paradigm of the sequential way that knowledge operates within most fields, disciplines, and trades. Those who work today build upon the knowledge of those who came before. Those who come after us will know things that we did not, and so on. Everyone stands higher and higher on the shoulders of evermore giants, a wonderful (if rickety) tower of progress.

If this is the case, then the unknowable is the gust that sways the tower.

The unknowable is not disruption for disruption's sake. To understand the unknowable, you must abandon the comforting fantasy of facts and information as things that can be picked up or put down like boxes of cereal on a grocery shelf. You must be willing to entertain the idea that knowing is not so straightforward. It can be a murky, quiet, loud, shadowy, difficult, contradictory process. To understand the unknowable, you have to shift your focus away from information and towards the knowers. What *you* know defines what *you* cannot know. What you have internalized to the point of naturalizing—the kind of knowledge that infuses your whole life, self, and orienting structure—defines what you cannot know.

The unknowable is that which demands you change the very way you make sense of yourself or the world around you. It lies just beyond the frameworks that structure your understanding of the world. This is why it is so difficult to perceive: you simply are not used to doing so. This is why it is so inherently discordant: if it weren't, it would merely be unknown, not unknowable.

2. The full quotation from which the phrase comes, from then–Secretary of Defense Donald Rumsfeld: "Reports that say that something hasn't happened are always interesting to me, because as we know, there are known knowns; there are things we know we know. We also know there are known unknowns; that is to say we know there are some things we do not know. But there are also unknown unknowns—the ones we don't know we don't know."

The unknowable is confrontational and dissonant by design. It's the thing that requires a massive rearrangement of your structure of understanding to grasp. It's the grave that you grew up with in the town that couldn't let you know it existed. The unknowable is all of the information which, although it isn't hidden, cannot be acknowledged or assimilated due to the contradictions it poses to the fundamental precepts upon which your system of knowledge rests.

We—whoever your "we" is (or as Nandita Sharma puts it, "the 'we' that both celebrants and dissidents recognize themselves as belonging to"; 165)—are the ones who make a thing unknowable.

•

I am searching for a practice of detecting the unknowable.

In reality, this means that I'm searching for a way of detecting the boundaries of the structures of understanding I've been raised in. The reason why I search has much to do with what the unknowable holds: the ability to restructure everything.

I'm drawn to the unknowable because I am still in the wake of the grave in my hometown. What the presence of that grave finally shouted out is the extent to which Sugar Land, Texas, was home to some of the most violently racist forced labor systems that the United States has ever seen. This unknowable truth could only be whispered while I was growing up. Today, the city is diverse and thriving, full of upwardly mobile immigrants in search of a safe place to raise families within the richest country in the world. They are able to be there, in part, because of the fortune raised through the industries that defined a town once known as "the hellhole on the Brazos."[3] And while I distantly felt the brutality of Sugar Land's history while growing up, seeing it be clearly acknowledged has rearranged me.

My Nigerian parents brought me to Texas when I was nine and I left as soon as I could at age eighteen. I never publicly claimed to be from there, and retained few ties to the place. But the grave changed my relationship to my hometown. When your feet have trudged a land for nine years, over soccer fields and parks, through gas pedals and bike tires, with friends and family and sometimes alone, how can you pretend that you exist outside of it?

---

3. "The Brazos" refers to the Brazos River, which is the longest river in Texas and flows through my hometown.

The grave undermined the way that I was raised to think about my hometown—as sleepy, perfect, uniquely "Texan"—and it allowed for a new understanding that was somber and painful, yet more expansive. It was an understanding that felt like it could include everything, even the difficult bits. The massacres of Indigenous people, the heaving racism, the blood-stained battles, the hot and cold violence, the swamps and the plains, the layers of migration, the ever-shuffling industries: everything. I hadn't realized that the city's bullheaded and narrow projection of itself was what had left me convinced I had nothing to do with it. But once the sanitized story of my hometown crumbled, I could see it as it was. Paradoxically, I could finally see myself as part of it.

Endings and beginnings: these are what the unknowable threatens and promises. I have the sense that we need both, especially now. Author Dougald Hine argues that in the wake of irreversible climate change, an end to the type of world that brought about such devastation is required. "The end of the world as we know it is also the end of a way of knowing the world," he writes (5). Theorist Sylvia Wynter says that as we grapple with the imperialism that has shaped the modern world, we need "a new mode of experiencing ourselves in which every mode of being human . . . is a part of us" (197), rather than just a minority of experiences (and people) being upheld over the many. Whether we search for new ends or new beginnings, the keys to both lie in pulling the strings that might unravel the structures that organize what we presently know the world to be.

All this said, detecting the unknowable is an enormously difficult thing to do. Consider how much easier it is to discuss the formerly unknowable than the currently unknowable. The formerly unknowable has already been incorporated into collective understanding, so it's possible to perceive it in a way that feels like a triumph, not a challenge.

A classic example is Galileo Galilei, the sixteenth- and seventeenth-century Italian astronomer. Galilei brought the unknowable of his time to the forefront when he supported the Copernican theory that Earth revolved around the sun. In doing so, he implicitly challenged the Aristotelian beliefs that were prevalent at the time. The Aristotelian description of a sun that rotated around Earth implicitly justified the powerful political position of the Catholic Church. Therefore, in supporting the Copernican theory, Galilei struck at the very foundations of seventeenth-century Western European society.

In response, high-ranking cardinals fretted about the societal implications of Galilei's writing. He was sentenced to house arrest and put on trial for beliefs that were revolutionary in the most basic sense of the world.

As a child within a Western tradition of education, I learned about Galilei in grade school. It was so easy to hear his story as an important and mostly inoffensive historical tale. Today when I reflect on the events, it strikes me that Galilei must have felt afraid.

Perhaps I think this because of the fear that I feel. There is danger threaded through the act of searching for even a way of sensing the unknowable. Who would have thought that the question of whether the sun or Earth moved was a political one? Structures have churning logics of their own. Like a snake that hisses and strikes when stepped on, these logics become dangerous once transgressed. The unknowable is always destabilizing, and there are consequences for even the smallest attempt to find it.

For this reason, it feels easier to search for the unknowable from outside of an order. Distance protects. Just as every language reveals its gaps in the concepts it cannot translate from another (*saudade, pura vida, ji sike*), holding multiple structures alongside each other makes the unknowable in each easier to see. This was the approach called for in many of the African, Asian, and Caribbean nations that achieved independence in the 1950s, '60s, and '70s. They were able to pinpoint the gaps in the worldviews of their former colonizers because of the ways these worldviews had been crudely stamped atop their own. Édouard Glissant famously called for opacity, an insistence on multiplicity that would not devolve into hierarchy. Today, Oyèrónkẹ́ Oyěwùmí argues from a similar positioning for the use of the term "worldsense" rather than "worldview." The former is a nod to specificity and the decreased primacy of the visual in Yoruba West African culture (Oyěwùmí).

The truth, though, is that for all of its hard-won wins and clarity, the postcolonial approach didn't entirely work. As a member of one of those nations, I know well how many of us are still in the afterlife of colonization, the full impact of which remains unknowable, at least to some extent. And in a time where hyper-globalized markets and the internet have jumbled much of the world together, I doubt that there really is an *outside* from which to sense the unknowable. It reminds me of the 1956 Conference of Negro-African Writers and Artists in Paris, organized around the question of how African nations could rebuild Indigenous cultures within and despite the degradation of colonization. Of the participants, James Baldwin would later write that "they were all, now, whether they liked it or not, related to Europe, stained by European visions and standards, and their relation to themselves, and to each other, and to their past had changed" (68).

If there is no outside, then we are all left with no option but to determine the unknowable from a compromised position within. I think of it like playing a game of tag in the dark: hands outstretched, reaching for a surface that still prompts a jolt of surprise once felt. Risky, wary, and exhilarating. But as N. Katherine Hayles writes, "Although there may be no outside that we can know, *there is a boundary*" (qtd. in Barad 42, original emphasis).

The boundary I'm searching for exists in a place where a structure meets the reality it cannot hold. Thomas Kuhn, in writing about how new paradigms of thought emerge in scientific research, said that a deep awareness of the existing structure of understanding makes it possible to detect when something is off. "Novelty ordinarily emerges only for the [person] who, knowing *with precision* what [they] should expect, is able to recognize that something has gone wrong" (65, original emphasis).

Put differently: it's the combination of being in the structure and possessing a measured willingness to entertain difference that makes it possible to detect the unknowable. Multiple fluencies—not in languages, but in understandings—are required.

And you're never really alone in the act. There are always people whose lives are connected to unknowability, whether they would say so or not. There are people whose very presence complicates a nation's idea of itself, or the narrative it is keen on projecting. They exist, and in doing so, they carry histories that threaten to undo hegemonic narratives (Said and Mohr).

There are organizers and researchers whose commitment to their work pushes them to challenge narrow precedents. Their devotion to investigating at all costs sees them pushing past conventions, and in doing so, they begin the process of inviting in the unknowable.

In my hometown, there was an activist and historian named Reginald Moore who regularly went to county meetings to tell officials about the presence of our mass grave. He was summarily dismissed every time. Today, Rice University has acquired his archives of research in a collection that bears his name and celebrates his labor.

It is the willingness of so many to exist in that shadowy in-between place that gives me strength. They are like a lighthouse in the water when others choose to stay on land. They stand tall, trusting that one day the great many will climb into the boat.[4]

If it is the greater "we" of society that creates the structure that depends on denying the unknowable, the much smaller "we's" are the ones who can rearrange it. And when we do, we risk a more precious reward: rearranging ourselves as well.

---

4. I think of poet-theorist Christina Sharpe's description of "the wake," the place of fundamental contradiction where one "occup[ies] and [is] occupied by the continuous and changing present of slavery's as yet unresolved unfolding" (13–14).

Works Cited

Baldwin, James. *Nobody Knows My Name: More Notes of a Native Son.* Vintage Books, 1993.

Barad, Karen. *Meeting the Universe Halfway.* Duke University Press, 2007.

Burke, James. *The Day the Universe Changed.* Little, Brown and Company, 1995.

Department of Defense. "DoD News Briefing—Secretary Rumsfeld and Gen. Myers." 12 Feb. 2002, https://archive.ph/20180320091111/http://archive.defense.gov/Transcripts/Transcript.aspx?TranscriptID=2636.

Glissant, Édouard. *Poetics of Relation.* University of Michigan Press, 1997.

Hine, Dougald. *At Work in the Ruins.* Chelsea Green Publishing, 2023.

Kuhn, Thomas S. *The Structure of Scientific Revolution.* University of Chicago Press, 2012.

Oyěwùmí, Oyèrónké. *The Invention of Women: Making an African Sense of Western Gender Discourses.* University of Minnesota Press, 1997.

Said, Edward W., and Jean Mohr. *After the Last Sky: Palestinian Lives.* University Press, 1999.

Sharma, Nandita. "Strategic Anti-Essentialism: Decolonizing Decolonization." *Sylvia Wynter: On Being Human as Praxis,* edited by Katherine McKittrick, Duke University Press, 2015.

Sharpe, Christina. *In the Wake: On Blackness and Being.* Duke University Press, 2016.

Wynter, Sylvia. "The Re-Enchantment of Humanism: An Interview with Sylvia Wynter." Interview by David Scott. *Small Axe,* vol. 8, 2000, pp. 115–207.

CHAPTER 2

Emily Jungmin Yoon's Archival Poetics

"Comfort Women" Testimonies and Literary Justice in *A Cruelty Special to Our Species*

MARTIN JOSEPH PONCE

On August 14, 1991, Kim Hak-sun became the first survivor to testify publicly about her experiences as a former "comfort woman" subjected to systematic sexual slavery by the Japanese military during World War II. Her courageous decision to speak openly about her harrowing experiences encouraged other survivors to come forward and tell their stories and prompted sympathetic intellectuals to pursue the research necessary to historicize and validate their claims (Min 64–68; Yoshimi 34). The survivors' collective testimonies, along with the work of redress by activists and scholars, not only ended the silencing and shame that former "comfort women" endured in both Japan and South Korea after the war, they have also inspired a profusion of "comfort women" literature, art, and films produced by Korean American authors and artists in the United States.[1]

While the most well-known literary renderings of this history and its aftermath remain the novels *Comfort Woman* (1997) by Nora Okja Keller and *A Gesture Life* (1999) by Chang-rae Lee, this essay focuses on Emily Jungmin Yoon's more recent debut poetry collection, *A Cruelty Special to Our Species* (2018). The seven poems in the book's second section, "The Testimonies," renarrate the stories of the former "comfort women" whose names title each piece. Whereas Keller and Lee were influenced by listening directly to survivors speak about their experiences,[2] Yoon's connection to the "comfort

1. For overviews of "comfort women" cultural production, see Kang; Son; Stetz.
2. See, respectively, Farley; Garner.

women" takes place through accounts published in three English-language anthologies: Keith Howard's edited *True Stories of the Korean Comfort Women* (1996), Dai Sil Kim-Gibson's edited *Silence Broken: Korean Comfort Women* (1999), and Sangmie Choi Schellstede's edited *Comfort Women Speak: Testimony by Sex Slaves of the Japanese Military* (2000). As Yoon notes in the acknowledgments, the testimony poems "draw upon documentary materials" in these collections "used in combination with my own language," adding that "the transcribed, translated, and transliterated testimonies are all from *Comfort Women Speak*" (viii).

The acknowledgments not only serve to abide by copyright rules but also highlight Yoon's awareness about her poetry's relationship to these archival materials. In the author's note that follows, she positions herself as someone who is two generations removed from the former "comfort women's" wartime experiences (born in 1991, the same year as Kim Hak-sun's historic testimony) but is simultaneously invested in "return[ing] to my departed ancestors" and their experiences "from the Japanese occupation to the turbulent years in Korea before my birth" (xi). For Yoon, poetry serves as the vehicle through which "one can transcend the sense of belonging confined by temporal and geographical lines" (xi). Recognizing both her distanced relationship to the "comfort women" as well as poetry's capacity to "transcend" those divides, Yoon remarks further on the difference between the survivors' testimonies and her own poems. Whereas the survivors "were speaking from within, not for, a community" when sharing their accounts, Yoon aspires for her "poetry to serve to amplify and speak these women's stories, not speak *for* them" (xi).

Examining *how* Yoon endeavors to execute this task, this essay dwells on the conundrums that arise when Yoon's stated intentions seem to conflict with the formal techniques—especially her poetics of erasure—she uses to carry out those goals. At the level of public culture, Yoon's practice of drawing on the archive of "comfort women" narratives as the key repository mediating this history enacts a version of what Michael Leong calls "documental" poetics: the contemporary process of "refashion[ing] and recirculat[ing] preexisting documentation—from news reports to testimonies to governmental records—in order to make claims upon and about our cultural memory" (1). In this respect, Yoon's testimony poems "recover forgotten or marginalized information" (2) and remember those whose lives are quickly coming to an end: "the insistence on redocumenting marginalized lives is a resistance to their social deaths, to their public erasures" (5).

At a more granular level, however, the formal means by which she "transform[s] overly familiar texts" (2) into testimony poems operates, I suggest, not according to a logic of reductive appropriation (as one might infer from the poems' elisions) but through processes of selective extrapolation, metaphorical resonance, and temporal rearrangement that implicitly address the commodification of "comfort women" prose narratives since the early 1990s. In this regard, I interpret Yoon's archival poetics as not so much contributing directly to the redress movement (see Min and Son) but rather as performing an intimate mode of literary justice that seeks to recognize and affirm the survivors' experiences—during World War II but especially in the haunted present.

At first glance, the "experimental" techniques that Yoon uses in the testimony poems—jagged line breaks, uneven white spaces between fractured phrases, vertical columns—and the resulting condensed narratives appear to contradict her aim "to amplify and speak these women's stories." The prose accounts that extend three to seven pages in Schellstede's *Comfort Women Speak* are reduced to relatively short poems that barely exceed a single page in *A Cruelty Special to Our Species.* One consequential act of erasure occurs in the first testimony poem, "Hwang Keum-ju," which begins: "a draft notice for girls, who was going to go?" (15). Yoon excises the opening paragraphs of Hwang's prose account describing how she voluntarily responded to the "draft notice" to spare the three daughters in her foster family from being conscripted (Schellstede 4). Most significantly, Yoon inserts a space between "Everybody crying" and "I went" (Yoon 15) to indicate the erasure of this crucial information: "So I went. *I wasn't kidnapped, I was officially drafted.* I dressed nicely and went to the Hamheung train station" (Schellstede 4, my italics). In the longer testimony published in Kim-Gibson's *Silence Broken: Korean Comfort Women,* Hwang emphasizes that her experience of holding "an official draft notice," unlike most "women who registered as former comfort women," disputes Japanese denials of systematic recruitment by the military: "My case is significant because it points directly to official lying by the Japanese government" (Kim-Gibson 22).

In these and other instances, Yoon's poetics of erasure—the empty spaces alluding to the "whiting out of selected language of a source text" (Leong 17)—seems to mute, rather than "amplify," important details of the survivors' stories. Marking the differences between the testimonial archive and Yoon's poetry, these changes align with Jennifer S. Cheng's definition of "erasure poetry" as that which "translates an old document into a new one, and in doing so disrupts, interrupts, modulates the original." The "meaning" of the "new work," she suggests, is informed "by the shadow of the old document and the act of obfuscation that transforms it." Cheng thus argues that "the removal of language as either defacing or disremembering" is "always inherently a political act": "If erasure is a historical tool of the oppressor, can it ever be artistically innocent?" Given that imperial Japan sought to erase evidence of military sexual slavery by destroying documents related to the "comfort women" system and the women themselves, how are we to read Yoon's formal disruptions, interruptions, and obfuscations that seem to diminish further the voices of this counterarchive? After all, the "information" contained in the survivors' testimonies reveals "the stark realities that never appear in military and government documents, reports, or statistics" (Yoshimi 100). Whereas other contemporary women poets of color like M. NourbeSe Philip in *Zong!* (2011), Solmaz Sharif in *Look* (2016), and Layli Long Soldier in *Whereas* (2017) perform acts of erasure and extrapolation on the colonial "oppressor's" archival materials, Yoon employs the process on the once-subjugated women's own testimonies.

Clearly, Yoon is not keen on "defacing or disremembering" the survivors—quite the opposite. One way to account for this apparent discrepancy is to consider the opacity resulting from the poetic experiment as not so much an obfuscation of the prior text's meaning but as a deliberate effort to interrupt the easy consumption of what Kay Schaffer and Sidonie Smith refer to as the survivors' collective "ur-story of childhood poverty, abduction, forced sexual slavery, and lonely survival" that human rights "activists require for their activism and expect from their informants" (137). Indeed, Schaffer and Smith single out the anthology *Comfort Women Speak* from which Yoon derives her testimony poems as particularly complicit with reinforcing this "ur-story" because of its "common format of multiple (in this case, nineteen) abbreviated testimonies" (137).

Yoon's techniques of erasure and chronological reordering disrupt and modulate the "narrative template" required by human rights discourse and thereby interrogate the *form* such testimonies are expected to take (Schaffer and Smith 137). In shifting from the putative factual linearity of the prose accounts to the metaphorical, elliptical, nonlinear distillations of her testimony poems, Yoon exploits the gestural possibilities of white space. The empty spaces on the page point toward the silences that are constitutive of even these acts of self-revelation—what remains unspoken because of the constraints of what C. Sarah Soh analogously calls "the familiar master narrative, or the feminist humanitarian paradigmatic story" that emphasizes "young girls forcibly recruited by the military into sexual enslavement" (xiv), or because certain traumatic experiences are too painful to recall and rearticulate.

These gaps take on acute implications when dealing with the politics of representing sexual violence. Writing during the 1990s when survivors' testimonies were being collected and publicized for redressive purposes,

Chungmoo Choi laments how "the sum total of a comfort woman's life has unwittingly been reduced to nightmarish experiences of slavery for public consumption" and worries that the "intense focus on the repetitive sexual acts and abuses" might end up "serving voyeuristic curiosity" rather than political outrage (x). For the most part, Yoon's testimony poems avoid lurid depictions of sexual violence that cater to such prurient interests.

The poem "Kang Duk-kyung" provides a dramatic example of this practice. After running away from a factory because of lack of food and wages, Kang is picked up by a military police officer, raped on the mountainside, taken to a hut, then later brought to a "comfort station" along with six other Korean women (Schellstede 17). Yoon's poem clips this narrative into a series of short phrases and lines ("Kobayashi / took me / to a hut") that transmute the "repetitive" abuses into cumulative abstractions:

> Every evening
> soldiers
> countless soldiers   on the wild mountainside. (18)

Here, and in poems such as "Jin Kyung-paeng" and "Pak Kyung-soon," Yoon's cuts and condensings "avoid showcasing exploitative images of sexual violence that would further objectify a 'comfort woman'" (Reinares 385), instead alluding to the brutalities of serial sexual violence through the stark juxtaposition of short phrases.

As Yoon's acknowledgments indicate, however, her poetics not only erases and subtracts but also adds and reorders, endowing the words and phrases that *are* reproduced and inserted with increased significance. Again, these manipulations assume special importance when referencing sexual violence. For example, the poem "Hwang Keum-ju" removes the two paragraphs where Hwang expresses disbelief and indignation at a soldier's command to strip and he reacts viciously to her refusal. In their stead, Yoon interpolates a phrase extrapolated from Hwang's testimony in Kim-Gibson's *Silence Broken,* italicized here:

> Girls arrived   got sick   pregnant   injected
> with so many drugs   *nameless animals*
> *exploded on top of us.* (15, my italics)

Although this poem, as noted above, omits the circumstances of how Hwang was recruited, it nonetheless underscores the military's deceptive methods by repeating the word "factory" four times, stressing where Hwang thought she was going to work even when she is brought to a "comfort station" ("his kind of factory"; 15).

Even as Hwang's angry description of the Japanese soldiers as "nameless animals" inverts the dehumanization of Korean women (Soh 39–41), Yoon's poem implicitly connects the phrase to the war's end. The terse experiences of the "comfort women" ("arrived got sick pregnant injected") abruptly shift to the "day of liberation" as registered by the enjambed line "Suddenly, / no sound of horses" (15). The remaining soldier informs Hwang, "Your country is liberated, / and my country is sitting on a fire" (15). Yoon thus subtly links two forms of explosion: seminal ejaculations and the atomic detonations. Although she excises the latter from her version,[3] the poetic effect of the interpolated phrase ("exploded on top of us") suggests that the "fire" engulfing Japan is somehow retaliation for the sexual attacks. "Liberation," however, turns out to be cold comfort. Abandoned, the speaker walks "all the way to the 38th parallel," is sprayed by the Americans "with so much DDT / all the lice fell off me," and has since "lost [her] uterus" (Yoon 16).

Other testimony poems similarly manipulate endings to signal the ongoing effects of the survivors' World War II traumas and their unresolved grief. Notably, the only poem that registers the survivor's present feelings toward Japan is "Kim Sang-hi." The speaker acknowledges, "I should forget and forgive," but asserts, "I cannot":

> When my head turns toward Japan   I curse her
> I want to find solace   but I cannot
> When I wake up every morning   I cannot. (21)

Rearranging and deleting phrases while inserting horizontal spacing to create the right-hand column (see Schellstede 35), these closing lines articulate Kim's moral dilemma and sense of suspension. The last line in particular shifts the meaning in the prose account by deleting the final two words, "help it." Kim's compulsion to "curse" Japan every morning ("I cannot help it") turns into an inability to "wake up every morning," as though the "solace" that might be found by following the religious injunction to "forget and forgive" remains out of reach, thus rendering her unable to awaken fully from the nightmare of history.

---

3. Hwang's prose account explains, "Because of the atomic bomb his country was burning like hell, he told me, and I'd better leave quickly" (Schellstede 8).

Indeed, some of the most "poetic" transformations occur in the poems' endings, many of which gesture toward the persistence of haunting memories and dreams rather than political claims to restitution. The final lines of "Kim Yoon-shim," for instance, are Yoon's additions that express an elegiac lament for "a sick girl / who had been buried alive" and who haunts Kim's dreams because she was unable to "help her" (Yoon 23).

The close of "Kim Soon-duk" similarly eschews the politics of the present as articulated in the prose account and uses the dream trope to emphasize the survivor's persistent nightmares. Rather than end with Kim's criticisms of both the Japanese and Korean governments' failures to compensate the women and restore them to dignity (Schellstede 40–41), Yoon concludes the poem with her own interpolation: "when I was dreaming of legs that could not go anywhere" (27). The line parallels Kim's "dreaming / of suicide" when forced "to satisfy [the soldiers'] lust" at the comfort station (27), while also referring back to the "black powder" Kim was given "to reduce my bleeding from the vagina" (26). The manager's explanation that the concoction was derived "from a leg / of a Chinese soldier's corpse" becomes the source of ongoing nightmares:

> I dream of human legs rolling around   I dream it
>   to this day. (26)

What was grotesquely supposed to serve as a remedy for Kim's rape-induced injuries, the Chinese limb ground into black powder, resurfaces as the traumatic image that continues to permeate her dreams. Yoon's concluding rhetorical flourish—"legs that could not go anywhere"—again suggests a sense of suspension, the previously wished-for "suicide" unattained, the present haunted by dreams of severed legs rendered immobile.

By de-emphasizing the public's "intense focus on the repetitive sexual acts and abuses" (Choi x) in "comfort women" discourse while lingering on the painful effects of the survivors' past in the present, Yoon's testimony poems remember and rearticulate the testimonial archive during a moment when a formal apology and state-sponsored compensation from Japan have yet to be given. Rather than allow the survivors' narratives to remain buried in out-of-print anthologies and largely forgotten in the transnational public sphere, Yoon's documental poetics reactivates the archive and "function[s] as a counterhegemonic, unofficial, and demotic practice that authenticates marginalized experiences at the fringes of our cultural memory" (Leong 4). Such a practice of "citation" and "re-citation" (7) retrieves the experiences of "comfort women" from both historical amnesia and political denigration, addressing "the fundamental predicament that cultural memory is finite and that past documents are in constant need of recovery" (25).

In recovering and transforming the former "comfort women's" stories, Yoon's archival poetics refuses to "defer[ ] justice to some unknown future activation of records" (Caswell 38) and functions, I am suggesting, as an interim mode of literary justice that is distinct from both Japanese state reparations (that have been withheld) and the political activism of the redress movement (that is ongoing). This "unofficial" mode of recognition may be discerned in Yoon's effort at *constructing* rather than simply *claiming* kinship across "temporal and geographical lines." Ethically, this process occurs through Yoon's acknowledgment of the oral history projects, and thus the survivors' prior speech, that have made possible her testimony poems. By literally prioritizing that archive as their foundation, Yoon avoids "figuring the 'comfort women' as voiceless and as needing to be given a voice" (Kang 31).

Formally, the process of recognition that these poems undertake by revoicing the archive becomes evident through a palimpsestic layering of genres. Titling the poems with survivors' proper names announces, in dramatic monologue fashion, that the "I" is not to be conflated with the poet's persona as is customary with first-person lyrics. And yet, the formal revisions manifested on the page simultaneously make present the poet's "voice," as it were, instantiating Yoon's aspiration to "speak these women's stories." The formal manipulations reveal the poems' status as "actively mediated affiliations" that "resist[ ] the neat alignment of identity between" Yoon and the survivors (Kang 32). Avoiding a suspect mode of solidarity that rests on identification ("I am ___"; "We are all ___"), Yoon's poems speak *with* them (affiliation) rather than *for* them (appropriation) through the "stylistic eccentricities" of her poetic techniques (Kang 32).

The unresolved endings of Yoon's testimony poems, in particular, recognize and honor the women's precarity and resilience in the present. The impossibilities of forgetting, forgiving, or finding solace, the hauntings of corpses and limbs that torment the living—these are not conditions that can easily be redressed by "official" government reparations. But they can be evoked through the formal possibilities of "documental" poetry. Rather than emphasize the factual, evidentiary elements of the testimonies—especially the repetitive brutalities of imperial sexual violence—Yoon's elliptical, condensed, fractured, open-ended poems reimagine the archive by gesturing toward the unsaid, the implicit, and the durational that cannot be captured in the standardized "ur-story" of the "comfort woman" narrative, thereby pursuing an ethics of recognition that seeks to do poetic justice to the survivors' present subjectivities.

Works Cited

Caswell, Michelle. *Urgent Archives: Enacting Liberatory Memory Work.* Routledge, 2021.

Cheng, Jennifer S. "Erasure Poetry: A Revealing (i)." *Jacket2,* 1 Sept. 2016, https://jacket2.org/commentary/erasure-poetry-revealing-i. Accessed 9 Jan. 2024.

Choi, Chungmoo. "Guest Editor's Introduction." *positions: asia critique,* vol. 5, no. 1, 1997, pp. v–xiv.

Farley, Christopher Joh. "No Man's Land." *Time,* 5 May 1997, p. 101.

Garner, Dwight. "Adopted Voice." *The New York Times,* 5 Sept. 1999, section 7, p. 6.

Kang, Laura Hyun Yi. "Conjuring 'Comfort Women': Mediated Affiliations and Disciplined Subjects in Korean/American Transnationality." *Journal of Asian American Studies,* vol. 6, no. 1, 2003, pp. 25–55.

Kim-Gibson, Dai Sil. *Silence Broken: Korean Comfort Women.* Mid-Prairie Books, 1999.

Leong, Michael. *Contested Records: The Turn to Documents in Contemporary North American Poetry.* University of Iowa Press, 2020.

Min, Pyong Gap. *Korean "Comfort Women": Military Brothels, Brutality, and the Redress Movement.* Rutgers University Press, 2021.

Reinares, Laura Barberán. "Writing Unspeakable Things: Speechlessness, Abjection, and the Ethics/Aesthetics of (Not) Representing Sexual Violence in Three Korean American 'Comfort Women' Novels." *Journal of Asian American Studies,* vol. 24, no. 3, 2021, pp. 383–416.

Schaffer, Kay, and Sidonie Smith. *Human Rights and Narrated Lives: The Ethics of Recognition.* Palgrave Macmillan, 2004.

Schellstede, Sangmie Choi, editor. *Comfort Women Speak: Testimony by Sex Slaves of the Japanese Military.* Holmes & Meier, 2000.

Soh, C. Sarah. *The Comfort Women: Sexual Violence and Postcolonial Memory in Korea and Japan.* University of Chicago Press, 2008.

Son, Elizabeth W. *Embodied Reckonings: "Comfort Women," Performance, and Transpacific Redress.* University of Michigan Press, 2018.

Stetz, Margaret D. "Representing 'Comfort Women': Activism Through Law and Art." *Iris,* no. 45, 2002, pp. 26–29, 83–84.

Yoon, Emily Jungmin. *A Cruelty Special to Our Species.* Ecco, 2018.

Yoshimi, Yoshiaki. *Comfort Women: Sexual Slavery in the Japanese Military During World War II.* Translated by Suzanne O'Brien, Columbia University Press, 2000.

CHAPTER 3

Marginalia

IÑAKI BONILLAS

For this project, I worked only with photography books from my own library, in order to extract image fragments from them that allowed me to compose a collage that deals with a distinctive aspect of the life of photographic images in books: portraits of people on the move.

I have always been intrigued by the peculiarity of the paths, almost always white, that form around images in books. And here the equation was inverted so that the margins were the axis of the composition, and the photographic bits produced a random micronarrative around the labyrinth-like white trails that lead us from the Azteca Stadium in Mexico City to the streets of Rio de Janeiro in Brazil, passing through New York and Amsterdam, making a brief pause at the Houston airport, to continue the route on the way to Florence and Rome.

Follow the path, dear reader, that I propose throughout several pages of this publication, as if it were one of those old printed road maps, and approach the photographic act, but from the edges, moving away from the heart of the images to observe them obliquely.

FIGURE 3.1. (*following*) Marginalia, 2019. This work was part of a 2019 solo exhibition at kurimanzutto and was included in MoMA's online exhibition *Companion Pieces: New Photography 2020*. Used with permission from the artist.

CHAPTER 4

Caring, Keeping, and Kinship-Making

Unaffiliated Ancestors in the Space of the Archive

MELISSA ANNE-MARIE CURLEY

Recalling her work in the archives of San Francisco's GLBT Historical Society, Marika Cifor describes the startling experience of encountering human remains in the records: blood, hair, "bodily traces, fragments, and fluids" (33). Even when these remains belonged to people who were themselves long dead, Cifor discovered them "as lively" (33): "I propose," she writes, "that these traces of bodily matter are themselves animate, imbued in a new way with a kind of vitality or liveliness" (35). Focusing particularly on what it means to keep and care for the unaffiliated dead, this chapter tries to take the liveliness of bodily remains seriously.

What do I mean when I say "take seriously"? I mean recognizing the continuity between the living person and the traces of bodily matter that person leaves behind after death, and so recognizing a continuity between the life of the person and the liveliness of their remains. In other words, I mean understanding bodily remains not merely as matter that has a new kind of vitality all its own but as the persistent presence of a living person. We might pay attention here to a distinction suggested by Amber Aranui and Te Arikirangi Mamaku: Bodily remains are not (only) sacred objects but (also) Ancestors (94, 100). When we recognize bodily remains as persons or ancestors, we recognize them also as possessed of interests and capable of making demands—as having "power and agency in the present" (Supernant 269). In my own field of religious studies, this agency is sometimes understood in terms of boons and curses: the ways that ancestors and other such persons exercise their power in ways that help or harm, responsive always to how they are or are not being appropriately cared for.

Within rituals of memorialization, ancestors and other such persons may be cared for both by being called forth into the social world of their descendants and by being allowed to rest undisturbed. The idea of rousing the ancestors as an essential form of care resonates with critiques of norms around the collection of bodily remains that make "the museum a permanent warehouse of the dead" (Colwell and Nash 81), and more broadly with calls for what Michelle Caswell calls a "liberatory activation of records" (22). This chapter argues that allowing the ancestors to rest also constitutes an essential form of care, and that it is therefore worth thinking through how this might involve ritualized kinds of forgetting and leaving be that can be meaningfully distinguished from mere neglect.

With this focus in mind, the chapter takes up some contemporary efforts to care for the remains of the unaffiliated dead. The first part of the chapter describes a Japanese Buddhist memorial strategy for managing the remains of the ritually unclaimed dead, describing how this ritual—uncommon but effective—recasts the ossuary as an archive and turns lonely ghosts into public ancestors. The second part of the chapter considers an effort to care for ritually unclaimed ancestors in North America, looking at how this effort likewise involves a willingness to make kin out of strangers, expressed in terms of ritualized rest.

Caring for "Buddhas Without Relations"

A "bone buddha" (*okotsubotoke*) is a statue that commingles the cremated remains of thousands of dead people and incorporates those remains into the image of a buddha or Buddhist divinity. The most famous okotsubotoke in contemporary Japan are held at Isshinji, a Buddhist temple in the southern part of the city of Ōsaka. The first okotsubotoke at Isshinji was made in 1887; the fifteenth is set to be installed in 2027. Isshinji's okotsubotoke are cast out of ashes mixed with plant resin. Each statue incorporates the remains of anywhere between 120,000 and 220,000 people. The ashes included in the statue are given to the temple with the explicit understanding that they will be used in this way; the temple charges a small fee for this service. Isshinji is historically associated with Pure Land Buddhism, a mode of Buddhist practice oriented toward Amida Buddha, the buddha of infinite life; the okotsubotoke at Isshinji are cast in the image of Amida Buddha. The statues are arranged in an open hall at the heart of the temple complex, where visitors—sightseers as well as the personally bereaved—can offer prayers, incense, and votive offerings throughout the day. Makimura Hisako understands Isshinji's okotsubotoke hall as an example of the "communal urban graveyard," a burial strategy wherein individuals are interred together without regard to the family ties that have normatively organized graveyards in Japan (and elsewhere) (109). I want to suggest that the okotsubotoke work by both condensing and expanding the ritual logic of normative memorialization practices, and in this way they tell us something about archives.

Normative memorialization practices in Japan have two objectives.[1] On the one hand, they seek to integrate the deceased person into the sacred family of buddhas and bodhisattvas so that the deceased can enjoy a peaceful afterlife. On the other hand, they seek to re-establish the family relationships disrupted by the event of death, reintegrating the deceased into the ongoing life of the family as benevolent, boon-granting ancestors. In order to manage this complex transformation or rebirth—referred to as "becoming a buddha" (*jōbutsu*)—the family provides the deceased with a surrogate body (cf. Stephenson) in the form of the cremated bones or some portion thereof organized and placed in a reliquary urn, mimicking a fetus in a womb. Along with an *ihai* (a mortuary tablet with the posthumous name of the deceased written on it) and an *iei* (a memorial photograph of the deceased), the urn is brought into the household and attended to by the family for a period of forty-nine days—the length of time it is understood to take a spirit to travel from the world of the living to the world of the dead. At the end of that forty-nine-day period—when the temporary surrogate body has served its purpose—the urn is taken to the graveyard and interred in a family grave. The ihai and iei, however, remain in the household, placed in or next to the family's Buddhist altar, where the deceased can be engaged in conversation, given offerings of the things they particularly enjoyed in life, and participate in the life of the family as they learn how to be an ancestral spirit. The mortuary tablet and memorial photograph are, in principle, "retired" as part of a memorial service that takes place thirty-three years, fifty years, or one hundred years after death; at this time, they too are removed from the altar, deconsecrated, and taken to the temple to be ritually discarded. The deceased person is from this point on memorialized in perpetuity as one of the household's nameless tutelary ancestors, understood as collectively available both through the household altar and at the family grave.

1. On Japanese burial and memorialization practices, see the essential volume *Death and the Afterlife in Japanese Buddhism*, edited by Stone and Walter.

Memorialization of this kind involves remembering, but it also involves—indeed, requires—some ritualized forgetting. The remains of the deceased person's material body, which constitute one site at which their spirit might linger, have to be allowed to lose their specificity, merging with the material remains of all the other family members in the family grave and with the earth itself. The deceased person's name and image, which constitute a second site at which their spirit might linger, likewise have to lose their meaning, slipping out of personal memory. This ritualized forgetting serves the interests of the deceased person—it is what makes it possible for the dead to be fully released from the life they lived, and so it is what makes it possible for them to enjoy the peace of the afterlife. And this in turn serves the interests of the living: Because they are at peace, it is safe for them to be activated—to come back into this world, occasionally—as boon-granting ancestors.

In the absence of kin able to take on these rituals, the deceased person becomes instead a *muenbotoke*: "a buddha without relations." In this context, "buddha" is a euphemism—muenbotoke are not buddhas at all but lonely, unhappy ghosts, permanently trapped between this world and the next. Muenbotoke are traditionally imagined as having limited but meaningful agency—they make claims on the living by haunting them. In a secular framework, they might haunt us in a different way, as figural representations of what it is like to grow old and die in an increasingly atomized, deracinated society. The bone buddhas solve a practical problem by providing a place to deposit the material remains of those for whom burial in a family grave is not possible—first inside the temple and ultimately inside the statue. But they also solve a spiritual problem by providing a surrogate body that immediately and concretely effects the transformation of the deceased person's body into the body of a buddha. As surrogate bodies, the okotsubotoke make visible the same kind of transformation hoped for in normative memorial ritual: In a religious context in which sacred images are not just representations but living presences, we can be sure the deceased person has become a buddha because we can see it with our own eyes. At the same time, the okotsubotoke both condense and amplify the process of entering into the kind of collective presence that characterizes household ancestors.

The loss of corporeal individuality that happens slowly in the family grave over the course of many years happens swiftly and decisively at Isshinji, where the remains of tens of thousands of people together are mixed together. This dizzying massification is not something the temple tries to conceal—on the contrary, it is something the temple emphasizes as a significant and compelling feature of the okotsubotoke. And it runs in parallel with an immediate effacing of individual names and faces. The names of those persons incorporated into the statues are known to the temple, but they are not made known to visitors to the temple. This effacing of individual names and faces is part of why the statues work, ritually speaking: It means that when visitors engage with the statues—whether or not a blood relative is among the hundreds of thousands of people included in a given statue—they are consciously engaging with a collective presence, necessarily mostly strangers in life, offering that collectivity the same gestures of solicitude and care that one might offer one's own kin. In other words, the living agree to act as if the dead are their own ancestors. This is how the okotsubotoke pacify potentially dangerous muenbotoke: They create a context in which individuals without a familial kinship network can be knit directly into the larger and longer-lasting set of affiliations that has the temple as its center. This allows these spirits to rest and be cared for rather than to wander. At the same time, from within this state of peaceful rest, these spirits are alive in this world as agents of the Buddha of Infinite Life, making use of a vitality understood to persist within human remains. In other words, the dead agree to act as if the living are their own descendants.

It is in this way that the okotsubotoke function as an archive rather than an ossuary. Each statue gathers together the hundreds of thousands of people contained within it, affording them a surrogate body that has more permanence both concretely (because this body is closer to stone than flesh) and conceptually (because it is an instantiation of the limitlessly vast body of the buddha of infinite life). In being afforded this surrogate body, the individuals within it become available to the public, as public rather than private beings (cf. Derrida 10): available in the sense that strangers are called upon to care for them, and in the sense that they may be called upon to care for strangers. As a memorial strategy, the okotsubotoke thus generate something like what Alison Landsberg calls "prosthetic memories": memories that "are not natural, not the possession of a single individual," but which instead "conjure up a more public past" (149). Prosthetic memories are not our own; they come to us in mediated ways. But in that mediated encounter, they register on our bodies, and so they register for us as real. It is for this reason, Landsberg proposes, that prosthetic memories can be useful: "because they feel real they help to condition how an individual thinks about the world, and might be instrumental in generating empathy and articulating an ethical relation to the other" (149). Japanese Buddhism is oriented toward a particular articulation of such an ethical relation, grounded in an understanding that all beings exist in mutual dependence upon each other. An ethical relation to the other is one in which I feel the suffering of others as in some sense my own, and so one in which I take on the work of alleviating the suffering of others as my own urgent responsibility. Within this philosophical framework, by creating conditions in which we treat other people's relatives as though they were our own, the okotsubotoke open up a space in which we can practice an ethical relation to other beings. To the extent that we can understand the people interred in the statues as having real presence, we can understand this as alleviating their real suffering. But this is not a one-sided relationship. Contemporary urban life is for many people one in which the kinship bonds that define us are weak or strained—one in which we too are *muen*. By creating a framework in which we can care for others, the okotsubotoke also open up a space in which we can practice making kin and imagine being cared for as kin ourselves.

Caring for Other People's Ancestors

In settler colonial contexts, the bodies encountered in archives are almost always the unethically obtained bodies of colonized and subaltern people (Black and McCavitt 116). These are people that have been stolen from their proper resting places or denied a proper resting place, and sold, traded, or "donated" without the consent or authorization of their relatives and descendants. Within these kinds of memory institutions, these captive bodies are sometimes subject to careless treatment causing further injury. Carelessness can take the form of neglect and indifference. Lucy Bell describes finding Indigenous ancestors kept in museum archives "in all sorts of ways, from plastic bags to paper lunch bags," in bubble wrap, and in pill bottles, "stored as a mishmash" (Bell et al. 132); Maya Kassutto reports that remains believed to be those of Katricia Tree Dotson Africa and Delisha Orr Africa, children killed by the Philadelphia Police Department in the 1985 MOVE bombing, were retained by the University of Pennsylvania Museum of Archaeology and Anthropology and stored "in a cardboard box on a shelf." At the Denver Museum of Nature & Science, the remains of unaffiliated ancestors "sat on the museum's shelves for decades unvisited, unstudied, untouched" (Colwell and Nash 82). But carelessness can also appear as continued activation in the form of extraction and commodification. Material remains are broken up, damaged, and destroyed by researchers using techniques for carbon dating and DNA extraction. The bodies of Tree and Delisha Africa were used as instructional material for teaching forensic anthropology without acknowledging their lives, or even their names: a child turned "into a bare bone, ready to be objectified and used as data" (Clarke). Bodies are exhibited as entertainment or spectacle, in ways that reduce them to the status of specimen (Stephenson 16) or humiliate them—Ksenia Pimenova notes, for example, that the mummified body of a woman taken from the permafrost in the Altai Republic was displayed naked in a Russian museum in a way that caused even members of the museum staff to feel embarrassed (170).

Given all this carelessness, we might wonder if it is possible to properly care for ancestors within the space of the memory institution. Reflecting on the collection of unethically obtained human skulls held for decades by the University of Pennsylvania museum, writer and organizer aAliy A. Muhammad suggests that "the same institution that has been holding and exerting control for years over these captive ancestors is not the same institution that can give them ceremony" (Brewer). When ancestors are identifiable and affiliated with living descendants, it may be possible for them to be liberated from the archive, repatriated, reburied, and given ceremony—knitting back together a kinship network ruptured by their long years in captivity. Bringing the ancestors home is understood as a duty of care the living owe the dead; some museum professionals take the view that it is likewise a duty of care museums owe to the ancestors and their communities of origin (Aranui and Mamaku; Colwell and Nash). But what happens when kin cannot or will not offer ceremony?

This was the situation that arose when the touring exhibition *The Mysterious Bog People* came to the Canadian Museum of History (then the Canadian Museum of Civilization) in 2002. The exhibition included seven human bodies removed from peat bogs in northern Europe. Conditions in the bogs were such that the bodies had been mummified. In its stops at European institutions, the exhibition aroused no controversy, but ahead of its arrival in Ottawa-Gatineau, First Nations community members approached the museum with objections to the idea of putting the seven bog people—ancestors of "people associated with contemporary white Canadians"—on display (Gill-Frerking 73). CMH curator and exhibition coordinator David Morrison would later attribute this to cultural difference: "Europeans are comfortable with human remains. We have been putting them in reliquaries inside altars for 2,000 years. But aboriginal people are very sensitive about them, and so are some people in the larger community" (Conlogue). We might raise some objections here. It is not the case that in Europe it was commonplace to display the enfleshed bodies of the ordinary beloved dead—glass display cases are not reliquaries, and the bog people are not framed in the context of the exhibition as sacred bodies, commanding a special kind of respect. The suggestion that objections to the exhibition are a matter of some people being "comfortable" and others "very sensitive" positions these objections as fundamentally aesthetic rather than ethical. And the implication that First Nations people are not "comfortable with human remains" because they do not share a particular cultural history of putting them on display occludes the centuries-long history of museums stealing the bodies of Indigenous ancestors and putting them on display without the consent of either the living or the dead. When the bog people came to Canada, they became entangled in this history.

This was reflected in the way that the bog people's temporary dwelling space in the museum was eventually organized. The CMH invited First Nations ritual specialists to conduct a smudging ceremony, burning sweetgrass to purify the space and the people in it before the exhibition opened, and to request the forgiveness and guidance of the spirits (Gill-Frerking 73). The museum agreed that the bodies would be exhibited during the day but covered at night so that they could rest (Bruchac 345). And a Mi'kmaq elder who also worked on the museum's curatorial staff consented to "take responsibility for caring for these Dutch ancestral remains while they were at the museum" (Bruchac 345). These strategies reflect those developed in museum spaces to make them more hospitable to ancestors: on the one hand, holding open time and space for ancestors to receive visitors who offer them ceremony, song and music, formal greetings, and other kinds of direct address (rather than only spectators); on the other hand, holding open time and space for ancestors to rest quietly. These kinds of "Keeping Spaces" are designed to offer "better physical and spiritual care to the Ancestors" (Meloche et al. 7; Bell et al. 132). Where it has not yet been made possible to repatriate and rebury the ancestors, Keeping Spaces create a space inside the museum that is quiet like an archive without being a storage—recognizing the archive as a possible home, they nonetheless resist the archive's tendency toward house arrest (Derrida 10).

Framing the CMH case in terms of "the respect shown to the Indigenous Canadians who were . . . looking to care for European ancestral remains," Heather Gill-Frerking suggests that we find in it "a good example of how curators can meet the needs of communities in a respectful and ethical manner" (73). When we take the vitality of bodies in the archives seriously, however, it becomes less obvious that the First Nations people involved were expressing "needs" of their own. We might suggest instead that they extended themselves to address the needs of other people's ancestors, when those people's descendants were unable to do so. In this way, they were speaking to the questions storyteller and archaeologist Margaret M. Bruchac recalls asking herself when encountering a bog body on display in the Drents Museum: "Which neighbors were now asking after *her* well-being? Who was there to claim her, to lay her in a more peaceful place, away from the staring eyes of strangers?" (345).

For First Nations people in Canada, extending themselves this way for the bog people was not without epistemological risk—as Chip Colwell, Rachel

Maxson, and Jami Powell observe in a somewhat different context, Indigenous communities may hesitate to be perceived as "'taking' others' relatives," repeating the theft that led to these ancestors finding themselves in the museum in the first place (Colwell-Chanthaphonh et al. 32). Nonetheless, in the case of the bog people, as in other cases, Indigenous communities have taken on the responsibility of caring for other people's ancestors in circumstances in which kin capable of recognizing the need for ceremony proved difficult to find. This creates conditions in which those ancestors receive care and hospitality—in which they are recognized as persons. And it creates conditions in which the living descendants of those ancestors might at least potentially recognize those ancestors as such—that is, as agents capable of having interests and making demands, to whom the living bear some responsibility. Here too, then, ritual creates conditions in which one might practice an ethical relation to other beings. These are conditions in which one might meet one's relatives.

Conclusion

This chapter has described one case in which the ritual space of the ossuary becomes something more like an archive, in that it enables the production of prosthetic memory. And it has described one case in which the museal space, as a space where archival objects are put on display, becomes something more like the ritual space of the ossuary, in that it allows the dead to rest away from prying eyes. It has suggested that these shifts in both cases make it possible to counter estrangement, engaging with the dead as if they were our own ancestors. It has proposed that this act of imagination is a way of practicing kinship, both in the sense of actually caring for the dead and in the sense of learning how better to care for the dead.

When Colwell and Nash criticize the use of the museum as a "warehouse of the dead," they invoke a particular understanding of the archive as a space for storing objects; a sense that this is wrong—that bodily remains should be understood as more like subjects than as objects—is evident in their description of remains as having been left "unvisited" for years. One approach to addressing this wrong is to take the dead out of the archive and bring them back home, to a place where they can live with their kin. As Colwell and colleagues show us, a kind of repatriation is possible for the unaffiliated dead too, when there is a community willing to bear the responsibility of offering ceremony. But workers within the memory institution may also attempt to care for the unaffiliated dead within the walls of the archive. This can look like advancing disciplinary practices: individuating remains, improving physical care, and improving documentation (Hayflick and Robbins). To the extent that such disciplinary practices are bound up with disciplinary approaches to knowledge that render some human subjects "objects of science," however, they may yet remain entangled with "the disaggregation of the corpse from any sense of personhood or social relations" (Clarke).

The two cases we have considered here point to another form that care can take: not neglect but permitting the dead to rest a little. If strategies for activating the archive allow the dead to receive visitors, strategies for quieting the archive allow the dead to have their privacy—to be less than fully known. Not at odds with the activating strategies that allow the living to make kin with the unaffiliated dead, these moments of withdrawal or refusal may be understood as affirming the personhood of the dead who have to make their homes in the archive.

Works Cited

Aranui, Amber, and Te Arikirangi Mamaku. "The Importance of Kaitiakitanga (Guardianship and Care) and Rangahau (Research) for the Karanga Aotearoa Repatriation Programme." Meloche et al., pp. 91–102.

Bell, Lucy, et al. "Caring for the Ancestors at the Royal BC Museum." Meloche et al., pp. 127–35.

Black, Wendy, and Keely McCavitt. "The Southern African Human Remains Management Project: Making (P)reparations in Year One." Meloche et al., pp. 115–26.

Brewer, Graham Lee. "Penn Museum Buries the Bones of 19 Black Philadelphians, Causing a Dispute with Community Members." *NBC 10 Philadelphia,* 3 Feb. 2024, https://www.nbcphiladelphia.com/news/local/penn-museum-buries-the-bones-of-19-black-philadelphians-causing-a-dispute-with-community-members/3765737/.

Bruchac, Margaret M. "Indigenous Journeys: Splinterville, Drenthe, Amherst." *Indigenous Archaeologies: A Reader on Decolonization,* edited by Margaret M. Bruchac et al., Routledge, 2016, pp. 343–46.

Caswell, Michelle. *Urgent Archives: Enacting Liberatory Memory Work.* Routledge, 2021.

Cifor, Marika. "Stains and Remains: Liveliness, Materiality, and the Archival Lives of Queer Bodies." *Archives and New Modes of Feminist Research,* edited by Maryanne Dever, Routledge, 2019, pp. 32–56.

Clarke, Kamari Maxine. "The Geopolitics of Black Bones That Matter." *American Anthropologist,* 4 Aug. 2022, https://www.americananthropologist.org/geopolitical-lives/clarke.

Colwell, Chip, and Stephen E. Nash. "Why We Repatriate: On the Long Arc Toward Justice at the Denver Museum of Nature & Science." Meloche et al., pp. 79–90.

Colwell-Chanthaphonh, Chip, et al. "The Repatriation of Culturally Unidentifiable Human Remains." *Museum Management and Curatorship,* vol. 26, 2011, pp. 27–43.

Conlogue, Ray. "A Time Trip for the Ages." *Globe and Mail,* 18 Dec. 2002, https://www.theglobeandmail.com/arts/a-time-trip-for-the-ages/article1029077/.

Derrida, Jacques. "Archive Fever: A Freudian Impression." Translated by Eric Prenowitz. *Diacritics,* vol. 25, no. 2, 1995, pp. 9–63.

Gill-Frerking, Heather. "Showing Respect to the Dead: The Ethics of Studying, Displaying, and Repatriating Mummified Remains." *The Handbook of Mummy Studies: New Frontiers in Scientific and Cultural Perspectives,* edited by Dong Hoon Shin and Raffaella Bianucci, Springer, 2021, pp. 59–88.

Hayflick, Emily, and Helen A. Robbins. "Toward a Twenty-First-Century Model for the Collaborative Care and Curation of Human Remains." Meloche et al., pp. 103–14.

Kassutto, Maya. "Remains of Children Killed in MOVE Bombing Sat in a Box at Penn Museum for Decades." *Billy Penn at WHYY,* 4 Apr. 2021, https://billypenn.com/2021/04/21/move-bombing-penn-museum-bones-remains-princeton-africa/.

Landsberg, Alison. *Prosthetic Memory: The Transformation of American Remembrance in the Age of Mass Culture.* Columbia University Press, 2004.

Makimura Hisako. "The Creation of 'Communal Urban Graveyards' and the Trend Toward Cemeteries That Go Beyond Place Relations and Blood Relations." *Zōen zasshi,* vol. 5, no. 5, 1993, pp. 109–14.

Meloche, Chelsea H., et al. "Introduction: Working Together to Do Better." Meloche et al., pp. 1–17.

Meloche, Chelsea H., et al., editors. *Working with and for Ancestors: Collaboration in the Care and Study of Ancestral Remains.* Routledge, 2021.

Pimenova, Ksenia. "From a Museum of Others to a Museum of Selves: Repatriation, Affective Relations, and Social Values of Archaeological Human Remains." *HAU: Journal of Ethnographic Theory,* vol. 13, no. 1, 2023, pp. 159–78.

Stephenson, Jessica. "The Museum Mannequin as 'Body Without Organs.'" *Mannequins in Museums: Power and Resistance on Display,* edited by Bridget R. Cooks and Jennifer J. Wagelie, Routledge, 2021, pp. 12–27.

Stone, Jacqueline I., and Mariko Namba Walter, editors. *Death and the Afterlife in Japanese Buddhism.* University of Hawai'i Press, 2009.

Supernant, Kisha. "Decolonizing Bioarchaeology? Moving Beyond Collaborative Practice." Meloche et al., pp. 268–80.

CHAPTER 5

Archival Instabilities

From Ephemerality to Newfound Significance

AMY SHUMAN

Archives are both collections and reinventions. As Barbara Kirshenblatt-Gimblett observes in her essay "Anticipatory Heritage," archives and other collections are oriented not only to the past; they also sometimes anticipate their future audiences. Furthermore, in addition to the temporal processes of reassigning value to objects and documents, they can provide new status, for example by giving significance to otherwise ordinary or taken-for-granted cultural objects. My discussion, a comparison of three archives/libraries/collections in the same geographic region, exhibiting the same object in different ways, considers both the collections' temporal orientations and their (re) positioning of value and significance.

Kirshenblatt-Gimblett's essay describes what she calls "collecting the present" ("Anticipatory" 85). She begins with an account of the clandestine archive created by occupants of the Warsaw Ghetto in 1942. She writes, "They were experiencing the present as already historical and anticipating a future they would not live to see" (86). Emanuel Ringelblum, a historian, initiated the Warsaw Ghetto collection process. As it became clear that they would not survive, the Ghetto occupants endeavored to leave behind an archive that would survive them and "'scream their truth to the world' after they perished" (85). Kirshenblatt-Gimblett observes that collecting the present often includes the collection of ephemeral cultural practices (87; Franklin).

In this essay, I turn my attention to a different exercise in "collecting the present," the Museo dei Bozzetti, a museum containing the plaster models (maquettes) used by contemporary artists to create marble sculptures in

Pietrasanta, Italy. I discuss the Museo dei Bozzetti in the context of two other collections/archives that also include plaster model collections in the same region. The Museum of Work and Popular Traditions in Versilia includes plaster models in one of its eleven galleries, a gallery devoted to the production of marble sculpture in the area. The third collection, the *gipsoteca,* is more properly an archive housing the plaster models stored in stone carving studios for use by the artisans in their production of marble sculptures. Although the three collections are in the same geographic area, they are not part of a shared consciousness. Each responds to different needs and imagines a different audience. Each places the model/maquette in a different context of use and value. In all three collections/archives, models are both an integral part of the artistic process and relatively taken for granted as objects. Their display creates a shift in their significance from something that is otherwise left behind to being both notable and valuable.

I draw upon Susan Stewart's *On Longing: Narratives of the Miniature, the Gigantic, the Souvenir, the Collection,* which provides a framework for understanding different kinds of collections. Focusing on the principles of organization used to articulate the collection, she writes,

> It is not sufficient to say that the collection is organized according to time, space or internal qualities of the objects themselves, for each of these parameters is divided in a dialectic of inside and outside, public and private, meaning and exchange value. To arrange the objects according to time is to juxtapose personal time with social time, autobiography with history, and thus to create a fiction of the individual life, a time of the individual subject both transcendent to and parallel to historical time. Similarly, the spatial organization of the collection, left to right, front to back, behind and before, depends upon the creation of an individual perceiving and apprehending the collection with eye and hand. The collection's space must move between the public and the private, between display and hiding. (255)

Of particular relevance to my discussion, Stewart draws on Baudrillard to distinguish between collections and accumulations (153). She writes, "There are two movements to the collection's gesture of standing for the world: first the metonymic displacement of part for whole, item for context; and second, the invention of a classification scheme which will define space and time in such a way that the world is accounted for by the elements of the collection" (162). Each of the three collections/archives of plaster models I discuss depend on different metonymic displacements to assign significance to the models.

The objects in the collections I discuss are all plaster models of sculptures; that is, they are not the sculptures themselves but instead are metonymic displacements that reference, but stand aside from, the actual object, often invisibly. Some are copies, made from the actual object, but many are models, made *before* the actual object was created. I am interested in how these temporal displacements have been used to assign value to the models and the collections. Additionally, to better understand the particular value of these collections in Pietrasanta today, I consider them in the context of the larger "hostility toward [plaster] casts in the 20th century" (Winkler-Horaček, "Destroy" 529).

My larger research project focuses on the production of marble sculpture in the Italian town of Pietrasanta, located at the base of the Carrara marble quarries in Tuscany. Although marble was carved in Carrara in the fifteenth century, large workshops were established later, in the mid-1800s (Paolicchi 331). Pietrasanta and Carrara became centers for the reproduction of classical sculpture in the early 1800s; large studios of hundreds of artisan stone carvers produced sculptures of saints for the cathedrals of South America. As part of the process of reproducing sculpture, the artisans use plaster models or maquettes. When they are copying a famous sculpture, such as Michelangelo's *David,* they make the model directly from the sculpture. When they are making a more pedestrian sculpture, such as a sculpture of an angel for a grave, they begin by making a plaster version. Making a plaster mold is a skill in itself.[1] Plaster molds from the famous sculptures are highly coveted, and in Pietrasanta everyone knows which studio has an original, a mold taken directly from the sculpture rather than a copy of a copy.

When I arrived in Pietrasanta, in 1982, the enterprise of copying saints was on the wane, but dozens of contemporary artists had arrived, beginning in the 1960s, to have their work carved by the artisans (Shuman and McMartin, "Artist-Artisan"; "Folk Economies"; "Tradition"). The artists brought their clay or plaster models with them to be enlarged in stone. The contemporary studios, catering to the artists and the more traditional studios, existed side by side, and several studios carved both saints and contemporary works. A few studios also made (and continue to make) copies of Michelangelo's *David,* Canova's *Three Graces,* or other works by famous sculptors.

Plaster models have been part of marble carving and bronze casting since antiquity in Greek, Roman, and European sculpture production (Frederiksen and Marchand). Peter Rockwell suggests that there is evidence of the use of models in ancient Egypt; Rockwell describes the importance of models for complex architectural building. He writes, "The use of the model for carved

1. See Frederiksen and Marchand's extensive discussion of plaster-mold-making.

sculpture is that rarity in the history of technology, a revolution in technique that can be pinpointed in time. It happened twice, once in late sixth-century BC Greece and again independently in the Renaissance during the fifteenth century" (117). As Rockwell points out, although evidence of the use of models is conclusive, actual models from earlier periods are a rarity. Rockwell notes, "a clay model by Verrocchio survives" (117). In other words, although one might point to the frequent use of models, the models themselves do not exist. Under what conditions, then, are plasters conserved, and how does an archive of plaster models emerge? And furthermore, how does something that is commonplace, but not worthy of collection, become valued? Does this revaluing shift its position in history and/or its use value in the present?

The nineteenth century has been referred to as "the century of the cast and, in some cases, such as Germany, to the birth of the museum" (Winkler-Horaček, "Destroy" 530). In the nineteenth century, many museums displayed plaster casts as educational tools intended to show "the glories of the ancients from which they could learn and to which they could aspire" (National Gallery of Ireland). The Victoria and Albert Museum describes its collection similarly:

> The cast collection is a dramatic expression of Victorian ambition, and the strongest embodiment of the Museum's founding mission as a school of art education for both practitioners and the public. At a time when travel was difficult, the Courts brought copies of art and architecture from around the globe together under one roof, offering an encyclopaedia of international decorative styles. Collecting reproductions reached the height of popularity in the mid to late 19th century, and today new methods of digital replication encourage ongoing explorations into copying in the 21st century.

Even a travel website, *Atlas Obscura,* claims significance for the plaster archives, in this case a collection that combines these educational models, cast from completed sculptures, and plaster models used in the production of sculpture.

> The Gipsoteca Bartolini (Hall of Models) is a unique space where the museum's origins as a teaching gallery are on display. The Accademia Gallery was first created for students of the art academy next door to study the works of great artists. One of these greats was the 19th-century sculptor and academy professor Lorenzo Bartolini. The Gipsoteca, a loose recreation of his studio, holds a collection of more than 250 plaster models of Bartolini's sculptures, as well as those of his protégé, Pampaloni. Busts line the shelves of the plaster gallery, which displays models of prominent Italian figures such as

FIGURE 5.1. Gipsoteca at Studio Cervietti, 2006. Photo courtesy of Keara McMartin.

> Machiavelli and Brunelleschi, and casts of some of Bartolini's most famous works. The plasters were made of clay, treated with patina. Many appear speckled with dark spots where nails were used as reference points for transferring the cast to the marble block. Sometimes the plaster cast is accompanied by a photo of the finished piece, giving a fascinating, if slightly creepy, glimpse into the careful craft of building models for the era's elegant marble sculptures. (Neal)

Most of the plasters in collections referenced above were replicas, copies of completed marble sculptures.[2] By contrast, in Pietrasanta, plaster models are used in the production of marble sculptures (see figure 5.1). In Pietrasanta, the past is literally archived in plaster collections, called *gipsotecas* from the Italian word for plaster, *gipso*. Many studios in Pietrasanta continue to house such libraries/archives. They are not public spaces but rather occupy the attic of a studio, often accessible only by rickety ladders. One of the gipsotecas, owned by the Cervietti family, has the only original plaster cast of Michelangelo's *David* in Pietrasanta. An original is a first-generation casting, taken from the

2. See Annetta Alexandridis and Lorenz Winkler-Horaček's discussion of the terms replica and copy with regard to plaster casts (13).

original marble. Cervietti's gipsoteca also has first-generation Canova sculptures and others.[3]

The complete collapse of time and place in the gipsoteca is remarkable; for example, a plaster for a Botero is stored next to a Garibaldi, a Giambologna sits next to a bust of Ronald Reagan. A gipsoteca is an archive or library, not a museum. Like any archive or library, the gipsoteca carries history, in this case the history of the work done in Pietrasanta, where plasters of angels are stored comfortably next to plasters from famous works of art. The gipsoteca represents a tangible, nonchronological, history; it is a record of work done and does not make distinctions based on how the work was appreciated or used. The model/maquette is a tool, one of many tools used in the process of making sculpture. As such, the model/maquette by itself has little value. It is *stored* rather than *displayed,* and even if the models are no longer used, the principles of organization are designed to optimize use. The gipsoteca is not organized according to aesthetic principles of display. As a library, the gipsoteca is organized according to principles of access.

Although the gipsoteca is a well-defined category as a collection, it is never complete because there will always be additions, for example, new busts of politicians. The elements in the collection are supposedly singular; one would not need duplication. At the same time, to an outsider, the saints are similar enough to appear to be repetitive. When asked, the artisans point to the different gestures, nods of the head, or what the saint is holding—each saint is known for some particular, easily identifiable, visible object. The plasters, many of them, represent saints, and the saints are associated with particular narratives. But in the gipsoteca, the gestures represent not those narratives but instead the possibilities of the figurative sculpture. The principles of organization are different in the gipsoteca from, for example, in the church where the marble versions, the completed sculptures, are displayed. The gipsoteca represents a different principle of organization and thus a different history and a different memory, one closely attached to the artisans' embodied knowledge.

The gipsoteca makes the history of the community materially present through its display of different styles of carving. Each saint's hair, the clothing on the busts of the politicians, the chisel marks on the skin represent the historical knowledge of the artisans. The history of the community is materially present in this embodied knowledge, in the artisans' training and expertise in how to use particular tools to achieve particular effects. The artisans' knowledge includes differentiations between hair or silk carved according to

3. The gipsoteca at studio Franco Cervietti is the most extensive in the area and is included in the studio's website, https://www.cervietti.com.

Classical Renaissance, or nineteenth-century Romantic styles. In his book on stone carving based on observations of the Italian artisans, Peter Rockwell wrote, "There are recognizable differences between the methods of roughing a statue, for instance, and carving a molding. There are also differences that are much more difficult to recognize among the various methods for roughing a statue. Our problem in analyzing technology is that it is precisely these minor variations that are so important" (80).

The gipsoteca is a storehouse for embodied knowledge, but it is a kind of knowledge only available to an artisan who knows how to read the salient differences evident in the plasters and to transfer or translate that knowledge into marble.

By contrast, the plasters displayed at the Museum of Work and Popular Traditions of Versilia are part of a museum display, arranged for educational rather than work purposes. The museum occupies one floor of what was once a Medici palace and contains eleven galleries dedicated to agriculture, domestic life, and other categories, including both the excavation of marble and marble carving. The marble-carving gallery description points to the history and ongoing significance of marble production in the area:

> The efforts of Michelangelo Buonarroti to open up the quarries near Seravezza between 1518–1520 were carried out by Cosimo I de' Medici and by his successor Francesco I. However, it was only after 1820 that quarrying and working the marble became the main economic resource in Versilia, employing over two thousand people at the beginning of the XXth century. World-wide famous firms, important sculpture workshops have exported their works all over the world. (Museo del Lavoro e Delle Tradizioni Popolari)

The marble gallery displays all the tools used in carving marble, including plaster models. The museum website calls attention to the plaster models with photos of a plaster model of the bust of John Fitzgerald Kennedy and the figure of an angel, among others. Unlike the gipsoteca, the models/maquettes in the Museum of Work and Popular Traditions are not meant for use. To the contrary, they are displayed as historical objects, referencing the past. Ironically, until recently, just out the window of the gallery, thirty yards away, one could see a marble studio where very similar maquettes were being used to carve saints. That studio has since closed, though others exist in the area. Despite acknowledging the ongoing importance of the traditions of marble carving, the Museum of Work and Popular Traditions presents the past as past and grants value to plaster models as relics of that past.

The plasters displayed in the Museum of Work and Traditions document what are marked as traditional artisan marble-carving practices. Although they are visually prominent, the plasters are not more significant than any other carving tools represented in the exhibit. The use of plaster casts to copy saints or make other sculptures is taken for granted. However, the use of the same process in the production of contemporary sculpture is often startling to outsiders who have visions of sculptors carving directly into the marble, without the use of a plaster model. Even more startling is the fact that many artists today bring their clay models to artisans who carve them in marble. These clay models, part of the taken-for-granted process of carving marble, are on display in the Museo dei Bozzetti, where they have gained a new significance.

In contrast to the Museum of Work and Popular Traditions, the Museo dei Bozzetti is an example of what Kirshenblatt-Gimblett calls "collecting the present." In 1963 Erminio Cidonio, director of Henraux, a major stone studio, invited many of the most well-known sculptors in the world to come to bring their maquettes to Henraux, where artisans would enact them in marble. Henry Moore, Hans Arp, Henri Georges Adam, Isamu Noguchi, Francois Stahly, Emile Gilioli, Georges Vantongerloo, and others came, and many developed long-standing relationships with artisans who carved their work (Shuman and McMartin, "Artist-Artisan"). In 1982 Jette Muhlendorf, a Danish photographer, journalist, and art critic who lived in Pietrasanta, created an exhibition called *The Past and the Presence: For a Museum of Maquettes* (Il Passato el La Presenza: Per un Museo dei Bozzetti) including both maquettes and photographs by the prominent artists and others for display in the cloisters at the center of town. Her idea was to document the ongoing and explosive presence of contemporary artists who came to Pietrasanta to carve marble or give their models to artisans who would enact the carvings. As Chiara Celli later wrote in the catalog of the museum, Muhlendorf's idea was that "the maquettes could be a testimony of the presence of sculpture in Pietrasanta" (18). Their models, along with those of the many artists who arrived in Pietrasanta since then, are displayed in the Museo dei Bozzetti.

Displaying the maquettes of contemporary artists was a novel idea. As Claudio Rosati writes in the catalog, "The Museo dei Bozzetti was the first and perhaps the only museum established with the aim of shedding light on the importance of the maquette in the creative process" (8). Rosati notes that Muhlendorf's exhibition calls attention to the maquettes and "makes people discover a good that was under everybody's eyes" (8).

The *Past and the Presence* exhibit did make a claim for a connection between the plaster models of the 1900s displayed in art museums, the plaster models in the gipsotecas, and the artists' models of the second half of the twentieth century. However, it is a tenuous connection, based on the fact that all are collections of plaster models, but the collections had, and have, different purposes, different audiences, and different value.

The display of plaster models, so common in nineteenth-century art museums, was intended to supplement a museum's collection of ancient or classical art. Signaling hierarchies of value, today, when those museums have collections of actual marble sculpture, many have deaccessioned their collections of those plasters (Margolies). For example, the vast collection once exhibited at the Metropolitan Museum of Art now belongs to the Institute of Classical Architecture and Art.[4]

The curators of the Museo dei Bozzetti also note that today, unlike in the 1900s, giving status to maquettes requires an act of imagination. The maquette is an ordinary part of the life of a marble studio; until the creation of the Museo, maquettes had little significance for a public audience beyond the general display of tools, marking the past (as in the Museum of Work and Popular Traditions). To outsiders visiting Pietrasanta, the Museo offers a rare opportunity to see artists' models, the objects touched and shaped by the famous. The museum makes a claim to the local, to the idea that famous artists, from Michelangelo to Moore, are connected to Pietrasanta and its quarries.

The nineteenth-century collections were oriented toward the past; often their value is proclaimed as a teaching opportunity for students interested in sculpture. The gipsoteca is, or was, a working library, oriented toward the future. In his entry in the Museo dei Bozzetti catalog, Sergio Tedeschi writes, "Museo dei Bozzetti has always had its 'eyes' turned to the future. In any case, looking towards the future is just what its collection is about. Structurally in perennial growth, it is dedicated to witnessing the constant arrival of new acquisitions of works and documentation" (16).

The primary relationship of the nineteenth-century collections was a student learning with the aid of a plaster cast; the primary relationship of the gipsoteca is an artisan and the production of a sculpture; and the primary relationship of the maquettes in the Museo dei Bozzetti is artist and artisan. One could argue, as does Chiara Celli in her catalog entry, that understanding the maquette is a means for understanding an artist's process. She observes, "Maquettes differ greatly in their correspondence to the final sculpture. Some are precise and others generate ideas. . . . At times, the craftsmen who collaborated in the completion of a work left a certain interpretive freedom for enlargement" (24).

---

4. Institute of Classical Architecture and Art, "Plaster Cast Collection," https://www.classicist.org/resources/plaster-cast-collection/.

Conclusion

Each collection sets up different convergences, juxtapositions, and oppositions.[5] First, the three collections (and also the historical collections of plaster models displayed in art museums) suggest several instabilities. In one collection, the maquette is a historical tool no longer used; in another, it is a part of the ongoing production process; and in the third, a large collection of maquettes is worthy of a museum of its own. Additionally, the relationship between the model and the sculpture potentially destabilizes the status of copies and originals. One might argue, in the case of the maquettes in the Museo dei Bozzetti, that the models *are* originals, bearing the marks of the artist's hands, though they are not, yet, works of art. Whether as not yet realized works of art or as copies of existing works of art, the plaster models hold unstable value. They are only valuable, in the case of the gipsoteca, as tools, or perhaps as a material account of artisan traditions. Although the placement of the bust of Giambologna next to the bust of Ronald Reagan in the gipsoteca is a kind of temporal instability, the larger temporal instability is that chronology is not significant in the gipsoteca. Chronology is significant in the Museum of Work and Popular Traditions, but as I noted above, the museum itself betrays a temporal instability by displaying models as if they belong to the past, when, directly outside the museum, they are being used in the present.

In my view, the most interesting instability is not in misplaced temporalities but in the recovery of a relatively unrecognized object as an object of value, worthy of display. Exhibiting plaster models is an act of recovery. The Museo dei Bozzetti elevates the taken-for-granted through collection and preservation. Plaster models were never meant to be displayed; to the contrary, the plaster model becomes inconsequential as soon as the sculpture is made. Each of the collections assigns a different context to the plaster models.

Second, temporally, each of the collections I have discussed assigns models to a different place in the past, with a different purpose in the present, and a different legacy for the future, and in some cases, that past is ongoing and coincides with the present. Once a contemporary purpose is obsolete, for example in the nineteenth-century galleries of plaster models used by students of art, the object has little value. Or, to be more precise, the models need to be repurposed to have value. Repurposing depends on new contexts and new discourses. The Museo dei Bozzetti is exactly that sort of new context.

---

5. See Marie Després-Lonnet and Maryse Rizza's discussion of how the status of an object changes in the process of its documentation.

Importantly, unlike the nineteenth-century collections in art museums, the collection of plasters in the Museo dei Bozzetti depends on its local context.

Third, the collections have different relationships with local contexts and larger-than-local attachments. All archives require attention to local contexts, including the context of the collector, the collection, the cataloger, and the user. Of course, the objects in archives may also have global connections and value, but the local attachment is primary. In Barbara Kirshenblatt-Gimblett's terms, the models in the Museo dei Bozzetti have "value-added" through their attachment to a local context and to the memories of a designated past (*Destination* 151).

Archives also gesture toward the instability of objects in their local contexts, whether through the juxtaposition of objects from different time periods placed together or through the juxtaposition of the past with the present. This instability is explicitly evident in the three different archives in Pietrasanta/Serevezza, all displaying different juxtapositions and different contexts for the plaster models. As part of representing a past way of life, the Museum of Work and Popular Traditions relies on the idea of the handmade, and the display of looms and textile production corresponds to the handmade sculpture. The exhibit does not take up the question of things that continue to be made by hand. Although, of course, hand-weaving continues in the present day, it is not ubiquitous as it once was in the area. By contrast, the same marble tools on display in the museum as representatives of the past are still in use, and at one point, they could be observed in use in a marble studio visible through the window of the museum.

Fourth, the three archives are perhaps most differentiated by the relationships they establish and propose with the hand, the body, and more generally, the sensorium that encompasses bodies and nature. Objects in the Museum of Work and Popular Traditions are made by hand, and in some cases, photographs of the handwork are displayed. Made-by-hand technologies differentiate these objects from the present. In "The Work of Art in the Age of Mechanical Reproduction," Walter Benjamin argues against oversimplifying the distinction between the handmade and the mechanically reproduced. These temporal instabilities are not surprising, but the placement in the archives also grants the objects temporal stability, long-term assignments of meaning.

Fifth, and finally, each of these archives/collections assigns value to plaster models differently. Displaying the ordinary as significant requires a shift in imagination. In the process of granting value to the models/maquettes, otherwise taken-for-granted objects, each of the collections destabilizes the present from the past. In a discussion of "the imagination as a social practice," Arjun

Appadurai suggests that when the past is (falsely) unmoored from the present, it can be open to new configurations, including the rescue of a past signification (4–5). The Museo dei Bozzetti and the gipsoteca might contain similar objects, and to some extent, they can claim similar legacies in a historical past of plaster casts dating to antiquity. This claim to a legacy can be part of the claim to significance. However, the claim to the past, especially antiquity, also betrays several gaps, including the lack of actual continuity with the past and the ephemeral status of plaster models more generally, vulnerable to being overlooked.

Given all these instabilities, the recovery of the plaster model as significant in the Museo dei Bozzetti is all the more remarkable. I suggest that the model's ephemeral status contributes to it being available for recovery. The archivists and curators can make multiple claims for the significance of the plaster; even in its demolition, it acquires significance (Alexandridis and Winkler-Horaček). In positioning the Museo dei Bozzetti models in relation to the nineteenth-century plasters and to the plasters in the gipsoteca, the curators create an imaginary connection with a time in the past when those collections were valued. Although plaster casts were highly valued and were fundamental to many museum collections in the nineteenth century, most of those collections were destroyed in the twentieth century. As Annetta Alexandridis and Lorenz Winkler-Horaček observe in their mammoth edited book, *Destroy the Copy—Plaster Cast Collections in the 19th–20th Centuries,* both the creation and the destruction of plaster collections were complex, involving different purposes and values. As they observe in their introduction, in addition to their use in education and scholarship, "Plaster casts were also instrumental in globalizing knowledge of Western art" (4). Their destruction is variously attributed to a critique of the plasters as copies rather than originals (Schreiter, "Burnt" 234), to a lack of storage space in museums (Foster 385), and to their participation in colonialist discourses (Alexandridis 493). In any case, the editors of the volume point out that "the value of casts was constantly negotiated and renegotiated" (Winkler-Horaček, Introduction 223). Of particular importance to my discussion here, the collection and destruction of these museum plaster collections are part of a discourse of loss and replication that is central to the renegotiated value of the collections in Pietrasanta.

The gipsotecas in Pietrasanta today are particularly vulnerable collections. As working archives, they may soon be replaced, if they have not been already, by computerized imaging. Of course, all plasters are copies, subordinate in status to the actual sculpture. Each of these collections assigns value to the plaster models (or, in the case of the nineteenth-century collections, revokes that value). Relying on the local context of the production of marble sculpture, and drawing on an imaginary past of plaster model collections, the Museo dei Bozzetti grants significance to the otherwise overlooked and at the same time calls attention to its instability.

Works Cited

Acebal, Martin, et al. "The Performativity of the Archive from a Semiotic Perspective." *Southern Semiotic Review*, no. 22, 2020, pp. 31–47.

Alexandridis, Annetta. "'Classical' Plaster Casts in Enlightenment and Colonialist Discourses on Race." Alexandridis and Winkler-Horaček, pp. 527–83.

Alexandridis, Annetta, and Lorenz Winkler-Horaček. *Destroy the Copy—Plaster Cast Collections in the 19th–20th Centuries: Demolition, Defacement, Disposal in Europe and Beyond*, edited by Annetta Alexandridis and Lorenz Winkler-Horaček, De Gruyter, 2022.

Alexandridis, Annetta, and Lorenz Winkler-Horaček. Introduction. Alexandridis and Winkler-Horaček, pp. 1–17.

Appadurai, Arjun. *Modernity at Large: Cultural Dimensions of Globalization*. University of Minnesota Press, 1996.

Benjamin, Walter. "The Work of Art in the Age of Mechanical Reproduction." *Illuminations: Essays and Reflections*, by Walter Benjamin, Schocken, 1978, pp. 217–51.

Celli, Chiara. "Il Bozzetto: Come Nasce Una Scultura." *Museo dei Bozzetti "Pierluigi Gherardi" Pietrasanta*, edited by Chiara Celli and Valentina Fogher, Pacini, 2011, pp. 18–29.

Després-Lonnet, Marie, and Maryse Rizza. "When the Archive Embodies the Institution: The Role of Curatorial Files in the Documentary Making of a Fine Arts Museum's Museality." *Annales des Sémiotiques*, vol. 12, 2021, https://journals.openedition.org/signata/3151.

Dondero, Maria Giulia, et al. "Introduction: Semiotics of the Archive." *Signata: Annales des Sémiotiques*, vol. 12, 2021, https://doi.org/10.4000/signata.3275.

Foster, Sally. "Smashing Casts: Replication of Scottish Early Medieval Sculpture as a Case Study on the Fragility of Value." Alexandridis and Winkler-Horaček, pp. 375–400.

Foster, Sally M., and Neil G. W. Curtis. "The Thing About Replicas—Why Historic Replicas Matter." *European Journal of Archaeology*, vol. 19, no. 1, 2016, pp. 122–48.

Franklin, Ruth. "Writing Out of Annihilation." Review of *Warsaw Testament* by Rokhl Auerbach, translated from the Yiddish by Samuel Kassow. *The New York Review of Books*, 19 Sept. 2024, pp. 56–58.

Frederiksen, Rune, and Eckart Marchand, editors. *Plaster Casts: Making, Collecting and Displaying from Classical Antiquity to the Present*, vol. 18. De Gruyter, 2010.

Kirshenblatt-Gimblett, Barbara. "Anticipatory Heritage." *Journal of American Folklore*, vol. 137, no. 543, 2024, pp. 85–93.

Kirshenblatt-Gimblett, Barbara. *Destination Culture: Tourism, Museums, and Heritage*. University of California Press, 1998.

Margolies, Jane. "Move Over Marble; Plaster Gets Pride of Place." *The New York Times*, 2 Sept. 2016, https://www.nytimes.com/2016/09/02/arts/design/move-over-marble-plaster-gets-pride-of-place.html.

Museo del Lavoro e Delle Tradizioni Popolari della Versilia Storica Seravezza. Ufficio Informazioni Turistiche, n.d. Brochure.

National Gallery of Ireland. "Remembering the Gallery's History: Plaster Casts." N.d., https://www.nationalgallery.ie/explore-and-learn/plaster-casts-gallery.

Neal, Meg. "Gipsoteca Bartolini." *Atlas Obscura,* 15 Jan. 2018, https://www.atlasobscura.com/places/gipsoteca-bartolini.

Nora, Pierre. *Les Lieux de mémoire.* Gallimard, 1984.

Paolicchi, Costantino. *I Paesi Della Pietra Piegata: The Town Where Stone Was Tamed.* Container Editrice, 1981.

Rockwell, Peter. *The Art of Stoneworking.* Cambridge University Press, 1993.

Rosati, Claudio. "A Happy Necessity." *Museo dei Bozzetti "Pierluigi Gherardi" Pietrasanta,* edited by Chiara Celli and Valentina Fogher, Pacini, 2011, pp. 8–10.

Schreiter, Charlotte. "'Moulded from the Best Originals of Rome': Eighteenth-Century Production and Trade of Plaster Casts After Antique Sculpture in Germany." *Plaster Casts: Making, Collecting and Displaying from Classical Antiquity to the Present,* edited by Rune Frederiksen and Eckhart Marchand, De Gruyter, 2010, pp. 119–42.

Schreiter, Charlotte. "Burnt, Destroyed, Sold, Lost: The Fate of Cast Collections in the 18th and 19th Centuries." Alexandridis and Winkler-Horaček, pp. 225–37.

Shuman, Amy, and Keara McMartin. "Folk Economies and the Artisan Workshop." *The Folklorist in the Marketplace: Conversations at the Crossroads of Vernacular Culture and Economics,* edited by Willow G. Mullins and Puja Batra-Wells, Utah State University Press, 2019, pp. 252–70.

Shuman, Amy, and Keara McMartin. "Tradition and Embodied Knowledge in an Artisan Community." *Contexts of Folklore: Festschrift for Dan Ben-Amos on His Eighty-Fifth Birthday,* edited by Simon Bronner and Wolfgang Mieder, Peter Lang, 2019, pp. 287–98.

Shuman, Amy, and Keara McMartin. "De Relatie Tussen Kunst en Ambacht in Pietrasanta, Italie." Translation of "The Artist-Artisan Collaboration in Pietrasanta, Italy." De Relatie Tussen Kunst en Ambacht in Pietrasanta, Italie. Beeldengaerij, Het Depot, Studio Sem, 2012, pp. 27–97.

Stewart, Susan. *On Longing: Narratives of the Miniature, the Gigantic, the Souvenir, the Collection.* Duke University Press, 1993.

Tedeschi, Sergio. "Il Passato e la Presenza." *Museo dei Bozzetti "Pierluigi Gherardi" Pietrasanta,* edited by Chiara Celli and Valentina Fogher, Pacini, 2011, pp. 15–18.

Victoria and Albert Museum. "Cast Collection." N.d., https://www.vam.ac.uk/collections/cast-collection.

Winkler-Horaček, Lorenz. "Destroy the Copy? Destroy the Copy! A History of (Non-)appreciation." Alexandridis and Winkler-Horaček, pp. 527–83.

Winkler-Horaček, Lorenz. Introduction. Alexandridis and Winkler-Horaček, pp. 221–24.

CHAPTER 6

Archival Forethought

BRIAN EUGENIO HERRERA

Not long ago, I was taking my seat in an off-Broadway theater to see a buzzy new play featuring a celebrity-stacked cast. My seat was a good one, thanks to the fact that I was attending in my official capacity as nominator for an awards body. I was glad for this particular assignment, as there would have been no other way for me to see this production, which had sold through several extensions and boasted capacity crowds even as the show's ticket prices skyrocketed to dizzying heights.

As I surveyed the well-heeled matinee audience, a casual acquaintance took her assigned seat next to mine. I knew this person to be a well-regarded arts administrator, presently most known for her deft stewardship of several important programs at another major off-Broadway theater. We were exchanging brief hellos when her attention was caught by someone seated immediately behind me.

(I didn't intend to eavesdrop, but the conversation happened in public and at full volume directly over my right shoulder and, thus, my right ear. What follows is my recollection of my experience of the spirit and substance of the exchange, albeit with all the necessary caveats.)

The person seated behind me, whom I did not recognize, turned out to be another theater professional who worked in a similar capacity at a similarly significant not-for-profit theater but in a different major theater city. The exchange began in the manner of that familiar swap of lightly informational niceties that happens when artsy folk cross paths in artsy spaces, but it wasn't long before the conversation took a specific turn that caught and tuned my attention.

"Don't you love this?"

"Oh, the program card?" My seatmate flipped the oversized matte-finished postcard handed to her by the usher just moments before. "Oh, yes," she replied. "We've started doing the QR code thing for the full program too."

"But I like this one—with photos of the full cast and then the main artistic staff listed on one side of the card, with the QR code and the poster on the other . . ."

"We had an experience recently with one show that got really . . . Yes, being able to make necessary changes to the program information online without having to order rush reprints for everything every time . . . simplifies everything. None of those last-second hassles or rush expenses—and less paper waste too!"

"I totally agree. Might be the only thing I like about the changes in our industry coming out of COVID. Well. So nice to see you. So glad we got sent to the same show this afternoon!"

"Good to see you too."

My seatmate's attention returned forward. We smiled hello once again. I spoke.

"So you're liking the move to program cards over full printed programs?"

"I do. We're finding you can put so much more in and make updates without the limits of print. Do you like them?"

"They make me anxious."

My response clearly surprised her.

"Anxious? Why?"

"I'm a historian, both by training and by disposition, and I worry that we're setting ourselves up to lose the traces of a whole era of theater-making."

"What do you mean?"

"I save the link to every theater program QR code I open on my phone, and when I go back a few months or even a few weeks later, so many of the links are just dead or gone or they lead to the program information for an entirely different show. Do you happen to know if your organization has an archival strategy for the program information currently being housed online?"

"I don't."

"That's what makes me anxious. If the theaters aren't archiving this stuff, and history-minded packrats like me can't add the paper programs to our own personal hoards, I start to worry about the archival future of this theatrical moment."

My seatmate granted my point, noting that she hadn't considered digital programs in archival terms. Right about then, the lights dimmed and the season's latest hot-ticket show began.

As the audience's laughter began to flow in response to the precision-timing of the gaggle of TV stars assembled on stage, my thoughts wandered. "Have I become an archival scold? Why do I start ranting about the digital programs as archival threat at the drop of a postcard? Does any of it really matter?"

I did not answer myself that afternoon. Perhaps that is why I have felt those questions looming every time I've clicked on a theater's QR code since. I also now understand that my polite mini-outburst about digital programs is but one thread in a tangled knot of anxiety that I can feel tightening anytime I encounter a theater company or theater-maker treating their own archive as something for someone else to do some other time.

This habit of thought—that the archive is something to be constructed after the fact, by someone else, at some indefinite future moment—is not unique to theater-makers. Yet I find myself alert to the ways that it is particularly pronounced among them. I first began to find words for these concerns when contributing to the collaboratively authored "Latinx Theatre Commons Wallace Planning Grant Concept Paper for Archiving Latine Theatre." This white paper was composed by a "circle" of thirteen scholars (including myself) and sought not only to "define, historicize, and problematize the systems and ideologies that have categorized Latine theatre and Latine peoples" but also to offer relevant "histories, strategies, and suggestions for archiving Latine theatre in all its forms and technologies."[1]

One section of the white paper—"Challenges for Archiving Latine Theatre"—most animated my engagement. Indeed, the passage that most continues to resonate for me elaborates on how "the task of attending to the needs of the immediate past" functions both as "an afterthought" and as "a peculiar sort of magical thinking" (21). Here, the circle of scholars describes a habit of thinking wherein it is assumed "that archival work happens 'after'—after the show closes, after the season resolves, after the company reaches a milestone, after the theatre ceases or shifts operation, after the manuscript is delivered to the publisher, after the website is updated, after some librarian calls, after someone dies . . ." This habit of thinking also imagines that, in this presumptive future moment, "some unspecified someone will someday have the necessary time, resources, expertise, and commitment to go back and collect all the relevant materials and somehow put them into an archive somewhere" (21). Here, new media scholar Wendy Hui Kyong Chun's dual admonition that, on the first hand, "habits, for all their inflexibility, are also defined by their changeability" and that, on the next, "crises are opportunities for habit

1. For a discussion of and a link to the full white paper, see Della Gatta.

change" (85) seems especially relevant to the question of how to disrupt the habit of archival afterthought, perhaps especially for minoritarian performance histories.

As I revisit the circle of scholars' critique of the reliance on unspecified someones in this habit of afterthought in 2024, I am reminded of my 2016 published ruminations about "my own archival naiveté, or my misguided assumption that the familiar admonition 'the internet is forever' applies fairly, equally, and predictably" to all sorts of digital content (Herrera 47). Focusing on the challenges of archiving Latine theater, the 2024 white paper noted both the failure of institutional repositories to cultivate relationships with Latine theater-makers and also the enduring problem of gaps in cultural knowledge around the diversity of Latine cultural practice, especially with regard to linguistic biases and the imprecision of crowdsourcing and digitization (especially optical scanning) in capturing accurate renderings of Latine presence in theater archives. By contrast, my 2016 essay emphasized the "evanescence" of the recent queer-performance past by highlighting "how fleeting and easily lost the recent queer past can be" (47). The essay charted erasures effected by evolving internet platforms, the archival elusiveness of subcultural embodied performance practice, and the persistence of heteropatriarchal biases around end-of-life protocols for (and archives of) queer elders. (I might note that, as a collectively authored piece, the words in the 2024 white paper belong to the full circle of scholars, including myself, who collaboratively authored the piece. Even so, I find myself reaching for different possessive pronouns, oscillating between "my" and "our" when referencing the ideas and words in the white paper. Some of the ideas feel like mine, reflecting my own independent thinking on this topic, even as the ideas also emphatically reflect the collaborative process that went into developing the white paper.)

But as I think between the provocations offered by the 2024 white paper and my 2016 essay—one emphatically personal, one collaboratively collective—I am struck by the fact that these very different pieces are both centered on different, if intersecting, minoritarian performance communities that have been historically and structurally marginalized by traditional archival practices. I also note that in both works the consonance and persistence of the early twenty-first-century notion that "putting it on the website" was a suitable proxy for an archival strategy. Over the last ten or so years, I confess to being particularly alert to how web-hosted archival materials seemed especially vulnerable to a range of mundane hazards—ranging from a website becoming frozen (due to a lost password, domain ownership problems, or shift in personnel) to being inoperable or erased altogether (due to system software updates, the obsolescence of embedded video/audio code, or the shuttering of the webhosting platform altogether). For the archivally minded, the mortifying discovery that a long-valued cache of information had suddenly "disappeared from the website" increasingly seemed to me to be analogous to that sadly familiar horror of hearing that so-and-so's stash of personal papers had been destroyed by a house fire or tossed in a dumpster by uncaring relatives or roommates. And in early 2025, the particular vulnerability of online archival strategies was underscored by the brisk erasure of long-thought-secure digital channels of public information and data collection by the newly constituted Department of Government Efficiency (DOGE).[2] For by 2025, the structural vulnerability of web-housed archives seemed clearly to be a feature, not a bug.

Yet, because performance practice operates in the present or future tense, and because the hustle of fundraising and publicity also orients toward the future, a great amount of performance documentation is created in the conceptual space of what is happening "now" or "next"—with little thought to the fact that today's now is the future's past. This might explain why so much of the physical performance documentation typically available in traditional archives—programs, press releases, production photos, reviews, clippings, grant applications, et cetera—takes the form of outward facing materials originally crafted to stir interest or investment in a current or soon forthcoming performance. In such materials, the theatrical past is typically invoked—if it is invoked at all—through strategically placed and selective lists of past credits, productions, or accolades of the artists, companies, or funders involved in presenting the current or soon forthcoming performance.

A production program is perhaps the most familiar example of this "now" sensibility. Over the last century or so, the freely distributed printed program has become a routinely anticipated feature of attending a performance. The program might be a hand-folded photocopy, or it might be a glossy magazine-style publication. Whatever the format, the printed production program provides the anticipated audience member a detailed snapshot of the performance they are about to encounter. For some audience members, such a program might also become a personal keepsake or memento of the performance. But most performance programs are neither intended nor designed to be archival artifacts but instead a presumptively disposable (or recyclable) commodity designed to be of limited use for a specific window of time. Perhaps this explains why so many theater administrators regard printed programs as a retrograde waste of resources. If most contemporary audience members throw their programs away, often leaving them as trash on the theater floor,

2. For an account of the grassroots efforts to preserve archival data amid DOGE's evisceration of the government's informational infrastructure, see Lucas.

why put time, money, and materials into the fabrication of yet another disposable object?

Enter the program postcard with QR code—arriving as an apparently elegant solution, a deft adaptation of the traditional physical theater program within a contemporary, adaptive, and resource-mindful practice.[3] Yet my question to my seatmate remains. What archival strategy is in place to document the information previously, however haphazardly or ephemerally, captured on the performance program?

Because the QR code itself should also remind us of the particular archival precarity of digital ephemera. To explain, a "QR code" (shorthand for "quick response code") is a graphic image—often a cluster of black and white squares—that can be "read" or scanned by a smartphone camera to provide access, typically through a weblink, to information housed online. Each QR code typically activates a short sequence of virtual interfaces—from the graphic code to the smartphone camera to the internet and, with a final jump or three, to the intended online resource. Each juncture in this digital supply chain typically relies on a different platform or provider. If one link breaks—if there is a misprint or error in the QR code; if the QR code provider shifts linking protocol or ownership; if the destination website undergoes a redesign or changes domains—the entire sequence is vulnerable to collapse, with the QR code printed on the postcard maybe routing to an entirely different webpage, an error message, or literally nowhere at all. The contemporary trend toward QR codes on program postcards should then underscore the urgent ongoing need for performance-makers to develop forward-thinking archival strategies for digital ephemera. While some attention has been paid to digital archival strategies for digitally native collections, the challenge for capturing digital ephemera is ever-evolving. Alongside the reliance on QR codes and web-hosted programs, the recent proliferation of digitally native theatrical commentary—whether commissioned companion pieces hosted on this or that theater's website; or the essays published on digital platforms like *3Views, Howlround,* or Substack; or the constantly shifting circuits of "beyond print" commentary offered by podcasters, TikTokers, YouTubers, and the like—present a complex and confounding archival conundrum.[4]

3. For an illustrative account of the utility of QR codes in the temporal register of the "now," see Ozturkcan and Kitapci. For a brief description of the adaptive utility of QR codes for performance programs coming out of COVID-19, see the dedicated section in chapter 3 of Crawford and Hansen.

4. For a discussion of the necessary archival and accession strategies for digitally native performance materials, see Reside. For an example of how scholarship can itself actuate a form of digital archival practice, see Boffone, *Renegades* and *TikTok*. See also Harmony Bench's deft theorization of the distinction between "ephemera" as archival object and "the ephemeral tense" as archival mode in "'Complex Temporalities.'"

But what is to be done about this stubborn habit of archival afterthought? How does the archival afterthought exacerbate the vulnerability of particular archives, whether physical or digital? What of archives without infrastructural connection to the resources and expertise to preserve, cultivate, and advocate for the value of the archive itself? In the archiving Latine theater white paper, the circle of scholars noted haphazard reliance on the accident of "an individual theatre artist, researcher, or administrator [who] recognizes the need for an archive and unofficially deputizes themselves to hold onto the archivable materials" (21). Yet the particular material complexity (and concomitant vulnerability) of digital ephemera thwarts the sincere efforts—and I speak from experience here—of even the most dogged self-deputizing grassroots archivists interested in covering these inevitable digital-archival gaps.[5]

But what would it require to cultivate an ethical practice of archival forethought? Indeed, what might it mean for theater- and performance-makers to cultivate an archival sensibility that understood—in practical, material, and actionable terms—that any collateral developed for the show happening now or the show happening next might also stand as valuable documentation of what will soon be the show's past? What might it mean for performance scholars, archivists, and advocates to understand the priority of capturing the cultures of commentary and critique proliferating beyond print in the twenty-first century? And what might it mean if we were to take seriously my scolding concern that, say, shifting to postcards with QR codes—however expedient as practical adjustments to the exigencies of the "now"—might be inadvertently creating the conditions for a soon to be irretrievable theatrical past?

The archivally minded among us cannot lapse to that old notion that what we put "on" the internet will still be there forever. Over the last decade or so, we've encountered the precarity that follows relying on proprietary platforms to build or house grassroots archives when those platforms might be sold, shuttered, or "enshittified" per the unpredictable whims of platform capitalism.[6]

Archival forethought requires that performance-makers—whether individuals, companies, or institutions—intentionally integrate an archival strategy into the cost-efficiency calculus that guides their decisions about most public-facing documentation. What does this cost in terms of time and money? What

5. For a consideration of the digital-archival gaps in existing efforts to archive public-facing internet resources, see Hartelius.

6. For a discussion of "how the ease of changing how a platform allocates value [and] where a platform sits between buyers and sellers" can lead to the degradation of its utility to both those using and those subsidizing a digital platform, see Doctorow. For a broader consideration of the overarching structures of platform capitalism, see Jones, especially chapter 2, "Artificial or Care Work."

is the most efficient and effective way to meet this goal? Add to this calculus a simple step of how we capture this work within the archive that we are compiling. What would it take to make the simple but potentially consequential pivot to integrating archival forethought into the organizational practice of the "now" and "next" of your own performance-making and promotion?[7]

Is your performance worth the expedient risk of putting the question of archive off to later? Are you confident that a proverbial someone will loop back someday to assemble an archive from what traces—digital and physical—your performance might have left behind? Are you comfortable relying on the habit of archival afterthought? Or is your performance work worth the risk and the effort of integrating some archival forethought into your performance practice? Without a forward-thinking archival strategy, without cultivating a practice of archival forethought to counterbalance the entrenched habits of archival afterthought, and without an evolving infrastructure to accommodate and value as archival materials things that are not printed, whole generations of performance activity (companies, artists, subcultures) run the risk of contributing to their—and our—historical erasure.

Coda

I might add that I just went to the Notes app on my phone to click my saved link to the digital program for that recently-buzzy-but-now-already-mostly-forgotten off-Broadway comedy I mentioned at the outset of this piece. As I write this, it has been not quite five months since I took my seat and clicked the QR code published on that program postcard. The link still works. I note that the link reflects some changes to the cast listings apparently made after I saw the show. But most of the program information still appears to be there. For now.

Works Cited

Bench, Harmony. "'Complex Temporalities': Digitality and Ephemeral Tense in Adam H. Weinert's 'The Reaccession of Ted Shawn.'" *The Routledge Dance Studies Reader*, edited by Jens Richard Giersdorf and Yutian Wong, 3rd ed., Routledge, 2019, pp. 364–73.

Boffone, Trevor. *Renegades: Digital Dance Cultures from Dubsmash to TikTok*. Oxford University Press, 2021.

7. Of note here is the American Theatre Archive Project (ATAP), which developed a rigorous but resource and expertise intensive experiment in modeling best practices of archival forethought. See Brady and Koffler.

Boffone, Trevor. *TikTok Broadway Musical Theatre Fandom in the Digital Age.* Oxford University Press, 2024.

Brady, Susan, and Helice Koffler. "The American Theatre Archive Project: Carrying the Record of the Past to the Future." *Performing Arts Resources,* vol. 31, 2015, pp. 103–21.

Chun, Wendy Hui Kyong. *Updating to Remain the Same: Habitual New Media.* MIT Press, 2016.

Crawford, Brett Ashley, and Paul Hansen. *Raising the Curtain: Technology Success Stories from Performing Arts Leaders and Artists.* Wiley, 2024.

Della Gatta, Carla. "Latinx Theatre Commons Wallace Planning Grant Concept Paper for Archiving Latine Theatre." *Howlround,* Sept. 2024, https://howlround.com/latinx-theatre-commons-wallace-planning-grant-concept-paper-archiving-Latine-theatre.

Doctorow, Cory. "The 'Enshittification' of TikTok." *Wired,* 23 Jan. 2023, https://www.wired.com/story/tiktok-platforms-cory-doctorow/.

Hartelius, Johanna E. "The Anxious *Flâneur*: Digital Archiving and the Wayback Machine." *Quarterly Journal of Speech,* vol. 106, no. 4, Nov. 2020, pp. 377–98.

Herrera, Brian Eugenio. "Evanescence: Three Tales of the Recent Queer Theatrical Past." *Theatre Topics,* vol. 26, no. 1, Mar. 2016, pp. 47–51.

Jones, Phil. *Work Without the Worker: Labour in the Age of Platform Capitalism.* Verso, 2021.

Lucas, Julian. "The Data Hoarders Resisting Trump's Purge." *The New Yorker,* 14 Mar. 2025, https://www.newyorker.com/news/the-lede/the-data-hoarders-resisting-trumps-purge.

Ozturkcan, Selcen, and Olgun Kitapci. "A Sustainable Solution for the Hospitality Industry: The QR Code Menus." *Journal of Information Technology Teaching Cases,* June 2023, https://journals.sagepub.com/doi/full/10.1177/20438869231181599.

Reside, Doug. "'Last Modified January 1996': The Digital History of *RENT.*" *Theatre Survey,* vol. 52, no. 2, Nov. 2011, pp. 335–40.

PART 2

NETWORKED MEMORIES AND MINOR HISTORIES

PART 2 INTRODUCTION

PUJA BATRA-WELLS AND HARMONY BENCH

The second section of this volume, Networked Memories and Minor Histories, focuses on more familiar understandings of archives and collections. Some of the contributions draw from collections the authors themselves have created (Gonzaba, Bonds), while others narrate their experiences of archival meaning-making and historical interpretation (Marsden, Harnetty, Wood). An unexpected thread weaves through this section, as over half of the chapters bring regions from the central US into focus, challenging readers to consider how oft-overlooked noncoastal and rural communities are not merely beholden to history but active agents within it (Gonzaba, Marsden, Harnetty, Wood). These minor histories receive their due as the authors simultaneously reconsider what kinds of materials can be primary sources (Gonzaba, Harnetty), and how even seemingly conventional documents may hold unconventional histories within (Wood). We have brought these contributions together because of how they analyze the role of everyday objects in constructing communities and identities, how they understand that collections intended for one reason may nevertheless contain altogether different information, and how they employ digital collections to cut across the holdings of multiple archives and create new entry points. In this section, collections are put to use. Their contents are repurposed in creative projects and online databases as part of a strategy for recovering marginalized voices and histories. Together these contributions unsettle inherited categories of value, legitimacy, and authority to consider not only who is being remembered but also the shape of that remembering.

Eric Gonzaba has worked across a number of archives to gather images for his *Wearing Gay History* online collection, in which the humble gay bar T-shirt reminds us of how seemingly mundane objects are central to crafting identities and signaling group membership. Gonzaba shows how these T-shirts evidence queer US histories outside of the dominant coastal metropolises, and even mark broader shifts in the cultural landscape. Created for advertising and other prosaic purposes, these T-shirts "document events and communities that might otherwise remain hidden in conventional archives." As such, the T-shirts gathered in Gonzaba's collection make visible forms of historical data embedded in everyday objects. Leigh Bonds also gathers disparate materials in an online collection, in her case a bibliography of the writer Mary Robinson, who was well known in her day but was largely forgotten until the 1980s. Because it is impossible to search across archives, such focused clearinghouses of relevant source materials remain important for scholarly research. But even as Bonds commits to digital bibliography, she recognizes the "vulnerability of digital collections' infrastructure," pointing to the 2023 cyberattack from which the British Library had not fully recovered as of this writing, and the 2024 disruptions to the *Internet Archive.* Whether collections are physical or digital, precarity, it seems, is a shared condition. Nicole Wood presses this issue further in her analysis of environmental data found in archival documents. Noting the disappearance of climate datasets from federal websites during the second Trump administration, Wood pointedly remarks: "Archivists can only preserve data that exists." The kinds of data captured are subject to the whims of those in power, and digital datasets are all too easy to erase. But Wood shows how historical documents contain unintentional or "latent" environmental data prior to its formal collection by government or other agencies. Tracing the devastating spread of the American chestnut blight throughout Tennessee in the first half of the twentieth century and measurements of rainfall in California in the 1800s, Wood shows the value of data that resides in alternative sources, which may prove particularly vital for future research in our own era of disappearing data.

Brian Harnetty continues with the theme of precarity of both communities and environments in his sound art project *Forest Listening Rooms.* Appalachia has long been a space of resource extraction accompanied by national neglect. Pointing to how stewarding community memory is also part of stewarding the forest, Harnetty proposes that listening to place, to history, and to each other fosters conditions for healing communities and stimulating change in Appalachian Ohio. Sounds from the archive in the forms of oral history and nature recordings blend with co-present listeners, who serve as an audience for these "archival performances." Listening cultivates greater empathy and also prompts memory, as listeners recall their own experiences and histories with the land around them. Mariah Marsden likewise focuses on an underrepresented geocultural area of the US, but this time in conjunction with lesbian histories in the Ozarks. Countering "rural queer erasure," Marsden elevates the queer place-making that occurs outside large cities. In such places, inscrutability may be a survival strategy, or communities may draw different lines of affiliation beyond the dominant identity formations of city-dwellers. Similar to the gatherings represented in Gonzaba's T-shirt collection, here potluck events and newsletters allowed a lesbian community to cohere across distances, without requiring members of the group to manifest an identity in a prescribed way.

Representing a diverse set of approaches to archival engagement, the contributions in Networked Memories and Minor Histories reflect on such questions as: How can digital collections bring together voices and experiences that might otherwise remain hidden within more traditional archives? How do collections express a point of view, and how can gathering materials along new trajectories and especially across collections support alternate avenues of interpretation? How does the labor of archivists and collections managers inhere in how histories are written? If data can disappear and library access can be terminated, what are other modes of sustaining memory, for example through creative and sensory engagement? What roles do everyday objects and local contexts play in how social groups understand themselves through their practices of memory-keeping? And in what ways might participatory memory work unintentionally reproduce or reinforce social, cultural, or political asymmetries?

CHAPTER 7

The American Gay Bar T-Shirt

Understanding Queer Nightlife Histories with the *Wearing Gay History Archive*

ERIC GONZABA

In the late 1960s, a butch lesbian from California named Terry moved to Chicago and received anything but a warm midwestern welcome. Unlike her community back in the Golden State, Terry found Chicago in the late '60s to be more subdued, with the queer community relatively "closeted" upon her arrival. She even encountered difficulties while trying to secure an apartment. After viewing several places and submitting applications, she had no success in convincing a landlord to rent to her. Eventually, Terry asked a woman she was dating at the time to attempt to rent the apartment on her behalf; her girlfriend encountered no issues. "The only difference," Terry surmised, "was that I looked dykey and she looked straight. . . . They weren't exactly enthusiastic about renting to gays" (de la Croix 23).

Terry admitted that she wasn't much of a bar person, but upon moving to Chicago with a few friends, she thought hitting up the city's small lesbian bar scene would be fun. Her first Chicago lesbian bar was the Lost and Found nestled on Irving Park Road. She remembered the bar being dark (with "25-watt lights") and overcrowded, with women elbow to elbow in a compact space. During her first visit, Terry wanted to wear a comfortable (and butch) T-shirt, a staple of casual bar wear in the lesbian bars she frequented back in California. However, her friends warned her that the bar wouldn't let her in if she wore a T-shirt, like an unpublicized but enforced dress code. "[The Lost and Found] didn't want to have problems with [police] raids," she explained, "so anyone that had masculine looking clothes on [was] not allowed in. . . . When I went I had my collar buttoned up hiding the T-shirt." To Chicago lesbians, the seemingly innocuous T-shirt, despite its comfort, could not be worn even in public lesbian spaces; its connection to maleness identified the female body as "queer" and could invite unwanted attention not just from casual homophobic passersby but sometimes also from city police and vice squads.

Contrast Terry's experience with what Chicago's lesbian bar scene was like by the early 1980s: Patrons at bars like Paris Dance and Augie's & C.K.'s sported a wide range of attire, from casual bar and softball T-shirts to button-up shirts and overalls. The women in photographs published on the website *Block Club Chicago,* donated by lesbian bar owners, capture the essence of these 1980s lesbian bars. They are seen joyfully holding up their beers to the camera or huddling for group photos around pool tables. They appear unafraid and happy, seemingly wearing whatever attire they want. This was a far cry from the lesbian experience just a decade or two before at the Lost and Found. Dress, it seems, could signify evolutions in LGBTQ+ American life ("Chicago's Lesbian Bars").

Building on the vivid contrasts between Terry's experiences in the late 1960s and the more open atmosphere of the early 1980s, we see a narrative of progress and change within the Chicago lesbian bar scene. This evolution mirrors broader shifts within the LGBTQ+ community, especially in the aftermath of the Stonewall riots, the traditional historical starting point for the gay liberation movement in the United States. The post-Stonewall era was marked by a significant expansion of gay infrastructure and the birth of "gayborhoods" in American metropolitan centers, especially in gay nightlife. The number of documented gay sites like bars, bathhouses, cinemas, and cruising spots exploded by 1970s. Gay bars and nightclubs not only became havens for the gay community but also vibrant sites for expression, resistance, and camaraderie.

In this chapter, I contend that one way to make sense of this transformative period of queer nightlife is to use unconventional primary source materials. Traditional historical accounts have offered often utilized textual sources, such as gay newspapers, personal diaries and memoirs, and other forms of print culture. However, I argue that using dress is another way to investigate nuances in the queer American experience in the later twentieth century. That is, I argue that clothing (here, the common T-shirt) transcends mere fashion history and trendsetting; it can document events and communities that might otherwise remain hidden in conventional archives.

This chapter utilizes queer bar T-shirts gathered in *Wearing Gay History,* a digital archive and museum I began while a graduate student at George Mason University.[1] The T-shirts examined in this chapter largely come from my work

1. See https://wearinggayhistory.com.

collecting and documenting historical LGBTQ+ T-shirts in archives around the globe, beginning in 2012. I initially set out to build this digital archive to mitigate what I saw was the "bicoastal bias" of queer history by spotlighting the rich narratives from the American Midwest and South. I hoped for the site to underscore the diversity and interconnectedness across geographic and cultural lines within the LGBTQ+ community, while also bringing visibility to smaller, often overlooked queer archives. The project not only includes a broader spectrum of LGBTQ+ experiences, particularly those of queer people of color, bisexuals, lesbians, and transgender individuals, but also uses its digital platform to ensure that these histories are accessible and relatable to a wide audience. All in all, *Wearing Gay History* reimagines traditional archival practices by embracing T-shirts as unconventional yet potent historical documents. This approach not only preserves the tangible artifacts of queer culture but also highlights the everyday expressions and interactions that conventional archives might overlook.

After briefly describing the origins of the online archive, I explore the tangible and symbolic meanings that T-shirts can reveal about gay bars. These wearable artifacts, emblazoned with logos, slogans, and imagery, can sometimes encapsulate the challenges, triumphs, and lived realities of the wider LGBTQ+ community. Using T-shirts as a form of material culture placed alongside traditional textual and photographic sources, I argue, allows researchers and the wider public to explore the multifaceted ways queer culture has developed in the United States since the 1970s.

As a proud kid from Indiana, I attended undergrad at Indiana University, where I realized my ambition to become a historian of LGBTQ+ people. I thought a fun project would be to investigate the history of queer Hoosiers like myself, but I had no idea where to start looking for sources about gay folks in Indiana. I learned that Indianapolis, the state capital, hosted an LGBTQ+ archive at the Chris Gonzalez Library and Archives, which was open one day a week. (It has since closed.) I expected to find newspapers or records from gay rights organizations, but I became distracted during this visit when I saw boxes filled with old, somewhat musty T-shirts piled on the floor. I asked the archivist at the time if I could look through these unprocessed boxes, and with permission, I quite literally rummaged through them. What surprised me about the collection was that the T-shirts weren't all about LGBTQ+ pride or politics. Many captured less understood events, like gay TV watch parties, lesbian sports leagues, and many a bartender T-shirt. This visit and the rummaging through T-shirt boxes sparked my curiosity about other aspects of gay life I wasn't aware of, all through the lens of what people wore.

During my grad studies at George Mason University, I took this curiosity further by starting to archive, collect, and photograph LGBTQ+ T-shirts from different places in the US. Eventually, my collection grew to include items from other parts of the Americas, Europe, Asia, Australia, and Africa. In 2014 I launched *Wearing Gay History,* which has become the largest online archive dedicated to queer clothing culture. The website features nearly 5,000 historical LGBTQ+ T-shirts from over twenty archives worldwide, showcasing T-shirts from every US state and more than forty countries. Users can navigate the website in a variety of ways, via themes (like Pride, African American, or Politics & Elections), or geospatially, exploring T-shirts via their geographic origins. My goal with *Wearing Gay History* is to enrich our understanding of how these items of clothing have documented queer politics and culture on local, national, and international levels.

Before moving forward with this short analysis of *Wearing Gay History*'s queer bar T-shirt collection, it's crucial to recognize that T-shirts, like any piece of history, have their limitations as sources. T-shirts can provide only a glimpse into the complexities of gay, lesbian, trans, and bisexual experiences. Often, T-shirts lack necessary context, leaving historians without crucial details that can tell fuller histories. For example, few if any of the bar T-shirts in this chapter include dates or information about who created them. Furthermore, the survival of certain T-shirts, typically those produced in bulk, suggests that not all voices from the past are equally represented; many smaller bars (perhaps owned by less affluent queer entrepreneurs) lacked the means to publicize their nightlife establishments through T-shirts. The process behind T-shirts involves a wide range of contributors, from the creators and designers to the marketers, purchasers, and ultimately, the viewers. Understanding the full impact and significance of these garments goes beyond mere observation; it requires a deeper exploration into the various roles and contexts involved. Still, the T-shirt is one window into queer nightlife histories.

As of February 2024, the *Wearing Gay History* digital archive features nearly four hundred T-shirts under the "Bar and Nightclub" category, making up about 8 percent of the site's total collection. These T-shirts primarily hail from individual bars located in the United States and Europe, spanning the last forty years. At a cursory look, most of these T-shirts appear unremarkable. The predominant use of white or black fabrics is not surprising, given their cost-effectiveness for mass production. The design on these T-shirts is typically straightforward, often featuring the bar's name on the front or back, sometimes accompanied by the city, occasionally an address, and perhaps a small logo to promote the bar.

It's also important to ponder why gay bar T-shirts were created in the first place. Some of the reasons can be seen directly by viewing these bar T-shirts on *Wearing Gay History,* while others need more context. One of the most obvious reasons gay bars began printing T-shirts with their names and logos was for their bartenders and other staff. T-shirts were often an easy, recognizable uniform for bar staff, which assisted patrons in identifying who worked at the establishment. This was especially helpful in crowded or dimly lit bars; though Terry remembers no T-shirts allowed in the late 1960s Lost and Found, the dark "25-watt lighting" wasn't all that uncommon in the gay seventies discos or other gay taverns by the 1980s.

But gay bar T-shirts were not just limited to staff. By the 1970s, gay bars distributed (often at little or no cost) T-shirts for the simple reason of promoting their bars. Patrons wearing a specific bar's T-shirt outside that venue were essentially walking billboards, bringing attention and publicity to that establishment. This was especially true for patrons wearing gay bar T-shirts within gay villages (or gayborhoods) or within other LGBTQ+ establishments; since many T-shirts had few symbols or words marking their bars as gay, to be understood as a gay bar shirt, the viewer of the walking wearable billboard had to somewhat already know that such an establishment existed. In a way, branded gay bar T-shirts might have fostered a sense of community and loyalty among patrons. Wearing gay bar T-shirts might've made customers feel part of the burgeoning queer community beginning in the 1970s.

In many ways, the ubiquity of the gay bar T-shirt correlates with the rise of the gay and lesbian community in the United States post Stonewall in 1969. T-shirts became so ubiquitous to the American gay bar scene that bars across the United States began hosting "bar T-shirt" nights; by the early 1980s, many gay bars across the US South, for example, poured alcohol freely to those wearing cotton billboards across their chests. In 1981 at P's, self-described as "Atlanta's original levi/leather bar," patrons wearing any bar T-shirt got cocktail hour prices all Thursday night long. If you wanted those same prices on a Friday night, however, you had to be wearing a specific P's T-shirt (or leather would work). That same year, the gay bar Lafitte's in New Orleans advertised 75 cent beers on Mondays, provided patrons wore "any bar T-shirt." A few years later, Houston's gay bar The Barn publicized in the local gay press that Mondays in 1984 was "T-shirt night," which gave patrons happy-hour prices if they specifically wore a Barn T-shirt.

This trend highlights the gay bars' strategic use of T-shirts not only as a promotional tool but also to build a loyal customer base. The willingness of these establishments to offer perks for wearing T-shirts from any bar indicates a broader strategy to foster a collective gay identity and solidarity. These events encouraged patrons to celebrate their community and support various gay bars, not just the ones offering the deals. It was a clever way to weave individual bars into the larger fabric of the gay (and later wider LGBTQ+)

community, encouraging a culture of inclusivity and mutual support that transcended the walls of any single establishment.

Gay bars also promoted themselves via T-shirts and supported the LGBTQ+ community by helping fund queer social activities, particularly gay and lesbian sports leagues. By the late 1970s, gay and lesbian sports leagues were common in several cities across the United States. For example, queer sports lovers in 1977 formed the North American Gay Amateur Athletic Alliance (or NAGAAA) to encourage "the participation of gay men and lesbians in organized softball competition." The proliferation of leagues in major US cities required financial backing, and gay institutions like bars and nightclubs often stepped in to assist with funding equipment and uniforms (including T-shirts). It did not hurt that several of these bars could rely on the patronizing of league members in their bars following matches, a smart business practice.

Several T-shirts in the *Wearing Gay History* archive highlight historical queer sports leagues. One T-shirt from the gay and lesbian bar EJ's displays the bar's name within a large yellow softball, accompanied by two images of the state of Texas. The words "Houston, Texas" are featured at the top and bottom of the shirt, which is photographed alongside a color-coordinated skirt, signaling EJ's support for a softball team. Another T-shirt from Houston, red with white shoulders, promotes the Montrose Softball Association as the 1984 South Division Champs. However, the most prominent feature on this shirt is the oversized text "Copa Houston" that covers more than half the front, indicating the sponsorship by the iconic Houston gay bar Copa. Copa was opened by Gene Howle and his partner Lynn Ganey in 1979.

Moving north, a yellow T-shirt from 1980 in Chicago showcases a pictogram of figures playing volleyball, identifying the Lincoln Park Lagooners team at the "2nd National Invitational Volleyball Tournament." Beneath the tournament details, the shirt prominently displays "Carol's Speakeasy" alongside the bar's streetlamp logo, indicating the bar's sponsorship of the team (see figure 7.1). Not every sports league T-shirt explicitly mentions its connection to the sport. For instance, a cream-and-green T-shirt for Kindred Spirits, a popular Houston lesbian bar operational from 1981 to 1989, features only the bar's name and logo with the subheading "A Woman's Alternative." Yet a photograph on the bar's history page by Houston historian JD Doyle captures twenty women in the 1980s on a softball field in a team pose; they are all dressed in the team's uniform for that year, which includes distinctive green softball pants and the aforementioned cream-and-green Kindred Spirits T-shirt. These examples illustrate how sports league T-shirts from gay and lesbian bars not only promoted the establishments but also underscored their

FIGURE 7.1. T-shirt from "Lincoln Park Lagooners 1980 Tournament." Chicago, Illinois, May 24–25, 1980. Co-sponsored by Carol's Speakeasy. Collection: Gerber/Hart Library and Archives—Chicago, Illinois. Image used with permission from *Wearing Gay History*, accessed March 25, 2025, https://wearinggayhistory.com/items/show/594.

integral role in supporting and fostering community sports teams. The inclusion of bar sponsorships on team apparel highlights the bars' commitment to the LGBTQ+ community's social and recreational activities, and thus social cohesion of the rising and now quite visible queer community.

One way to examine queer bar T-shirts is to look at how they promoted their establishment, particularly in terms of how visibly "gay" or "queer" the T-shirt appeared. Few bar shirts explicitly stated "gay bar" or "lesbian bar" (consider, for example, Kindred Spirits' subheading "a woman's alternative"). Nonetheless, the visibility of gay or queer identity on bar T-shirts ranges widely, from overt displays to more subtle cues. Choosing subtlety in their T-shirt design, such as by including only a bar's name without any revealing images or symbols, could enable patrons to acknowledge their patronage of queer bars to those within their queer communities while remaining discreet in the broader public. Conversely, a more "in your face" design might be worn only by the most openly proud members of the community, or perhaps exclusively within the confines of gay bars themselves. Regardless of the approach, the design choice of a queer bar's T-shirt was strategic; a design that was too overtly "gay coded" could expose patrons or bar staff to personal and social risks.

Some of the more obvious gay bar T-shirts included images of just men, usually shirtless or with minimal clothing on. The T-shirt for Club Rendezvous in San Francisco includes the bar's name on a white shirt with blue trim, but the giveaway image is the profiles of two men looking at each other mere inches apart, both with '70s-style shaggy long hair and one with a prominent mustache. The black T-shirt from famous Chicago leather bar Gold Coast (open from the late 1950s until the late 1980s) featured an image, likely by artist Dom Orejudos, of a shirtless, hairy-chested man in tight leather pants and a leather jacket and leather hat. It's unlikely that any man attempting to project straightness would don this sort of shirt, a sign that its wearer was likely gay. A nightclub T-shirt even more revealing was After Dark, which the Darmon gay travel guides in the late 1970s noted was an after-hours cruisy bar with "flicks, [a] game room, [and a] pool table." Its design featured two muscular men in an intimate embrace, with exposed buttocks, alongside the bar's name and locations in Atlanta and Houston.

Sometimes, a bar's explicit link to gay men was represented not by images of men but through phallic symbolism. For example, the white 1986 T-shirt promoting Toronto's Toolbox featured the tagline "the Bar with Balls," incorporating a stylized phallus emerging from the two o's in the bar's name, encircled by chains. These designs not only promoted the bars but also boldly asserted a sexualized gay identity, unlikely to be worn by someone aiming to appear heterosexual. Through these T-shirts, bars communicated more than their existence; they signaled bar spaces for all-male sexual fraternization.

More subtle queer bar T-shirts often employed coded symbols, with the pink triangle being one of the most notable. Originally used by Nazis during the Holocaust to identify gay men, akin to the yellow Star of David for Jews, this symbol was reclaimed and became closely associated with the radical queer politics of the 1980s and 1990s, particularly during AIDS activism and with groups like ACT UP. The first consistent use of the pink triangle by gay bars began in the early 1990s. For instance, a blue shirt from Superior, Wisconsin's Main Club, around 1990 features the bar's name above a simple pink triangle. Similarly, the black T-shirt commemorating the thirteenth anniversary of Jacksonville's The Phoenix in 1990 displayed just the bar's name, the anniversary mention, and a pink triangle. Later in the 1990s, some pink triangle T-shirts combined minimalistic symbols with more overtly sexualized imagery. A 1999 shirt from Des Moines, Iowa's, gay bar Blazing Saddle showcased the bar's name and horse logo atop a pink triangle on the front, and on the back, it featured a more explicit connection to gay identity with a full-sized image of a bare male torso with a pierced nipple, all above a pink triangle with the Blazing Saddle tattoo (see figure 7.2). Gay bars' embrace of the pink triangle symbol shows both the way the symbol was reclaimed from one of persecution to empowerment and a reminder of how queer people embraced codes even into the more progressive end of the twentieth century.

Sometimes, physical modifications to preprinted bar T-shirts can reveal deeper insights into the broader gay community. Consider the T-shirt from Over the Rainbow, a gay bar in St. Paul dating back to the late 1990s. The bar's T-shirt is seemingly unremarkable at first glance. It features the bar's name, a direct nod to Judy Garland's iconic musical number in *The Wizard of Oz*, which has long been associated with the gay community, printed above a wavy rainbow—a symbol of LGBTQ+ identity. However, this otherwise plain white T-shirt bears handwritten messages in pen, including expressions like "Love the new bar!" and "Best Wishes, Over the Rainbow. Tina + Skippy 6-7-1997," along with playful inquiries like "Who's your Daddy?" These personal annotations transform the T-shirt from a simple piece of memorabilia into a document of social interaction and community support within the gay bar scene. They not only celebrate the establishment's significance but also chronicle personal connections and moments of joy within the space.

Physical alterations to preprinted T-shirts highlight the significance of integrating textual sources with material culture. Consider a T-shirt from the Chase, a renowned gay dance bar and club situated in the heart of Indiana's capital, established in 1975. *Blueboy*, a prominent magazine for gay men, once

FIGURE 7.2. T-shirt from "Blazing Saddle 1999." Des Moines, Iowa (Male physique). Collection: Formerly held at the Chris Gonzalez Library and Archives—Indianapolis, Indiana. Image used with permission from *Wearing Gay History,* accessed March 25, 2025, https://wearinggayhistory.com/items/show/219.

ranked the Chase among the top ten discos nationwide. Indianapolis local Mary Byrne reminisced, "It was the ultimate bar. That's where I learned to dance and where I came out." The Chase's T-shirt, similar to many in the *Wearing Gay History* collection, features no explicit or hidden symbols, merely the bar's name in bold on a black background. Yet an unknown individual marked this T-shirt with a painted circle and an X over the name. The reasons behind this graffiti remain unclear, both on the T-shirt and in archival records. In a conversation with Michael Bohr, archivist at the Chris Gonzalez Archives and former manager of the Chase, I uncovered that Bohr himself had collected the T-shirt, providing insight into its unique mark. He shared that a patron, on the bar's last night in 1983, had marked the shirt, expressing sadness and possibly anger over the bar's closure. The local gay publication, *The Works,* lamented the Chase's closure, terming it "Paradise Lost." Guides from the early 1980s suggest that while Indianapolis hosted several smaller gay bars, it lacked another large dance venue. Tom E. Green, a writer for *The Works,* observed, "very few bars can compare to the 'class' of The Chase." Without Bohr's insights, the T-shirt's alteration could have been misconstrued as a protest or grudge, masking the genuine sentiment of loss. This revelation emphasizes a crucial lesson: T-shirts, while seemingly simple, encourage us to dig deeper, posing questions and uncovering new paths of exploration. What rendered the Chase so special for many? Does this T-shirt amplify the narrative that its closure marked a substantial loss, echoing "paradise lost"?

From Terry's initial experience with Chicago's subdued queer scene in the late 1960s to the more openly expressive gay bar culture in the US by the 1990s, T-shirts reveal significant insights into the dynamics of queer nightlife history. Gay bar T-shirts served not only as practical uniforms for bar staff and promotional tools for establishments but also as a means for the broader queer community to express their identities and foster a sense of unity. The messages conveyed through these T-shirts, whether through coded symbols or explicit imagery, illustrate the complex ways in which the queer community navigated issues of visibility, pride, and discretion. Viewing historical T-shirts not as mundane items but as artifacts that offer deeper insights into the nightlife and broader social experiences of LGBTQ+ individuals helps us to better understand overlooked historical trends and experiences.

Works Cited

"Chicago's Lesbian Bars Vanished for Years, but Sapphic Spaces Are Making a Comeback." *Block Club Chicago,* 15 June 2023, https://blockclubchicago.org/2023/06/15/chicagos-lesbian-bars-vanished-for-years-but-sapphic-spaces-are-making-a-comeback/.

Damron, Bob. *Bob Damron's Address Book.* Bob Damron Enterprises.

de la Croix, Sukie. "Chicago Whispers." *Outlines: The Voice of the Gay and Lesbian Community,* 18 Nov. 1998, p. 23.

Gonzaba, Eric. "Wearing Gay History." *Wearing Gay History,* https://www.wearinggayhistory.com/.

NAGAAA (North American Gay Amateur Athletic Alliance). *NAGAAA,* https://web.archive.org/web/20140101135709/http://www.nagaaasoftball.org/.

CHAPTER 8

Archival Encounters

Lesbian Newsletters and Rural Visibility

MARIAH E. MARSDEN

When I visited the Ozark Lesbian and Gay Archives (OLGA) at Missouri State University in 2021, I was a returnee. I'd come home to nearby Jasper County during the COVID-19 pandemic and was working on my dissertation exploring print culture in the Ozarks. When I arrived on campus in Springfield, OLGA boxes waited for me, arranged by a cheerful archivist who greeted me with suggestions and open-ended offers for help. At a table next to mine, a student worker was making their way through more OLGA boxes, reorganizing and logging new materials in their growing collection, some for digitization and online access. At the end of the day, I chatted with the archivists who'd wander by, enjoying their stories and updates on the collection. They talked glowingly about the late drag queen who was so often featured in Tri-Life, a local newsletter from the early 2000s; they recommended work from the local scholar whose work initiated and energized the OLGA project; they spoke about the work of leaders at the GLO Center, a present-day community space for LGBTQ+ Ozarkers. I got the sense of OLGA as a living collection, actively growing under purposeful and enthusiastic archival attention and deeply embedded in the present. The archivists were thrilled I was there and that I had come with a purpose: to explore their collection of *Blossom* newsletters, which made up a comparatively small part of the OLGA collection and up to that point had received little critical attention.

Blossom—an acronym for "Brave Lesbians Organizing Some Saturdays of the Month"—was a women's potluck and social group that first gathered at the Springfield Unitarian Church in 1992 in an event organized by Linda Thomas, later dubbed "Mother Blossom." Later that year, the group began to circulate a newsletter with details on social events as well as discussions of life experiences and political struggles. Though editorship changed hands throughout the years, the publication remained in circulation until 2001.[1] A collection of these newsletters now remains as part of Missouri State University's Special Collections, along with proofs and loose pages from the editorial production process, and this archival record stands as a compelling example of how newsletters, as a media technology, allowed lesbian and feminist groups to informally create community through the postal network—no small feat, given the history of restrictions surrounding the Comstock Laws criminalizing the circulation by mail of material deemed obscene.

But beyond a black-and-white record of group events and historical information, these newsletters offer us the opportunity to consider how print, as an informational and creative technology, mediated the lived experiences, traditions, and legacy of a group of women often situated on the margins of the rural Ozarks and, more broadly, the imaginative moves that scholars and researchers can make as they encounter social artifacts in the archive. Newsletters are tools that translate experiences and organize them into recognizable forms. Events, news, and lore are reframed and recontextualized within the pages, situated as a part of the group's collective culture, sense of history, and plans for the future. Here, I trace my own encounter: situating Blossom's story within the context of the Ozark region and unpacking how members navigate visibility and presence through print and records.

Blossom in the Ozarks

> The Ozarks' National Scenic Riverway of the Current River became the playground of seven BLOSSOM women who camped out and floated. . . . We took a different direction, watched the wizardry of the laser light, were mesmerized by the fire's ember and the Milky Way; shared a wonderful adventure, a baby bird, the pineapple-eating bee, and the deep recesses of a cave; and observed the chilly kayakers revolutions.
>
> —Gina, "Fall Float was fantastic," *Blossom Newsletter,* November 1992

"When I left this year's retreat on Sunday afternoon," writes Linda in the May 1994 issue of the *Blossom Newsletter,* "I was waiting to come home and immediately write a love letter to every woman who'd been there." On that cool

1. Blossom later transitioned into the Ozark Mountain Pearls Women's Group and was listed in the GLO Community Spotlight until 2006.

and drizzly weekend in May, a group of local lesbians gathered for the second annual Blossom Retreat held at Camp Wakahni about forty-five miles northwest of Springfield, Missouri, in the wooded Ozark region. That weekend, Marideth, an established folksinger, crooned beside the campfire in the evening, while Ande led workshops on healing foodways and natural medicine during the day. There was Mitch with the insightful tarot readings, Pat's pottery showcase, and storytelling and political insights from "Mom" out on the cabin patio. Linda glowingly recounts these memories and more in her report, a testament to the skills of the individual attendees and her affective connections with the group at large: "This retreat strongly confirmed for me that we are a group of incredible women, with amazing talents." In that same issue, details for the upcoming Blossom Float Trip on the Niangua River and the annual party at Hawk Hill run beside the group's financial reports and dates for their team's softball games. The newsletter for Blossom shows that the group had a robust social schedule, from large-scale organized events to smaller gatherings listed in the "Coming Attractions."

Queer histories of the Ozarks often center larger cities in the region, as demonstrated by historian Holly A. Baggett's account of the city of Springfield, Missouri. In "The Creation of Community: A History of Gay and Lesbian Springfield, 1945–2010," Baggett outlines not only the cultural climate of conservatism and evangelicalism in the region but also the significant events that shaped LGBTQ+ communities in the Ozarks. From national headlining news such as the backlash to a local production of Larry Kramer's play *The Normal Heart,* to hate crimes and attacks outside of local bars, Springfield was host to controversies and violence against LGBTQ+ individuals and groups.[2] These events were moments of intense public visibility for local and regional LGBTQ+ communities, which simultaneously grappled with this overexposure even as they were frequently erased from the rural landscape.

Rural queer erasure is not specific to the Ozarks. Jack Halberstam's breakdown of migratory metronormativity and Scott Herring's reclamative queer anti-urbanism point to the ways in which analytical and historical focus prioritized metropolitan spaces, fostering the perception of queer absence within rural geographies.[3] Colin R. Johnson continues this "rural turn" in *Just Queer*

2. In 1989 the Department of Theatre and Dance at Southwest Missouri State University in Springfield (currently Missouri State University) produced Larry Kramer's *The Normal Heart,* which explored the AIDS crisis and impact at the time. Local conservatives, ministers, and Missouri state representatives mounted an outraged resistance, culminating in arson on the opening night of the performance and gaining national attention. Baggett notes that these events galvanized LGBTQ activists and communities in the area (317–18).

3. Other writers, including Mary L. Gray in *Queering the Countryside: New Frontiers in Rural Queer Studies,* have urged scholars to rethink metronormative assumptions regarding gender and sexuality. Gray notes that equating queerness with urbanity further reinforces a

Folks: Gender and Sexuality in Rural America, where he takes a queer historicist approach to deconstruct predominant understandings of queer pasts across the United States. "The discourse of sexuality in the modern United States is a profoundly spatial one," Johnson argues (13). He joins the call for greater attention to how genders and sexualities are constructed within and through rural spatial discourse as well as bodily enactments, and the Ozarks makes for a compelling region of study in light of this scholarship.

Historically, the Ozarks proved an attractive destination for lesbian intentional communities. The isolation of the Ozarks—while limiting access to economic and cultural resources—did allow for a more covert presence. Moreover, Amin Ghazianai's 2015 mapping of lesbian geographies indicates a notable preference: Same-sex female couples tended to live in less urban areas than same-sex male couples (62). In the Ozarks, Baggett notes three women's communities—Hawk Hill, Dragon Wheel, and Diana's Grove—in southern Missouri, some of which were home to Blossom members. Diana's Grove, in particular, listed their retreats in the newsletter and was regularly included in the list of affiliated community groups. Hawk Hill utilized the *Blossom Newsletter* to share invitations to parties and other social gatherings onsite near the small town of Ava, Missouri. Blossom member Susan Wiseheart discusses her move from Grand Rapids, Michigan, to take over Hawk Hill under the Ozark Regional Land Trust as a part of her interview with the OLGA Oral Histories collection:

> And I think it took some doing to get us here, behind the scenes here. People who had been trained by Suzanne Pharr. . . . She's a feminist lesbian who started the Women's Project in Little Rock, and she wrote a really fabulous book about homophobia and she did trainings, and people here, women here—because the women in the Ozarks have gotten together for a really long time as women—they took her training. . . . When there was some, you know, concern about lesbians coming to live here, they said, "Get over it." . . . They got it, they really got it, and that was fifteen years ago.

As Wiseheart points out, homophobia was not a static element pervading all spaces and places in the Ozarks. Groups interceded and provided education and opportunities for activism, supporting groups like Hawk Hill through the acquisition and security of land. Wiseheart's story harks back to one of the points of Johnson's *Just Queer Folk*: Heteronormativity and homophobia are

---

spatial hegemony that distinguishes what Karen Tongson calls the "enlightened liberal subject [who has emerged] from out of the darkness" from rural queer subjects who remain unenlightened and in the dark (qtd. in Gray 14).

not inherent elements of rurality but are constantly being constructed, questioned, reinforced, and contested.

Many Blossom members migrated to the Ozarks from more urban spaces, as recounted in interviews given to the OLGA Oral History Collection, but there were also local women who joined throughout the years. Blossom was made up of Springfield residents, some intentional community members, some outlying townsfolk, and still more who lived on farms in the surrounding region. Some had been born in the area, including women from Greene and Barry Counties, while others traveled to the region from Maryland, Colorado, New Mexico, and New Jersey. Even those who were born in the area had traveled a great deal before settling in Springfield at the time, often spanning coast-to-coast. The *Blossom* newsletters themselves recount the migratory journeys of many members, some who left the area and even some who later returned.

A notable feature of Blossom was its mobility. There was no central location, no organizational meeting place, but rather a map of connected sites that shifted and changed over time. "Mobility has always been important in the small town, rural, or regional 'city' gay experience," Baggett writes (307). And, indeed, the women of Blossom seemed to embrace that mobility, socializing at Springfield bars such as Martha's Vineyard while also trekking to an out-of-town farm for Mayfest '95 or stopping on the banks of the North Fork during the annual Blossom Float; visiting nearby Hawk Hill and Diana's Grove while also traveling as a contingent to the Michigan Womyn's Festival and Marches on Washington. Even after the establishment of the GLO Community Center, a queer space shared by other LGBTQ+ organizations, Blossom continued to host events at a variety of places and spaces. This mobility meant that the community centered itself around a kind of event—specifically, the potluck—rather than a site of meeting.

Accounts of the previous Blossom potlucks are preserved within the group's printed newsletter along with plans for future gatherings, and print was a convenient medium at the time for this simultaneous recordkeeping and mobilization. In this way, both the potluck and the newsletter become technologies of gathering for a community dispersed across a regional swath. Moreover, Blossom's use of print demonstrates how the group integrated more diffuse and remote interactions on paper alongside event-based interactions, like the potluck. Newsletter contributors transform events into stories and narratives: tales of skinny-dipping at the lake, enthusiastic square dancing, and brutally competitive volleyball games. Some depictions are artful and poetically rendered, such as Gina's descriptions in the epigraph of this section. "Narratives are fundamental to our lives," write Deborah Schiffrin and Anna de Fina in *Telling Stories: Language, Narrative, and Social Life.* "We dream, plan, complain, endorse, entertain, teach, learn, and reminisce by telling stories. They provide hopes, enhance or mitigate disappointments, challenge or support moral order, and test out theories of the world at both personal and communal levels" (1). In the *Blossom* newsletters, rather than sharing individually driven personal narratives, contributors and editors tell collective stories, highlighting the sociality of potlucks, the companionability of float trips, and the camaraderie of camping retreats. Print allows Blossom members to narrativize their traditions and do the imaginative work described by Schiffrin and de Fina that is integral to the management of the group. But print, as a material technology, brings up questions of visibility. The *Blossom* newsletters might be understood as a process of materialization, translating embodied experience into textual and archival memory. Writing makes these real-time experiences accessible to new audiences, and the circulation of the newsletter makes these once-bounded experiences visible to new witnesses.

Visibility is a nuanced concept within ongoing rural queer studies. Carly Thomsen's *Visibility Interrupted: Rural Queer Life and the Politics of Unbecoming* argues that calls for LGBTQ+ visibility "comprise the backbone of gay rights activism—a strategy emboldened by positing visibility as an uncontestable social good, as that which everyone *everywhere* desires" (viii, original emphasis). She points out, however, that this celebratory take on visibility can further marginalize rural LGBTQ+ people, who may have a different experience of what visibility entails and the stakes of being visible. "Calls for visibility," she points out, "create 'authentic' gay subjects as those who are 'out, loud, and proud' in a prescribed manner; position those who are not visible in such a prescribed way, as well as the places that ostensibly prevent such ways of being, as anachronistic; conflate coming out, being out, and being visible" (x). The in/out binary has always been an imperfect one, and the conflation Thomsen identifies bears further consideration in the case of Blossom.

Blossom members reflect a more ambivalent attitude about lesbian visibility. After a 2004 interviewer posed a question about what "out" means to the community, Rose DeGray answered: "That's a tough one. Because I never really considered myself that out." DeGray articulates "outness" as an issue of degrees: How "out" might one be? In what circles? Under what circumstances? Outness is often situational for rural queer people, and while some strive for clear-cut recognition, others seek to negotiate different levels of visibility. The formal and textual elements of the *Blossom Newsletter* help lesbian members navigate that visibility, as we explore more concretely in the examples that follow.

But it is important to note that, while lesbianism is marked—overtly and covertly—as the heart of the *Blossom* newsletters, the contributors, editors, and responding readers demonstrate a contested, intersectional, dynamic, and emplaced view of what lesbianism signifies. It is a scattered identity marker, encompassing a plurality of orientations and ideas. Contributors like "Mom" write candidly about their experiences with disability. Other members advertise and recommend lesbian antiracist periodicals. Some took a hardline attitude in favor of lesbian separatism, whereas others were morally opposed to it. Editorial columns demonstrate an intense awareness of place, exploring both the affordances and the drawbacks of rural life while also reflecting on the writers' previous experiences living in cities along the East and West Coasts. In a February 1993 issue, Cruz writes:

> The ties that bind us may not be the strongest or the most glamorous or even for that matter recognized by each of us as being the same thing. None the less, WE ARE HERE and we meet at gatherings to be with each other and we hope that we as well as those we met return home feeling more positive about ourselves and this life.

Indeed, within the newsletters Blossom members seem less interested in codifying an idea of what "a lesbian" looks like than in showing up together to share knowledge, skills, and stories. In this way, meaning is generated not through stabilizing lesbianism but through sharing space and time together. "WE ARE HERE," as Cruz asserts.[4]

Blossom's presence is felt not only through in-person gatherings but also on the page. Folklorist Dorothy Noyes writes of "rituals of seeing" and "rituals of sharing" in festival events that navigate the murky waters between individual personhood and the collective communal body (88). In a similar way, the composition, publication, and dissemination of the newsletter might also be understood as rituals of seeing and sharing, where differing perspectives

4. While the newsletters often reflect a positive picture of Blossom, there are other elements of the group to be reckoned with, as well. The rhetorical roots of trans-exclusionary feminism can be traced within the separatist discourse that Blossom members debated. While some members engaged with antiracist activism through reading discussions and calls to action, others expressed their disappointment in failing to invite more Latina and BIPOC participation. Former members noted the all-too-often cliquish social dynamics (Vaugine). For all its goals on paper, Blossom was still subject to intragroup fault lines, gatekeeping, and internal stigmas. We find these counternarratives, too, in the archives at Missouri State University as part of the OLGA Oral History Project. The newsletters are not the only record of authority here, and the wider context of the collection situates the group within a particular place and time.

are juxtaposed, members are visible to one another, and attention is drawn to the collective rather than the individual. The newsletter form offers a useful means to coordinate those efforts, focusing on shared experiences and action above conceptual reflections.[5]

These publications offered members a means for covert circulation and control of information. One of the central tenets of the group was its public avoidance of putting "Blossom" alongside "lesbian." Publicly, Blossom was labeled a feminist women's potluck group, masking the "lesbian" identifier within an innocuous acronym. Linda makes this disassociation explicit in her 1996 direct address to members in "Linda's Back—Explains Why Potlucks Monthly Again, But Newsletter Not." She describes how Blossom will attempt "active outreach," distributing event flyers to allied bars and bookstores while contacting other LGBTQ groups. "Don't panic thoug[h]," she assures. "Our standard operating policy of discretion will still apply and the name, 'BLOSSOM,' will never appear publicly with the word, 'lesbian.'" Here, lesbian visibility is a textual concern: Linda seeks to assuage member worries about the semiotic association between "lesbian" and "Blossom."

Blossom, as a collective, illustrates the complexities of the in–out continuum. The columns, content, and events covered in the newsletter make the queer-leaning orientation of the group clear, but one would need access to either the newsletter or Blossom event spaces to confirm this connection. Visibility politics play out as Blossom and its affiliated groups navigate attention within the community at large. Further care is taken within the newsletters themselves: Contributors usually sign off with their first name, sometimes with a last-name initial, and sometimes as simply "Anonymous." Even as Blossom members debated the benefits and drawbacks of visibility and outness, the newsletter staff took pains to limit identifying information so that only those with insider knowledge might glean the significance of the text.

Ultimately, the *Blossom Newsletter* creates community through a calendar, one that reflects the logic and priorities of the group. What events are

5. The newsletter is a historical genre tied to community formation and imagination. Communications scholar Kathleen L. Endres charts the evolution of early print genres like the newsletter, from handwritten pages that detailed civic business as well as gossip in the Roman Empire (*Acta Diurna*) to the post-office circulated papers of government news during the T'ang dynasty in China (*ti-pao*) (91–92). Endres also notes the legacy of newsletters in Europe, such as the *Schanbriefe* (or *Serienbriefe*) of Germany, noting how such publications often incorporated both oral and written elements to accommodate audiences regardless of their literacy skills. And she notes that newsletters were difficult to control and regulate across the continent: "Threats of capital punishment, exile, and harassment could not and did not rid Europe and the city-states of the newsletters" (93). Endres attributes this endurance to their small-scale circulation, allowing such publications to operate beneath the notice of government entities and public officials.

worth marking in the historical record? Where are they located within social and cultural landscapes? What is flagged for member attention? In this way, Blossom's network becomes diffuse, shifting even as editorial leadership and designers change the features and layout of the publication. The text itself—a collaboratively composed document—becomes the dominant translating voice for the group even as it remains a site of contestation and debate. While this certainly erases individual differences and voices within the group, it nevertheless affords Blossom something very compelling: a sense of collectivity that masks individuality, when to be singled out is to risk unwanted attention and even violence.

Conclusion

> [I] never have said to you what a swell thing it's been to watch Springfield dykes come together and find each other through BLOSSOM and related stuff. What great occurrences for a town/region where homophobia still holds so strong. What acts of bravery for you all to come together to find strength and pleasure from the company of other lesbians . . . so important and necessary.
>
> —Anonymous, "From You to Us," *Blossom Newsletter*, May 1993 (ellipsis in original)

It is important to note the impact of the archive in this exploration of Blossom. While the newsletters initially circulated within a localized group, their collection and preservation within the Ozark Lesbian and Gay Archives shift their visibility status. No longer records for the group alone, they are reframed by OLGA's mission: "to document the lesbian, gay, bisexual, and transgender (LGBT) experience in the Ozarks region" ("Ozark Lesbian and Gay Archives"). In this way, Blossom's topographical traces are temporally complex, leaving a mark on the region's history in meaningful and revelatory ways. The newsletters gain a new translative dimension within the context of the archive: They make these covert histories visible to later generations and historians. While frequently described as a homogenous conservative region, the rural Ozarks have been home to LGBTQ+ groups and activists that have been marginalized or erased from the landscape but who, nonetheless, came together through "acts of bravery," as described in the epigraph above. Now, these archived newsletters provide the basis for a queer topography that spatializes Blossom's social history and maps their traces across the Ozark terrain.

In fundamental ways, this archive and my own archival research are imaginative. Blossom members used print to imagine their community—not unlike the "imagined communities" outlined by Benedict Anderson that form around the circulation of print.[6] "Communities are to be distinguished," Anderson writes, "not by their falsity/genuineness, but by the style in which they are imagined" (6). As demonstrated here, Blossom's stylistic strategies can be witnessed in their newsletters: Their imagined community is a complex negotiation of visibility and invisibility, presence and absence, the overt and the covert—all mediated through print. This technology allows for collaboration, multiplicity, gathering, and negotiation. Like Anderson, we have noted the stylistic and creative choices within the newsletters, highlighting how editors and contributors elevate the collective "Blossom" and obscure individual identity in the process—in this case—through the act of writing, printing, and circulating their newsletters. Technologies of writing transform abstract thoughts, reflections, or concepts into material texts, and the materiality of these inscribed objects is powerfully relevant. The *Blossom* newsletters become historically significant artifacts when located within the special collections of OLGA. They remain as evidence of a covert and sometimes-veiled organization, enduring long after its dissolution, and remain as the central voice continuing to represent the Blossom experience.

As others encounter Blossom through its archival records, they, too, will imagine a community of the past. My own imaginative process unfolded spatially, topographically. When I first encountered Blossom through their newsletters, I felt the urge to trace: trace its history and origins, trace its legacy across time, and trace its footprint across the region (see figure 8.1). I'd recognize place names and local landmarks mentioned in the newsletters, spaces that I suddenly saw in a new light through queer history. Mapping Blossom across the Ozarks was revelatory, liberatory, and troubling. This process required me to critically reconsider my own imagined geographies. To re-evaluate my expectations about rural LGBTQ+ cultures. To reckon with my identity as a rural queer woman whose regional experience had been marked by both discovery and repression, who struggled with her own questions about visibility and "outness." Tracing Blossom through the archives meant navigating conceptions of self and community, place and space, visibility and erasure, an imaginative practice that continues with every new archival encounter.

6. Anderson focuses on large-scale communities imagined around ideas of nationhood, but I argue that some of the mechanisms through which these communities are wrought—especially print—still operate in smaller scale groups, such as Blossom.

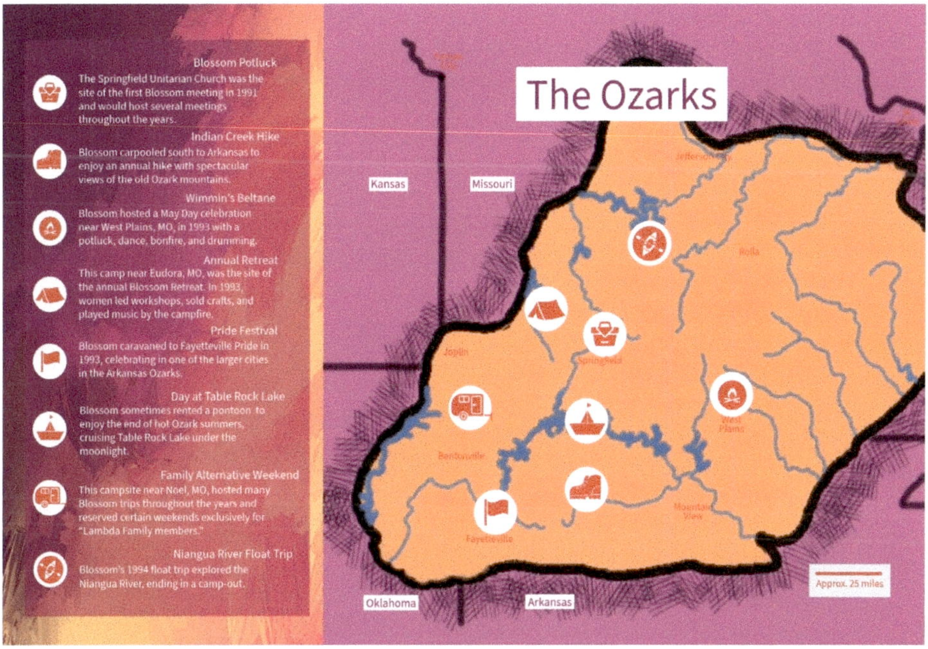

FIGURE 8.1. Map of Blossom events from the early 1990s, showing locations and activities across Missouri and Arkansas. Illustrated by and used with permission from the author.

Works Cited

Anderson, Benedict. *Imagined Communities: Reflections on the Origin and Spread of Nationalism.* 1983. Verso, 2006.

Baggett, Holly A. "The Creation of Community: A History of Gay and Lesbian Springfield, 1945–2010." *Springfield's Urban Histories: Essays on the Queen City of the Missouri Ozarks,* edited by Stephen L. McIntyre, Moon City Press, 2012, pp. 305–40.

Blossom Newsletters. Series 1, box 1. Ozark Lesbian and Gay Archives Collection [M018], Department of Special Collections and Archives, Missouri State University, 1993–2001.

DeGray, Rose. Oral history interview. *Ozarks Lesbian and Gay Archives Oral History Project,* Special Collections and Archives, Missouri State University, August 2004.

Endres, Kathleen L. "Newsletters, Newspapers, Pamphlets." *Encyclopedia of Life Support Systems: Journalism and Mass Communications,* edited by Rashmi Luthra, EOLSS Publishers, 2009.

Ghazianai, Amin. "Lesbian Geographies." *Contexts,* vol. 14, no. 1, 2015, pp. 62–64.

Gray, Mary L. *Queering the Countryside: New Frontiers in Rural Queer Studies.* New York University Press, 2016.

Halberstam, Jack. *In a Queer Time and Place: Transgender Bodies, Subcultural Lives.* New York University Press, 2005.

Herring, Scott. *Another Country: Queer Anti-Urbanism.* New York University Press, 2010.

Humphrey, Theodore C., and Lin T. Humphrey. *"We Gather Together": Food and Festival in American Life.* Utah State University Press, 1988.

Johnson, Colin R. *Just Queer Folks: Gender and Sexuality in Rural America.* Temple University Press, 2013.

Lewin, Ellen. "'Natural' Achievements: How Lesbian and Gay Families in North America Make Claims to Kinship." *The Cambridge Handbook of Kinship,* edited by Sandra Bamford, Cambridge University Press, 2019, pp. 253–75.

Linman, Becky. Oral history interview. *Ozarks Lesbian and Gay Archives Oral History Project,* Special Collections and Archives, Missouri State University, 8 June 2009.

Miller, Isabel. *Side by Side.* Bella Books, 1990.

Noyes, Dorothy. *Fire in the Plaça: Catalan Festival Politics After Franco.* University of Pennsylvania Press, 2003.

"Ozark Lesbian and Gay Archives." *Missouri State University Libraries,* Missouri State University, 20 Oct. 2025, https://libraries.missouristate.edu/OLGA.htm.

Thomas, Linda. Oral history interview. *Ozarks Lesbian and Gay Archives Oral History Project,* Special Collections and Archives, Missouri State University, 6 July 2007.

Thomsen, Carly. *Visibility Interrupted: Rural Queer Life and the Politics of Unbecoming.* University of Minnesota Press, 2021.

Schiffrin, Deborah, and Anna De Fina. *Telling Stories: Language, Narrative, and Social Life.* Georgetown University Press, 2010.

Vaugine, Shelley. Oral history interview. *Ozarks Lesbian and Gay Archives Oral History Project,* Special Collections and Archives, Missouri State University, 22 Nov. 2004.

Wiseheart, Susan. Oral history interview. *Ozarks Lesbian and Gay Archives Oral History Project,* Special Collections and Archives, Missouri State University, 30 Sept. 2004.

CHAPTER 9

Forest Listening Rooms

Sound, Archives, and Social Engagement in Appalachian Ohio

BRIAN HARNETTY

The Sonic Forest

I walk into the forest with a dozen people. Single file, spread out, silent. It is late spring, warm, and the canopy of trees is already full. As we climb a hill, we listen: footsteps, a soft breeze, a far-off dog, a swooping warbler. We arrive at a grassy clearing. A circle of chairs is there, placed in front of a shallow cave.

Still silent, we sit down and listen together. We listen inward, paying attention to our breath and hearts as they slow down. We listen outward, too: the swish of a pant leg, a creaking chair, a buzzing bee. As we settle, the forest becomes louder. Trees sway, water drips and echoes inside the cave, the hollow thud of a woodpecker sounds in the distance. We become aware of everything, and we disappear.

An archival recording begins. Long, quiet tones of clarinet, saxophone, and strings. The instruments seem to come out of the forest, overlapping and merging with the natural sounds around us. An old man begins to speak. For a brief moment, we are startled. Is that someone in the group? Is it a ghost? It is a recording, and the man talks of the place we are sitting, of secret meetings and labor strikes, of an underground fire. We hear other recorded voices, too. A woman sings an old local ballad. A girl describes insect patterns in a fallen tree. A man emotionally talks of escaping a coal mine explosion.

We come out of the silence, and begin to tell our stories. One person speaks of memory, of how she used to play in the forest as a child. Others talk about how they are feeling in that moment, noticing the complex sounds and sights all around. A man makes note of the continually changing land, and how the forest is returning over his lifetime. A woman tells a story of how the land might change in the future, and how she hopes her family can stay and thrive. (See figures 9.1 and 9.2.)

As we walk out of the forest, our pace is faster, our feet lighter. We fall into pairs and groups. Conversations continue; someone near the back laughs. We arrive again at the starting point. I thank everyone for coming, and our listening session is over.

The story above is a glimpse into *Forest Listening Rooms,* a socially engaged sound art project.[1] Launched in 2018 and continuing through today, the project shows how a group of people can gather, walk, sit, listen, and talk together in nature. It also reveals how the sonic forest begins to change us and how we understand one another.

This listening session took place at Robinson's Cave in the Wayne National Forest in Appalachian Ohio. After two centuries of extraction and ninety years of hard-fought recovery, the land is beginning to heal. At the same time, several ecological, economic, and social developments threaten these efforts: ongoing environmental destruction; new iterations of energy extraction, including gas, oil, and hydraulic fracturing (or "fracking"); a widening gap between wealth and poverty, and between urban and rural communities; economic struggles taking place in the small towns throughout the region; and an encroaching gentrification and development that rarely considers the land or local residents.

The forest has a much longer Indigenous history. The area where our listening sessions take place, for example, was known for being the hunting grounds of Shawnee chief Tecumseh in the late eighteenth century (Bashaw et al. 10–12). During the first decades of the nineteenth century, the Shawnee and other Indigenous tribes were systematically and brutally removed from the region (first to northern Ohio, and then out of Ohio altogether). By the time many of the coal mining towns were established in the 1870s, most of the tribes had been gone for decades. This makes Appalachian Ohio an important location for understanding the complex past and present landscapes of the forest.

The *Forest Listening Rooms* project acknowledges these tensions and struggles, and offers a simple yet radical proposal: to listen. Here, listening is a

1. "Socially engaged art" (sometimes called "social practice") refers to a type of art that is not based on the creation of objects but is instead focused on relationships built with communities of people. Socially engaged art is participatory, experiential, and has a goal of enacting social change.

FIGURE 9.1. A small group of listeners sitting quietly in a clearing during a *Forest Listening Rooms* session at Tecumseh Lake, Shawnee, Ohio. Photo by Julian Foglietti, used with permission.

FIGURE 9.2. A large group of listeners sitting quietly in a circle at a *Forest Listening Rooms* session at Robinson's Cave, New Straitsville, Ohio. Photo by Julian Foglietti, used with permission.

method of paying attention to past and present sounds to consider their contexts. Both vulnerability and strength, listening acknowledges that what may happen next is unknown, yet this leads to new ways of understanding. This at first might seem like a naive or reductive way to address complicated problems. And yet, the long-term work of listening to places, archives, and each other is a compelling method for connecting with a shared love for the land, and to enact social and environmental change.

Forest Listening Rooms, then, invites residents living in the forest to gather in outdoor spaces to listen. The goals of the project are to consider the land and how it is used; to help bridge the divide between rural and urban communities; and ultimately to help end large-scale extraction in the forests' public lands. The project asks: What does social change sound like? What are the stories of the forest and the people who live there? Through listening, how might people change personally, and how might they change the forest? At first, my answers to these questions were focused on environmental activism, and I saw the ending of fracking in the forest as the project's solitary goal. Now, I see this change in much smaller, personal increments, of individuals working together over generations, and of the land's own subtle, slow healing.

I began working in Appalachian Ohio in 2010, doing ethnographic research with a focus on sound. Many years later, I keep coming back to the forest. It has profoundly changed the way I work. Originally trained as a composer and sound artist, I now also incorporate methods from ethnography—including social engagement, observing, participating, listening, and writing—as part of my practice. I continue to experiment, make creative projects, and take part in community events and organizations.

Archival sounds are an integral part of *Forest Listening Rooms,* be they discussions, oral histories, field recordings, or local songs. Often, the recordings are of people from the past who lived and worked in the spots where we listen. The recordings not only have a haunting quality; they also allow listening to situate archival voices in the contexts of the present-day forest. We listen to traces of the past, and we are given clues for how to change the future.

Over the years, I slowly became attuned to the sonic forest. I noticed the sounds of nature and society, of damage and recovery. The forest became a welcoming place to walk into, a naturally built (and human built) environment where I could be quiet. As I spent time in the forest, listening became my main tool for understanding it. I developed and adapted many listening and community-based techniques, some of which I share below. They draw from music composition, sound art, socially engaged art, ethnography, meditation, and mindfulness. With these prompts and tools, you can also create your own "listening rooms," wherever you are.

An Anatomy of a *Forest Listening Rooms* Session

A simple definition of a "forest listening room" is any outdoor place one intentionally visits and pauses to listen. It is a place where you listen in context: paying attention to the past and present of where you are and the people who live there. It can be in solitude, or with others. Being in an actual forest or woods is ideal, but this is not always possible. A local park, a town square, or even sitting next to a lone tree in a parking lot all work, too. It does not need to be fancy or formal: If you designate a place to be so, then it becomes a "listening room."

Forest Listening Rooms is structured around five activities, all connected to sound and place: walking and listening, silent listening, archival listening, discussion, and return. This structure is flexible and can adapt to many situations and groups of people. When done with others, a listening room can open up unforeseen connections. When I first started working with communities in the forest, for example, I noticed their kindness and determination. I had a yearning to walk and sit with them, quietly listening and letting the forest strengthen these ties. I observed how adding archival recordings to the sessions allowed participants to connect more directly with the past; they were listening to the voices of their ancestors. I also had a hunch that this kind of activity might lead toward some kind of social change; not quick and dramatic, but slow and deliberate. Below, you can find a more detailed account of a listening room structure.

Walking and Listening

We begin and end each *Forest Listening Room* session with a soundwalk.[2] Soundwalks have a long history. Composers such as Annea Lockwood, Hildegard Westerkamp, Pauline Oliveros, John Cage, and the sound art collective Ultra Red have all contributed to this form of concentrated listening that is combined with movement over time and in a given place. In *Forest Listening Rooms,* this environmental listening is intentionally brought together with additional elements—the forest's rich, complex soundscapes[3] of extinction, extraction, degradation, and recovery—where events of the past still affect us today.

2. Hildegard Westerkamp broadly defines a soundwalk as "any excursion whose main purpose is listening to the environment" (18).

3. "Soundscape" refers to the environmental and human sounds of a given place or immersive environment—in short, the "sonic environment" (Schafer).

We gather in a parking lot or alongside the road within the forest. Because most participants are local residents, I note that their perspectives may be different from my own, and from each other. Contrary to many stereotypes of the region, the people who live in Appalachian Ohio are not homogenous and have knowledge and viewpoints across political and cultural spectrums.

We start walking in silence, and we focus on our listening. Immediately, I hear the other participants moving, falling into their own walking patterns: rhythms of feet shuffling, jackets swishing, gravel and coal sliding underfoot, an occasional twig snapping. Slowly, our ears adjust, and the forest introduces itself to us. Akin to the practice of "forest bathing," the trees affect our senses and change us, such as reducing stress hormones, boosting immunity, and lowering blood pressure (Aubrey).

The walk is usually not too long, fifteen to twenty minutes or so. Sometimes it is with many people, sometimes one. Walking into the forest—and later walking back out—situates each listening session as a ritual. It focuses us and concentrates our perception. The physical movement stimulates the body, yet quiets our inner voices. It begins the process of building trust among participants, and defining our presence in the forest.

Silent Listening

After the soundwalk, we arrive at a "listening room," a predetermined site within the forest for dedicated listening. It is temporarily prepared with chairs or places to sit, and audio speakers for archival listening. If possible, we sit in a circle. Sometimes we sit on a bench, or a fallen trunk soft with moss, or a grassy clearing, or we are positioned near a lake or a stream reclaimed from acid mine drainage. Other times we are close to an oil pump, or near an old coal mine entrance, or a fracking wastewater-well site. The "rooms" are often beautiful (and sometimes not), and all have historical meaning.

We sit quietly and listen in silence for a short while, twenty minutes or so. As we settle in, the forest becomes louder. The trees make the wind audible, and water from an earlier rain shower drips from the leaves. Cicadas and crickets sing their ever-present drones. A truck rumbles in the distance. Birds call antiphonally across a field. As we listen, we are making a space in the forest and defining our presence. We notice what is there, what is not, and the change between the two over time.

Listening to the forest in silence as a group can be a shocking experience. It is different from listening alone. It takes on a communal quality, a felt presence, one shared with the surrounding trees and plants and animals. It reminds me of Quaker religious traditions, where congregations are comfortable sitting in silence together.

The trees participate along with us. They are quietly changing us, and we strain to hear what they say. I call this practice "contemplative listening," where there is an inner sense of letting go, and a simple awareness without analysis, commentary, or argument. This approach encourages a sense of opening up to each other and to the world.

Archival Listening

We then turn to archival recordings of past and present residents.[4] Some of the recordings are of people long gone. They talk of their work as miners and shopkeepers, their pride in the land, social activities, jobs disappearing, towns vanishing. The recordings were often made decades earlier in the same places where we are listening now. Everything blurs together: Was that bird in the tree or on the tape? Was that voice from the past, or from someone sitting next to me?

These archival recordings are imbued with their own agency. The grain of voices long gone, together with the hiss and warble of the old media, deeply affect the listeners. This is what Jane Bennett calls "vibrant materiality," where objects have their own "trajectories, propensities, or tendencies" (viii). When played in the forest, the recordings are perplexing, like hearing ghosts from the past. Participants, in turn, observe the disparity between what is being spoken and what they observe around them: what has recovered, stayed the same, or gotten worse.

"Do you know how the mine fire started?" asks local historian Dot Dishon on an old cassette tape. "Well, I know what has always been heard," answers local resident Jim Bath. "I don't know if it actually started that a-way. But uh, over in Straitsville, there's a holler over there, they call 'Lost Holler.' It had a mine down in there. Uh, [it was] one of the miner's and mine owner's disagreements. A bunch of the miners loaded up a car of coal . . ." This story of a local mine fire continues with a different recording, this time from resident Judd Matheney in the 1970s. "It's pretty definitely accepted that the miners poured oil on a loaded car of coal," he begins, "and pushed it down

4. Historic recordings are from the *Little Cities of Black Diamonds* archive in New Straitsville, Ohio, and contemporary recordings are made by the author. All recordings are used with permission.

FIGURE 9.3. Perry County resident Joelene Dixon talks with Brian Harnetty while he makes an audio recording at Essington Lake, Ohio. Photo by Kevin Davison, used with permission.

the slope and it coasted a-way back in the mine and caught the seam on fire. There's apparently no doubt about that. One of the men that helped perform that act, after he'd seen what he had done . . . he said he never got it off his mind. It troubled him all his life, to think he was a party to the ruination of that [land]." When we hear these recordings, there is a disconnect between the bucolic soundscape and landscape around us, and the knowledge that directly underneath is a maze of abandoned mines and a fire that has burned for generations.

Other recordings feature voices of those who participated in earlier listening sessions (see figure 9.3). They often express their connection to the land, and their fears and hopes for the future. One participant notes, "It's definitely a meditative space for me personally, but it's also this really dense, complex, layered historical place that I don't fully grasp or understand." Here, the participant describes how the forest influences him in the present and acknowledges that the history of the place affects him, too: They are entwined and cannot be untangled or ignored.

Through archival listening, we hear the recordings in the context of the forest, where natural and archival sounds mix to create something new. It is this addition of archival recordings into the format of a listening session that helps it become what I call an "archival performance," where archival materials are reinterpreted and activated in the present moment as a way to connect with sonic memory.

Discussion

After the archival recordings, we begin a discussion, which lasts for about twenty minutes. I record the discussion (with the participants' permission) and often select one or two comments to include in future listening rooms iterations. The remaining recordings are saved as an archive, mapping the sounds and people of each place.

Most often, participants talk of the land, how they live on it and use it, and how they would like to see it change. At this point, we have all been actively listening with intention for fifty minutes or so, and our ears have sharpened and attuned to the forest. Now, our listening shifts to include the other participants, as we address these questions: Are we truly listening to each other? What does the forest tell us? How might we work together to make things better for us and for the forest?

For local residents, this discussion almost always begins with memory. There is a strong sense of connection between their childhoods and the forest, and the participants are allowing it to inspire them as it did when they were young. This type of listening—to one's own past—can act as a reminder of one's connection to the land, and a commitment to help it recover. During one listening session, a woman recalls her childhood walks through the forest, and her adult struggle to keep it from being mined for coal. She states, "My parents are gone. And after my dad died . . . I wasn't quite ready for the feeling of being an orphan. And something about being in an area that is familiar to you, that reminds you of your childhood, reminds you of carefree days, is comforting. I don't know how else to say it, it's just comforting. It's home." For this participant, the forest has become family, quietly standing in for her lost loved ones.

A *Forest Listening Rooms* discussion is also a space of critical thought, as we move through the messy process of working toward social change. During one discussion, a local hunter states, "When you look at public land, it's no secret that people are pretty divided today. But this is something that both sides of the political spectrum agree on. I feel like it's such a thing that can unite so many different factions that otherwise may not agree on many things." Astonishingly, the forest here becomes a mediator between participants. It is actively working to change us. Another participant notes, "The forest is winning the battle again; it's coming back and taking over. I've decided it's a good thing [for it] to reclaim this land."

Finally, the listening room is a place of understanding. Or, as one participant put it, "a space to think and feel." It changes our tone, our inner voice, and the way we talk with each other. Even if participants are from different towns or backgrounds, the sessions have not been argumentative. I attribute this conviviality largely to the forest and its emotional effect on us. I am convinced that our conversations would be less meaningful if we had not undergone a mutual listening experience together. It is at this moment that we become aware of a deeply shared interest in and love for the land; we are literally finding common ground.

Return

The discussion concludes, and we walk back together to the starting point. Ritual plays a part here, too, of both return and release: The intense listening process is over, and there is a sense of lightness in our steps and conversations. The walk is open, noisy, faster. Talk spills over from our earlier discussion, and I hear laughter in participants' voices. I should also say the listening does not stop here. It has shifted along with the mood, becoming celebratory. Listening reminds us that, when done as openly and objectively as possible, it is a radical act of attention, of trust, even love.

Over time, returning again and again to these places and residents is a process of social change. It is deliberate, slow, and complex, and often feels lost or misguided. Each time, however, something grows and some small connection is made. We witness and reflect on the land and its past, and work toward changing the place, to even heal it. At the same time, it is changing us, too.

Conclusion

After our listening session at Robinson's Cave is over, we walk down the hill and into a local history building for lunch. There are sandwiches, coffee, fruit, and sweets. We sit on creaky chairs at folding tables among archival photos, mining tools, maps, books, memories. I find myself still listening, attuned to conversations blending into one another. The sounds are relaxed, polite, inquisitive. Some people are getting to know one another; others have known each other all their lives.

I sit next to a man who happens to work at the Ohio Environmental Protection Agency. I ask him: How long will it take for the forest to recover? When will the effects of mining end? "About a century, give or take fifty years," he says. "The mines need to flush out the acidic metals over time. And once that happens, the waterways will recover fairly quickly. But we need to be patient, and persistent. We need to keep working to keep the water neutral, so that life can come back. But eventually we hope we won't be needed, and the streams can recover on their own."

I am impressed with the man's sense of time. He is not thinking in terms of a few years, but in generations and centuries. It strikes me that this is something he would not get to witness in his lifetime. He is not alone: In the 1930s, many people helped transform the barren hills here back into a forest, which they did not get to fully witness either. The man continues, "You'll probably still be taking your grandkids to see these streams and our efforts to make them better, to help fix all the damage mining did to this land."

In this man's comments, I see a clear-eyed yet optimistic way to move toward a recovering forest. He is describing the persistent, unglamorous, yet glorious rhythms of reclamation. Not one, but many people together enact these rhythms. They are steadily allowing the land to sound again: trees and animals, birds and insects, water and wind, life and decay. The past reveals its own rhythms, too. Through archival recordings, we hear the pride of labor, the joys of community, and the cautionary tales of extraction and disaster. Holding these often conflicting realities together—of recovery on one hand, and destruction on the other—and then finding ways to move forward is at the heart of my listening practice, and my hopes for the future of Appalachian Ohio.

Heard together, these rhythms are a reminder that social change is often imperceptibly slow, and hard to observe: It is in the voices of protesters and political movements, and it is also in the hearts of residents who want to make a better place for their children, or in the actions of a government worker making the water clean again, or in the words of a historian remembering the stories of the past, or the actions of a community organizer seeking ways to create an equitable and just economy.

These rhythms echo author Wendell Berry's words: He once called land that humans destroyed and then healed a "geography of scars" (7). It is a poetic and sober reminder that we cannot undo the harm done, but we can move forward to make the land better.

Works Cited

Aubrey, Allison. "Forest Bathing: A Retreat to Nature Can Boost Immunity and Mood." *National Public Radio*, 17 July 2017, https://www.npr.org/sections/health-shots/2017/07/17/536676954/forest-bathing-a-retreat-to-nature-can-boost-immunityand-mood.

Bashaw, Andrew, et al. *At the Glacier's Edge: An Environmental History and Field Guide of the Little Cities of Black Diamonds Microregion*. Sunday Creek Associates, 2007.

Bennett, Jane. *Vibrant Matter: A Political Ecology of Things.* Duke University Press, 2010.

Berry, Wendell. *What Are People For?* North Point Press, 1990.

Schafer, R. Murray. *The Soundscape: Our Sonic Environment and the Tuning of the World.* Destiny Books, 1994.

Westerkamp, Hildegard. "Soundwalking." *Sound Heritage,* vol. 3, no. 4, 1974, pp. 18–27.

CHAPTER 10

Countering Environmental Narratives with Archival Latencies

NICOLE WOOD

On January 31, 2025, news organizations began to broadcast the disappearance of numerous public datasets from United States federal agency websites, which were suppressed in response to executive orders from the Trump administration. Affected agencies, departments, and divisions ranged from the Centers for Disease Control to the Administration for Children and Families (Singer; Kurtzleben; Steenhuysen and Hesson). These orders, targeting diversity, equity, and inclusion initiatives, raised an immediate outcry over concerns for government transparency. At the same time, with less fanfare, environmental datasets were disappearing from data.gov. By the time the media began reporting this state-sponsored censorship, over two thousand datasets had vanished—disproportionately sourced from the Department of Energy, the National Oceanic and Atmospheric Administration, the Department of the Interior, National Aeronautics and Space Administration (NASA), and the Environmental Protection Agency (Koebler). The administration silently removed web pages from the US Department of Agriculture (USDA) and the US Forest Service (USFS) that documented climate change; while the USDA's Climate Hubs remained active, other sites, including the USFS Climate Change Resource Center, the Climate Action Tracker, and the National Roadmap for Responding to Climate Change, went dark (Canon; Colman and Brown). The White House Office of Science and Technology also issued stop-work orders for upcoming publications, such as the federal government's first National Nature Assessment, a document intended to offer information on how nature supports the US economy, national security, and the health and safety of its residents (Doyle).

This act of censorship echoed efforts by the first Trump administration to purge federal websites of information on climate change. According to Nost et al., between 2016 and 2020, references to the term "climate change" on environmental agency websites decreased by 38 percent ("Visualizing"). Webb and Kurtz posit that Trump's "war on science" was instrumental in helping the administration "advance its deregulatory agenda . . . by casting doubt on the need for climate regulations" ("Politics"). The Environmental Data and Governance Initiative (EDGI) documents the connection between this concealment of information and resulting deregulatory policies, such as the removal of web pages, fact sheets, and financial incentives related to the 2015 Clean Power Plan, which occurred a mere five months before Scott Pruitt, the Trump-appointed EPA administrator, announced the formal process to repeal the plan (Nost et al., "EDGI"). Government censorship of climate change has been so extensive that a number of organizations in addition to EDGI have developed environmental justice and regulation rollback trackers, such as Harvard Law School's Federal Environmental Justice Tracker, Columbia University's Climate Backtracker, and the Brookings Institution's Reg Tracker.

After Donald Trump was elected for a second term in November 2024, environmental justice groups, archivists, and researchers scrambled to preserve this data before the inauguration. The White House Council on Environmental Quality, Control, and Justice Screening Tool (CEJST) disappeared from government websites but found a new home with the Public Environmental Data Project (Quinn). The End of Term Web Archive preserves federal government websites at the end of a presidential administration through the Wayback Machine in a collaborative effort of the Common Crawl Foundation, EDGI, Internet Archive, Stanford University Libraries, and the University of North Texas Libraries (Miller). Other environmental groups are archiving biome- or location-specific datasets, such as the Urban Ocean Lab, which now collates data relevant to coastal ecosystems and offshore renewable energy. However, "this data archiving work is a temporary Band-Aid," according to Christina Gosnell, the co-founder and president of Catalyst Cooperative. If these datasets are no longer updated, they become "increasingly stale and thus ineffective at informing decisions over time" (Mulligan).

Archivists can only preserve data that exists, and the impending four-year gap in government-sponsored environmental data collection may encourage archivists to explore creative alternatives for capture and preservation. In this essay, I probe the concept of archival collections as a latent source of environmental data, drawing from Kristin Veel's description of latency in

Thylstrup et al.'s *Uncertain Archives*. I then argue that methodologies drawing from archives as a data source should incorporate both close and distant readings to confront sociohistorical bias in archival acquisition practices and to counter any dubious narratives that can arise from using subjective sources when attempting to draw objective conclusions. The essay concludes with practical examples of archives used as latent sources for environmental data creation through case studies that sought to track the spatiotemporal spread of the American chestnut blight in Tennessee and an effort to collate an authoritative dataset of historical rainfall totals in California prior to the systematic establishment of rain gauges across the state.

Archives as Latent Data

Information has existed since the genesis of the universe. Shockwaves from the Big Bang remain measurable in cosmic microwaves, sometimes referred to as "fossil radiation" (European Space Agency). Although the thermometer was not invented until 1654, over three billion years of the Earth's temperature fluctuations are recorded in climate proxies, such as sedimentary rocks and polar ice sheet layers (National Aeronautics and Space Administration). Ecofacts, such as mineral deposits, seeds, and bones, offer evidence of prehistoric human culture, and later developments have been preserved in the artifacts scattered across archives, museums, and the storage closets of university archaeology departments. This information, in its variety of forms, serves as evidence and supports research efforts in fields ranging from geography to historiography. Libraries and archives are responsible for preserving this evidence in tangible forms, referred to as documents, which first emerged from cave markings and, over time, transformed into imprints on clay tablets, inscriptions on papyrus, prints made from woodblock and moveable type, and, finally, text typed on a keyboard. The comparatively recent digital turn transformed the way these documents are assessed, described, organized, accessed, interpreted, and visualized, allowing researchers to use the information stored in these digitized and born-digital documents as a source for big data analysis.

Researchers utilize these technologies to construct their own datasets from collections. Thurstan et al. collated over 1,600 records published over 350 years to map the historical presence of European flat oyster reef habitats across their biogeographic range along the coasts of the United Kingdom, France, Ireland, Denmark, Spain, Germany, the Netherlands, and sections of Italy. The records included popular books, scholarly papers, government reports, customs accounts, oyster licensing records, travelogs, naturalists' accounts, newspaper articles, nautical charts, and scientific surveys. Wan and Wu used historical topographic maps and satellite imagery to model the evolution of ecological patterns of China's Poyang Lake wetland over the past 100 years. Zhang et al. identified historical distributions of black grouse in Northeast China using local gazetteers, fauna surveys, nature reserve scientific surveys, published scientific papers, and interviews. In the humanities and social sciences, scholars visualized social network analyses from collections of letters and art auction records (van Vugt; Fabiani and Marrone).

In *Uncertain Archives,* Kristin Veel refers to the "latent uncertainties" of big data archives as "the unknowns or unknowables that we are blind to and therefore do not think to harvest" (315). While this can refer to the human-produced archival silences perpetuated by selective preservation practices, it could also apply to information within a record that might be overlooked because of mundanity or perceived irrelevance. Documents are drafted to communicate a specific message, but auxiliary information slips in. Other definitions of latency cited by Veel include dormant, "present but not yet producing symptoms," and "something hidden from view that we expect to emerge into visibility at some point in the future" (313). *Oxford Reference* defines latent as "existing in a potential, dormant, or suppressed form but usually capable of being expressed or evoked." A latent variable is an "unobserved or not directly measured variable" that can be inferred from observed or measurable variables. This term is often interchangeable with a proxy variable or a "variable used instead of the variable of interest" when the variable of interest cannot be directly measured (Hashimzade et al.).

Agostinho et al. posit that archives have always been uncertain, with post-structuralist, feminist, queer, postcolonial, and critical race theories challenging the authority of the archive as a "reliable repository" and critiquing the archives' capacity to "produce truth, offer evidence, and categorise human identities" (423). The digital turn, with the introduction of big data in archival practice, is merely the next destination in the long timeline of archival selection, exclusion, authority, lacunae, and silence. Statistical aggregation, reductive datasets, and algorithmic bias can also extend and reify existing archival norms (422–24). This must be considered when consulting archives as latent sources for data, even for seemingly objective disciplines like environmental or climate science. In a study on the potential for unconnected oral history collections to inform understandings of climate change, Olson and Pinto da Silva propose a balance of small data approaches to big data to preserve the cultural insights and context that mitigate the risk of "decontextualization, oversimplification, and attention to mechanical relationships and mere correlations" when analyzing patterns and associations across collections, as Lahsen warns (qtd. in Olson and Pinto da Silva 334). The consultation of both small and big data approaches reveals "deeply cultural understandings, perceptions, and histories of environment changes" (340).

The concept of collections as data is an "orientation to collections that renders them as ordered information, stored digitally, that are inherently amenable to computation" (Padilla et al. "Final" 7). Users of collections as data are professionals sharing a common desire "to leverage computational methods like machine learning, computer vision, text mining, visualization, and network analysis" (7). When collections are transformed into data, the information within can be browsed, searched, and read at scale through text mining. As the extracted data are visualized using computational methods, connections can be drawn between persons or topics that would not have been easily identifiable when reviewing materials manually, and historical trends can be plotted over time (George; Padilla). While applying computational methods to archival collections has many benefits, including opening the archive to quantitative research methods, ethical considerations are emerging. The Vancouver Statement, released as part of the Institute of Museum and Library Services–funded Collections as Data project, includes a set of principles to support the responsible development and computational use of collections as data. One principle addresses the need to "work[ ] against historic and contemporary inequities represented in collection scope, description, access, and use" (Padilla et al. "Vancouver" 2). Large-scale data extraction may "obfuscate what is hidden or missing in the histories they [the collections] are perceived to represent" (Padilla et al. "Final" 14).

The datafied, decontextualized archive, or the "archive as data to be mined" (Moss et al.), is the natural offspring of Paul Otlet's "monographic principle," in which documents are dissected into their constituent components, "the whole document, chapters, sections and so on, down to facts," to be indexed as subject headings on cards for quick information retrieval and redistributed into amalgamated documentary files of similar information (Rayward 7; Otlet 185–86). Ludwik Fleck, a contemporary of Otlet, expressed concern about this reduction and summarization, arguing that the process omitted vital contextual information. According to Fleck, facts are socially constructed and understandable only with prior knowledge of and a shared cultural context within a community of thinking (Buckland 4).

Methodologies implemented in studies drawing data from archival collections often reflect the monographic principle, extracting atomic facts from various heterogeneous sources for reconciliation into a dataset to answer a specific question. The potential to aggregate fragmented collections and make connections across materials separated by looting, war, or simply by the necessity of format, as is often the case with letter correspondence, provides an "egalitarian vision of a unified digital memory of the world" not dissimilar to Paul Otlet's Universal Bibliographic Repertory (Dickerson and Eagle Yun 1). However, there has not been and cannot be a unified memory. Dickerson and Eagle Yun emphasize that "archives are people, and people are more than the records (and data) that document them" (2). Archival records carry the shadows of their subjects' agency, offering evidence of social norms, preferences, agendas, personal experiences, and expectations. The records are personally and socially created and curated, and "omissions, misrepresentations, and erasures" have been and likely will always be present in collections. "From the catalog to the archival finding aid," archives have "a long legacy of bias" (2).

Dickerson and Eagle Yun present a distinction between digitization and datafication, noting that datafication requires structure: "Structured data involve some element of loss, reduction, and/or essentialization of context," similar to critiques of Otlet's efforts to establish a universal truth for classification (2). If datafication is essentially reductive, Dickerson and Eagle Yun argue, "we will always need archives that are rooted in personhood and ethical engagement with the people being represented in these records" because "objective, structured, all-knowing, complete data" accommodates the viewpoint of the predominant culture in power and is at odds with the social justice imperative of elevating the voices of those marginalized in the historical record (2). Archival records containing latent environmental data are inherently personal, subjective, biased, and political. Care must be taken to properly contextualize the resulting output when treating humans as environmental sensors.

Latent Environmental Data in Ambiguous Archives

Viewing collections as data offers nontraditional sources for dataset compilation and an opportunity to present counternarratives to datasets published by so-called authorities. My research centers on case studies utilizing archives as sources for environmental and climate data to understand the extent to which disparate collections can be collated for environmental modeling. In the summer of 2023, I received funding from the University of California, Los Angeles (UCLA) to develop a methodology to compile and analyze diverse documents drafted between 1904 and 1950 to plot the spatiotemporal spread of the American chestnut blight in Tennessee. While some consulted materials were produced with the intention of documenting the American chestnut blight, such as the indisputably titled 1927 *Tennessean* newspaper article "Chestnuts Are Doomed," other sources contained what could be called latent environmental data. For example, a 1915 University of Chattanooga yearbook advertised a freshmen chestnut hunt, implying that local trees remained healthy and fruit-bearing (97). By contrast, a 1933 *Smoky Mountains Hiking Club Handbook* program for a January hike to Newton Bald describes a view of "three or four high peaks which, with the exception of a few dead chestnut trees, are completely bare" (14).

Spatiotemporal plotting of the dataset created from available primary source references to American chestnut trees or stands at a specific date, location, and condition (alive, blighted, or dead) reveal a potentially nonlinear trajectory of blight spread, with early warnings appearing in western Tennessee, followed by the east, and a year later in the middle portion of the state, deviating from the expected path of a blight dispersed via wind and animal encounters. An early newspaper article published in Huntingdon, Tennessee, located closer to Arkansas and Missouri than blight-infested Virginia, encourages readers to plant chestnut trees as a "civic duty" to fight the spreading blight ("Duty Devolving Upon Us All"). In the following years, blight warnings began appearing in newspapers largely in west and middle Tennessee. It was not until 1925 that a definitive reference to the chestnut blight along the East Tennessee–Virginia border can be found in the available archival record—an announcement in the *Knoxville News-Sentinel* that "all hope of saving chestnut timber" in the Cherokee National Forest had "been abandoned" ("Looking Back" 36). If the information contained in these records is considered latent sources for environmental data, it is worth interrogating manmade causes of blight spread, such as interstate nursery stock transportation and conflicting interests of the Chief of the Plant Quarantine and Control Administration and the American Association of Nurserymen (Pauly 152), which delayed the passage of the Plant Quarantine Act of 1912 until "it was too little, too late for the American chestnut" (Davis 148).

I am now expanding this methodology in a comprehensive effort to create an authoritative dataset of rainfall totals across California prior to the installation of rain gauges in the mid-1850s (Conner, "Los Angeles" 15 and "Sonoma" 4; Lynch 7) and as a supplemental data source prior to the collection of continuous, reliable rainfall measurements across the state. The final product will present a model of the large-scale extracted information accompanied by a close reading of the texts to confront and contextualize missing voices, dubious accounts, and the sociohistorical bias in record collection. Unlike the American chestnut blight project, in which a minority of sources (34 of 274) contained latent data, the majority of references to rainfall in California before official, widespread measurement can be considered latent or dormant. While Spanish mission priests maintained systematic rainfall accounts to inform planting practices (Lynch foreword), most measurements are sprinkled across the letters and diaries of farmers, homemakers, migrants, miners, loggers, and ice harvesters.

Take, for example, the personal letters of Franklin Augustus Buck, a sawmill owner and ice harvester in Weaverville, California, a mining town that began maintaining precipitation records at the Weaverville Ranger Station in 1894 (Western Regional Climate Center). In his correspondence, Buck documented six weather events between 1852 and 1866 in which measurements are extractable. On December 18, 1852, in a letter to his sister, Buck described an "incessant snowstorm" that laid approximately two feet of snow across the region. On September 18, 1853, nestled between reflections on manifest destiny and a gubernatorial election, Buck briefly remarked on a heavy thunderstorm that caused the local rivers and creeks to rise by four to six feet. In a letter written on April 6, 1862, Buck announced his daughter's birth and his brother's death, and he also mentioned a four-inch snowfall. Other observations include a three-foot measurement of snow at a local sawmill (December 14, 1856), a Christmas morning snowstorm (December 25, 1860), and a snowy day that reminded Buck of his childhood in Maine (January 18, 1866).

Miners E. C. Dunn ("Dunn Diary") and Jacob H. Engle (Grabhorn) also recorded specific precipitation measurements in diaries and letters written during their time in Weaverville. For most Californians, water was vital for earning income, and, as such, its presence and absence are heavily documented in the archival record. Miners used water to separate lighter sand from the heavier gold deposits; flowing creek beds were essential when sifting sediment through pans and sluice boxes. Farmers naturally relied on rain to water their crops. Loggers and sawmill owners needed flowing rivers to transport lumber downstream to potential buyers. Ice harvesters, by necessity, required a generous supply of water to freeze in the mountains long enough for warm-weather extraction. When interpreting these texts, it is necessary to consider the intent and authority of the author in recording water levels. For example, a farmer's diary would likely reflect rainfall measurements as accurately as possible to inform planting and harvest decisions. However, a miner working at a particularly profitable section of a river might send false news to nearby towns to protect their claim. Additionally, some documents consulted for data collection were published by businessmen and civic leaders who may have had vested interests in presenting an overly optimistic report of rainfall and crop growth to attract profit from an immigration influx, as evidenced in multiple references to the idea that "rain follows the plow," a now discredited theory that encouraged pioneers to settle in the Great Plains (Barnett).

Personal narratives as a source of latent environmental data inherently require using subjective accounts to draw objective conclusions. However, even authoritative environmental sources have always been swayed by bias. During the California Water Wars of the early twentieth century, familiar names like Theodore Roosevelt, Frederick Eaton, and William Mulholland voiced support in favor of "rich members of the San Fernando syndicate" controlling the surplus water of the Owens River at the expense of "thousands of homesteaders" who relied on the river for subsistence. During the water wars, Theodore Roosevelt went so far as to create the Inyo National "Forest," to cordon off the nearly treeless Owens Valley in accommodation of the Los Angeles Aqueduct (Reisner 93), explaining that the "water is more valuable to the people of Los Angeles than to the Owens Valley" (92). The people living in the Owens Valley would likely offer a counternarrative: that Mulholland employed "chicanery, subterfuge, bribery, a campaign of divide-and-conquer, and a strategy of lies" to acquire water for Los Angeles (72).

The California Water Wars' conflicting federal and local accounts echo through present-day environmental management practices. For example, the United States Forest Service describes itself as "a world leader in forest research" with a "renowned fire management organization" that provides "critical expertise in making communities and infrastructure safer" ("About"). When the Forest Service advocates for chopping down trees as a forest fire prevention tactic, does it matter that the agency is also balancing demand to meet annual timber quotas mandated and determined by Congress through the National Forest Management Act? If web pages are properly archived, future researchers will be able to gather and analyze the cacophony of relevant communications in bulk, such as federal government websites, peer-reviewed research that argues for and against forest thinning as a fire prevention tactic (Barni et al.; Brodie et al.; Lindenmayer et al.), social media posts, and grassroots communication networks, such as the letters to the editor teams at the Sierra Club and the John Muir Project.

The Trump administration's censorship of environmental data leaves the concept of federal data as authoritative open to critique, but federal data and the resulting research outputs are not and have never been neutral; collection criteria can reflect the whims of whichever administration happens to be in office. As archives continue to rescue vulnerable environmental data and federal web pages, they can also serve as a source for latent environmental data that challenges the narratives passed down by those in power. The ability to gather sources at scale expands the scope of voices that can be consulted, allowing a multiplicity of potentially conflicting experiences, opinions, and beliefs to be heard. By conducting close readings of these sources before extracting or analyzing data, researchers can identify the assumptions and agendas that inform how and why a document is written and mitigate the risk of oversimplification when reducing cultural heritage materials to structured text in a spreadsheet. Comprehensive environmental data collection is a relatively recent development in human history, but proxy and anecdotal evidence abound in the natural and human-created archives. All people, regardless of location or era, experience and observe their environment. As we reassess the credibility of long-trusted institutions, it is vital to identify the alternative sources waiting to be tapped.

Works Cited

"About the Agency." *Forest Service, U.S. Department of Agriculture,* https://www.fs.usda.gov/about-agency. Accessed March 26, 2026.

Agostinho, Daniela, et al. "Uncertain Archives: Approaching the Unknowns, Errors, and Vulnerabilities of Big Data Through Cultural Theories of the Archive." *Surveillance & Society,* vol. 17, nos. 3–4, 2019, pp. 422–41, https://doi.org/10.24908/ss.v17i3/4.12330.

Barnett, Cynthia. *Rain: A Natural and Cultural History.* Crown Publishers, 2015.

Barni, Paulo Eduardo, et al. "Logging Amazon Forest Increased the Severity and Spread of Fires During the 2015–2016 El Niño." *Forest Ecology and Management,* vol. 500, 2021, article 119652, https://doi.org/10.1016/j.foreco.2021.119652.

Brodie, Emily G., et al. "Forest Thinning and Prescribed Burning Treatments Reduce Wildfire Severity and Buffer the Impacts of Severe Fire Weather." *Fire Ecology,* vol. 20, no. 1, 2024, https://doi.org/10.1186/s42408-023-00241-z.

Buck, Franklin Augustus. 18 December 1852. MssBuck box 1, The Huntington Library, https://oac.cdlib.org/findaid/ark:/13030/kt9b69p0c8/entire_text/.

Buck, Franklin Augustus. 18 September 1853. MssBuck box 1, The Huntington Library, https://oac.cdlib.org/findaid/ark:/13030/kt9b69p0c8/entire_text/.

Buck, Franklin Augustus. 14 December 1856. MssBuck box 2, The Huntington Library, https://oac.cdlib.org/findaid/ark:/13030/kt9b69p0c8/entire_text/.

Buck, Franklin Augustus. 20 January 1861. MssBuck box 2, The Huntington Library, https://oac.cdlib.org/findaid/ark:/13030/kt9b69p0c8/entire_text/.

Buck, Franklin Augustus. 6 April 1862. MssBuck box 3, The Huntington Library, https://oac.cdlib.org/findaid/ark:/13030/kt9b69p0c8/entire_text/.

Buck, Franklin Augustus. 18 January 1866. MssBuck box 3, The Huntington Library, https://oac.cdlib.org/findaid/ark:/13030/kt9b69p0c8/entire_text/.

Buckland, M. K. *Document Theory: An Introduction.* UC Berkley, 2015, https://escholarship.org/uc/item/87s642x7.

Canon, Gabrielle. "Trump Orders USDA to Take Down Websites Referencing Climate Crisis." *The Guardian,* 1 Feb. 2025, https://www.theguardian.com/us-news/2025/jan/31/trump-order-usda-websites-climate-crisis.

"Chestnuts Are Doomed." *Nashville Tennessean,* 17 July 1927, https://www.proquest.com/historical-newspapers/july-17-1927-page-4-50/docview/1898695190/se-2.

Colman, Zack, and Marcia Brown. "USDA Ordered to Scrub Climate Change from Websites." *Politico,* 31 Jan. 2025, https://www.politico.com/news/2025/01/31/usda-climate-change-websites-00201826.

Columbia University. "Climate Backtracker." *Sabin Center for Climate Change Law,* https://climate.law.columbia.edu/content/climate-backtracker. Accessed 8 Feb. 2025.

Conner, Glen. "History of Weather Observations in Los Angeles, California 1847–1948." *Midwestern Regional Climate Center,* 2006, https://repository.library.noaa.gov/pdfjs/web/viewer.html?file=https://repository.library.noaa.gov/view/noaa/1204/noaa_1204_DS1.pdf.

Conner, Glen. "History of Weather Observations in Sonoma, California, 1850–1911." *Midwestern Regional Climate Center,* 2006, https://mrcc.purdue.edu/files/FORTS/histories/CA_Sonoma_Conner.pdf.

Davis, Donald Edward. *The American Chestnut: An Environmental History.* University of Georgia Press, 2021.

Dickerson, Madelynn, and Audra Eagle Yun. "Critical Community-Centeredness: Ethical Considerations for Computational Archival Studies." 2023, https://escholarship.org/uc/item/9dj4n154.

Doyle, Michael. "Trump Team Junks a Major Nature Study." *E&E News,* 6 Feb. 2025, https://www.eenews.net/articles/trump-team-junks-a-major-nature-study/.

Dunn, E. C. "E. C. Dunn Diary, 1852, Dec. 14–1853, Jan. 30." MssHM 67919 box 2, Huntington Library, 1853.

"Duty Devolving Upon Us All." *Carroll County Democrat,* 29 Nov. 1918, https://www.loc.gov/resource/sn89058115/1918-11-29/ed-1/?sp=2&q=American+chestnut.

European Space Agency. "Cosmic Microwave Background (CMB) Radiation." https://www.esa.int/Science_Exploration/Space_Science/Cosmic_Microwave_Background_CMB_radiation. Accessed 20 Oct. 2024.

Fabiani, Michelle D., and James V. Marrone. "Transiting Through the Antiquities Market: A Social Network Analysis of Auctions." *Crime and Art,* vol. 1, edited by Naomi Oosterman and Donna Yates, Springer International Publishing, 2021, pp. 11–28, https://doi.org/10.1007/978-3-030-84856-9_2.

George, Crissandra. "Digital Collections as Data: An Untapped Resource for Researchers." *Choice 360,* 15 Apr. 2024, https://www.choice360.org/libtech-insight/digital-collections-as-data-an-untapped-resource-for-researchers/.

Grabhorn, Jane Bissell. "A California Gold Rush Miscellany: Comprising: The Original Journal of Alexander Barrington, Nine Unpublished Letters from the Gold Mines, Reproductions of Early Maps and Towns from California Lithographs." Rare Books 211190, Huntington Library, Grabhorn Press, 1934.

Harvard Law School. "Federal Environmental Justice Tracker." *Environmental and Energy Law Program,* https://eelp.law.harvard.edu/tracker-type/environmental-justice-tracker/. Accessed 8 Feb. 2025.

Hashimzade, Nigar, et al. "Latent Variable." *A Dictionary of Economics.* Oxford University Press, 2017, https://www.oxfordreference.com/display/10.1093/acref/9780198759430.001.0001/acref-9780198759430-e-3738.

John Muir Project. "Get Involved." https://johnmuirproject.org/get-involved/. Accessed 17 Mar. 2025.

Koebler, Jason. "Archivists Work to Identify and Save the Thousands of Datasets Disappearing from Data.gov." *404 Media,* 30 Jan. 2025, https://www.404media.co/archivists-work-to-identify-and-save-the-thousands-of-datasets-disappearing-from-data-gov/.

Kurtzleben, Danielle. "Some Federal Web Pages Still Down as Agencies Implement Order 'Defending Women.'" *NPR,* 1 Feb. 2025, https://www.npr.org/2025/01/31/g-s1-45887/trump-opm-gender-ideology-defending-women-websites-transgender.

Lindenmayer, David B., et al. "Logging Elevated the Probability of High-Severity Fire in the 2019–20 Australian Forest Fires." *Nature Ecology & Evolution,* vol. 6, no. 5, 2022, pp. 533–35, https://doi.org/10.1038/s41559-022-01717-y.

"Looking Back—10 and 25 Years Ago." *The Knoxville News-Sentinel,* 1950, https://www.proquest.com/hnpknoxvillenewssentinel/docview/2660215632/6F9317AEB913405BPQ/43.

Lynch, H. B. "Rainfall and Stream Run-Off in Southern California since 1769." The Metropolitan Water District of Southern California, Los Angeles, 1931, https://cepsym.org/history/RainfallStreamRunoffSoCA_since1769.pdf.

Miller, Naseem S. "Researchers Rush to Preserve Government Health Data." *The Journalist's Resource,* 30 Jan. 2025, https://journalistsresource.org/home/researchers-rush-to-preserve-federal-health-databases-before-they-disappear-from-government-websites/.

Moss, Michael, et al. "The Reconfiguration of the Archive as Data to Be Mined." *Archivaria,* vol. 86, 2018, pp. 118–51, https://archivaria.ca/index.php/archivaria/article/view/13646.

Mulligan, Scott. "Inside the Race to Archive the US Government's Websites." *MIT Technology Review,* 7 Feb. 2025, https://www.technologyreview.com/2025/02/07/1111328/inside-the-race-to-archive-the-us-governments-websites/.

National Aeronautics and Space Administration. "Interactive Timeline: Evidence for Earth's Past Climate." *Climate Change: Vital Signs of the Planet,* https://climate.nasa.gov/explore/evidence-for-earths-past-climate?intent=021. Accessed October 20, 2024.

Nost, Eric, et al. "Visualizing Changes to US Federal Environmental Agency Websites, 2016–2020." *PLOS ONE,* vol. 16, no. 2, 2021, https://doi.org/10.1371/journal.pone.0246450.

Nost, Eric, et al. "Why EDGI Is Archiving Public Environmental Data." *Environmental Data and Governance Initiative,* 16 Jan. 2025, https://envirodatagov.org/why-edgi-is-archiving-public-environmental-data/.

Olson, Julia, and Patricia Pinto da Silva. "Meaning Across Context: Oral Histories, Big Data, and Climate Change." *Weather, Climate, and Society,* vol. 16, no. 2, 2024, pp. 331–49, https://doi.org/10.1175/WCAS-D-23-0114.1.

Otlet, Paul. *International Organization and Dissemination of Knowledge: Selected Essays of Paul Otlet.* Elsevier, 1990, https://www.mondotheque.be/wiki/images/1/16/Rayward_International_organisation_and_dissemination_of_knowledge.pdf.

Padilla, Thomas. "Collections as Data: Conditions of Possibility." *Medium* (blog), 28 Oct. 2016, https://tgpadillajr.medium.com/collections-as-data-conditions-of-possibility-494805bf16be.

Padilla, Thomas, et al. "Final Report—Always Already Computational: Collections as Data." *Zenodo,* 2019, https://zenodo.org/records/3152935.

Padilla, Thomas, et al. "Vancouver Statement on Collections as Data." *Zenodo,* 2023, https://zenodo.org/records/8342171.

Pauly, Philip J. *Fruits and Plains: The Horticultural Transformation of America.* Harvard University Press, 2007.

Quinn, Ryan. "As Data Goes Off-Line Under Trump, Environmental Researchers Are Uploading Backups." *Inside Higher Ed,* 29 Jan. 2025, https://www.insidehighered.com/news/faculty-issues/research/2025/01/29/data-goes-line-under-trump-researchers-upload-backups.

Rayward, W. Boyd. Introduction. *International Organization and Dissemination of Knowledge: Selected Essays of Paul Otlet,* Elsevier, 1990, pp. 1–10, https://www.mondotheque.be/wiki/images/1/16/Rayward_International_organisation_and_dissemination_of_knowledge.pdf.

Reisner, Marc. *Cadillac Desert: The American West and Its Disappearing Water.* Revised and updated ed., Penguin Books, 2017.

"Resource Hub." *Urban Ocean Lab,* https://urbanoceanlab.org/resource-hub. Accessed 18 Feb. 2025.

Riddle, Anne. "Timber Harvesting on Federal Lands." R45688. *Congressional Research Service,* 2022, https://crsreports.congress.gov/product/pdf/R/R45688.

Sierra Club Grassroots Network. "Resources." *Stop Clearcutting CA,* https://www.sierraclub.org/grassroots-network/stop-clearcutting-ca/resources. Accessed 17 Mar. 2025.

Singer, Ethan. "Thousands of U.S. Government Web Pages Have Been Taken Down Since Friday." *The New York Times,* 3 Feb. 2025, https://www.nytimes.com/2025/02/02/upshot/trump-government-websites-missing-pages.html.

Smoky Mountain Hiking Club. *Handbook of the Smoky Mountains Hiking Club.* 1933, https://digital.lib.utk.edu/collections/islandora/object/smhc%3A10554#page/15/mode/1up.

Steenhuysen, Julie, and Ted Hesson. "US Health Agencies Scrub HIV, Other Data to Remove 'Gender Ideology.'" *Reuters,* 1 Feb. 2025, https://www.reuters.com/world/us/us-health-agencies-scrub-hiv-other-data-remove-gender-ideology-2025-02-01/.

Thurstan, Ruth H., et al. "Records Reveal the Vast Historical Extent of European Oyster Reef Ecosystems." *Nature Sustainability,* vol. 7, 2024, pp. 1719–29, https://doi.org/10.1038/s41893-024-01441-4.

Thylstrup, Nanna Bonde, et al., editors. *Uncertain Archives: Critical Keywords for Big Data.* MIT Press, 2021.

"Tracking Regulatory Changes in the Second Trump Administration." *Brookings Institute,* 3 Feb. 2025, https://www.brookings.edu/articles/tracking-regulatory-changes-in-the-second-trump-administration/.

University of Chattanooga. *The Moccasin.* University of Chattanooga, 1915, https://digital-collections.library.utc.edu/digital/collection/p16877coll3/id/1260/rec/173.

Van Vugt, Ingeborg. "Networking in the Republic of Letters: Magliabechi and the Dutch Republic." *The Journal of Interdisciplinary History,* vol. 53, no. 1, 2022, pp. 117–41, https://doi.org/10.1162/jinh_a_01800.

Veel, Kristin. "Latency." *Uncertain Archives: Critical Keywords for Big Data,* edited by Nanna Bonde Thylstrup et al., MIT Press, 2021, pp. 313–19.

Wan, Zhiwei, and Hongqi Wu. "Evolution of Ecological Patterns of Poyang Lake Wetland Landscape Over the Last One Hundred Years Based on Historical Topographic Maps and Landsat Images." *Sustainability,* vol. 14, no. 13, 7868, June 2022, https://doi.org/10.3390/su14137868.

Webb, Romany M., and Lauren Kurtz. "Politics v. Science: How President Trump's War on Science Impacted Public Health and Environmental Regulation." *Progress in Molecular Biology and Translational Science,* vol. 188, no. 1, 2022, pp. 65–80, https://doi.org/10.1016/bs.pmbts.2021.11.006.

Western Regional Climate Center. "Weaverville, California—Climate Summary." https://wrcc.dri.edu/cgi-bin/cliMAIN.pl?ca9490. Accessed 19 February 2025.

Zhang, Chao, et al. "Use of Historical Data to Improve Conservation of the Black Grouse (Lyrurus Tetrix) in Northeast China." *Ecosphere,* vol. 11, no. 3, 2020, article e03090, https://doi.org/10.1002/ecs2.3090.

CHAPTER 11

Imagining Digital Bibliography as Archival Intervention

LEIGH BONDS

With the proliferation of mass digitization efforts by libraries, archives, and museums worldwide, researchers now have access to digital surrogates of cultural heritage materials once only available in situ. Holdings in collaborative digital libraries are in the millions: *Internet Archive* holds 44 million books and texts; *HathiTrust,* over 18 million items; and *Google Books,* 10 million. Digital collections aggregators like *Europeana* provide access to digitized holdings in European institutions; national digital libraries provide access to their digitized holdings and some aggregate digital collections within their countries like *Gallica* and *National Digital Library of India*; and institutional digital collections provide access to their own unique holdings. Licensed collections by vendors such as Adam Mathew, Gale, JSTOR, and ProQuest further expand the amount of cultural heritage material available from partnering institutions across the globe. Collectively, these create a distributed network of archival materials—books, periodicals, newspapers, prints, paintings, and ephemera—for researchers working on subjects, topics, periods, or locations covered in these digital collections.

Navigating this vast network to find specific materials, explore the materials available, and monitor additions of newly digitized materials, however, can be daunting even to an experienced archival researcher. The network's distributed nature requires searching each collection for materials: No one collection is comprehensive, nor is searching across collections yet possible. The ever-increasing holdings across the network require regular, ongoing perusal, for most digital collections lack the ability to set up notifications when materials with specific titles, subject headings, or authors are added. Complicating this work further, materials in licensed collections are limited to libraries with the funding resources to subscribe to them and, thus, to researchers affiliated with those institutions. Each researcher, therefore, builds their own enumerative bibliographies—lists of existing materials—and their own collections of downloaded digital materials from the digital collections they can access across the network.

Admittedly, the digital collections themselves have limitations. Foremost, they have been limited in scope to the content in contributing institutions' holdings and to those institutions' digitization priorities and selection decisions (e.g., items, patron requests, or unique collections) and resources (e.g., funding, labor, equipment). Unfortunately, the biases within their physical collections and/or in selection decisions have been replicated in digital collections.[1] As other chapters in this volume attest, these decisions are most often made *for,* rather than *with,* researchers and communities. Furthermore, for textual objects specifically, matters such as the condition of the material object, quality of digitization, medium being digitized (e.g., print or microfilm), and typography have impacted the accuracy of optical character recognition (OCR)—with its own inherent limitations—which, in turn, limits full-text searching.[2] The OCR inaccuracy in some collections or in older digitized materials renders searching unreliable, requiring researchers to scan digitized materials in collections like Gale's *Seventeenth and Eighteenth Century Burney Newspapers* in the same manner they once scanned microfilm. That said, even inaccurate OCR produces some results, providing at least a starting point for locating materials. Addressing these limitations requires the kind of intentional interventions found in HathiTrust's 2024 strategic directions to "enable members to identify, digitize, preserve, and contribute their unique content to the collection—especially that of underrepresented and historically-marginalized voices and perspectives," "invite organizations engaged in mass digitization of book and serial content, that are not currently members, to contribute and preserve their collections," and "apply existing and emerging computational tools and methods in service of text and metadata improvement." For researchers reliant on these collections, such expansions and enrichments on the horizon hold promise.

Despite these challenges, however, digital collections create opportunities for researchers and communities to identify, collect, contextualize or

1. See Ziegler; Padilla 9, 16; Lorang 28; Cordell 34; Bonds for discussions of the biases replicated in digital collections.

2. See Tanner et al.; Prescott; Hill and Hengchen; Cordell 23–25 for discussions of optical character recognition (OCR) inaccuracy and limitations.

recontextualize, and share primary source materials from across the network without the limitations of print. "Editorial work has always been about democratizing access to primary materials, at least access to reporting on those primary materials," Martha Nell Smith explains. "The new technologies that provide digital surrogates enable us to provide a much more capacious range of objects to study and treasure for our audiences" (12). The digital environment affords the contextualization or "recontextualization" of digital collections' materials that adds value to each individual object by not only placing the object in relation to other objects but also "relocating the object to a new context . . . that could lend to reinterpretation of the object" (Kenfield et al. 388). In essence, bibliographies are no longer limited to listing materials on a subject, topic, period, or location: Digital bibliographies may now serve as portals to the range of interrelated materials available in digital collections and augment those materials by contextualizing them to aid other researchers.

Two years ago, I embarked on an experiment to do just that for the late eighteenth-century writer Mary Robinson (1757–1800). My work on Robinson began in 2009 with an enumerative bibliography and grew over the next four years with my dissertation research in textual studies. In the decade since, it has expanded with subsequent projects to include primary sources evidencing the social, cultural, and historical contexts in which Robinson and her work circulated (e.g., authorial editions and translations, periodical publications, reviews, advertisements, letters, portraits, caricatures, and newspaper notices or "puffs") and secondary material from the nineteenth century to the present (e.g., scholarship, reference resources, biographies, editions, memoirs and letters of others within her circle). With the goal of sharing all the materials amassed and the relations among them to further Robinson research, the experiment has required revisiting textual studies scholarship to determine the aims of such an undertaking. Likewise, it has necessitated considerations of data structure, platform affordances and limitations, and sustainability to determine the means.

Aims

The impetus for amassing such varied materials lies with Mary Robinson herself. Before dedicating herself to writing, she appeared on the stage of Drury Lane in 204 theatrical performances across four seasons (1776–80) and circulated within London's fashionable society. Her scandalous affair with the Prince of Wales played out publicly in the press, and for the remainder of her life, the press kept that public apprised of every aspect of her life—fashionable lifestyle, intimate relations, pecuniary troubles, political affiliations, publishing, and illness. Robinson holds the distinction of being the most reviewed woman writer of the period with "15 poetic works and collections, seven novels, six biographical sketches, two essay series, two comic operas, a comedy, a tragedy, a translation, a memoir, a political treatise (published under two titles), and 79 poetic pieces only published in newspapers and periodicals" attributed to her (Hawkins xiv; Bonds 415). In addition, she served as a "poetical correspondent" and poetry editor for *The Morning Post* (Byrne 335, 354). Yet the writer and her writing virtually disappeared for two hundred years until recovery efforts began in the 1980s. To interpret Robinson's writings, therefore, requires an understanding of the social, cultural, and historical contexts in which they were produced, read, dismissed, and recovered; and to understand that requires a wealth of primary and secondary materials.

These requisites derive from the textual studies theory and practice—broadly defined—which includes bibliography.[3] Robert D. Hume explains that "textual interpretation" requires investigation of "four fairly distinct realms connected to the contexts in which our text has come into the world": "genesis, production, dissemination, and reception" (199–200). To interpret a text, therefore, a researcher must take into account the author's "background, education, reading, friends, and circumstances when writing"—genesis; the material "process by which a manuscript moves into its circulatable form"—production; the publisher, format, price, buyers, distribution form, edition, reprint—dissemination; and the "recorded responses" of readers and reviewers—reception (201–2). Hume's "aims" resonated with me, echoing the work of other textual scholars that preceded it—Robert Darnton's "communication circuit," D. F. McKenzie's "sociology of texts," Jerome McGann's "textual condition," and Gérard Genette's "paratexts." Collectively, they impressed upon me the breadth of materials required to understand Robinson and her writing and set a course for my scholarship to follow.

The digital project I envisioned would provide other Robinson scholars that breadth to enable them to follow that same course—a bibliographical resource for literary and textual studies. "Bibliography is the foundation of literary research," Kate Ozment argues, "in that it gives us data to analyze using standardized practices, fostering analysis of authorship, attribution,

3. As D. C. Greetham explains, "Textual studies is a discipline drowning in a sea of terms: enumerative bibliography, systematic bibliography, descriptive bibliography, analytical bibliography, historical bibliography and textual bibliography, textual analysis and textual criticism, textual editing, documentary editing, and social textual criticism—to say nothing of older dispensations as epigraphy, paleography, codicology, and diplomatics, philology and historical criticism, higher and lower criticism, all of which may still be invoked by textuists" (1). For additional definitions of bibliography, see Bibliographical Society of America.

textual production, and reception" (106). It would build upon and extend the work on which I have depended: the four biographies by Robert D. Bass, Paula Byrne, Hester Davenport, and Sarah Gristwood; the publishing histories of her poetry by Judith Pascoe and Daniel Robinson; the reviews of her work indexed by William Ward, Antonia Forster, and the contributing editors to *Romantic Women Writers Reviewed*; and the portraits identified by Philip H. Highfill, Kalman A. Burnim, and Edward A. Langhans. Moreover, it would be extensible to allow the addition of newly digitized or discovered materials and new scholarship, affecting the potential means of sharing these materials.

Means

For anyone embarking on a digital project, sustainability must be a priority. Élika Ortega's quip, "There is nothing more ephemeral than a website," and Jessica Otis's metaphor, "DH projects are cars, not books," resounded in my mind as I began considering the options for my own project. Both distill the sustainability concerns voiced over the last ten years by Jerome McGann, Amy Earhart, Laura Mandell, and Cait Coker and Kate Ozment that have prompted several initiatives to address these challenges like *The Socio-Technical Sustainability Roadmap* and *The Endings Project.* In an ideal environment, the infrastructure would be available to build, publish, maintain, and preserve the digital bibliography regardless of the technology used, but the absence of such an environment forces acceptance of and preparation for a project's eventual end *from the beginning.* As I have repeatedly told researchers with whom I have consulted in my capacity as digital humanities librarian, digital projects often begin and end as spreadsheets. The value of the project I envisioned would be its content and context, not its platform.

The open-source content management systems for digital projects that I had previously explored or worked with on other projects met neither the envisioned project's bibliographical needs nor sustainability priorities. I, therefore, turned to "minimal computing," an approach that focuses on necessity rather than innovation, for which Alex Gil has long advocated. The questions he and Roopika Risam pose guided my thinking: "1) 'what do we need?'; 2) 'what do we have'; 3) 'what must we prioritize?'; and 4) 'what are we willing to give up?'" (para. 5). Considering these seemingly basic questions provided clarity. The project required a database to share the primary source materials (e.g., representative images, metadata about those materials, and links to external digital collections) and the relations among them. The variety of materials necessitated flexibility, for each object type (e.g., works, reviews, portraits, caricatures) would need different metadata fields, and, of course, sustaining the project for the long term would be imperative. Essentially, the project would prioritize content delivery over creative design and dynamic functionality. CollectionBuilder, "an open-source framework for creating digital collection and exhibit websites that are driven by metadata and powered by modern static web technology," fit these requirements.

The Mary Robinson Project

Work on the project began in early spring 2023. With research funding, I enlisted the help of collaborators: Sofia Racevskis, an undergraduate research assistant, to work with me on the bibliographic data, and Olivia Wikle, a member of the CollectionBuilder team, to guide me through the process of learning and using the framework for this project and to make adjustments to accommodate the project. Together, we explored the possibilities for the archival intervention imagined and how that could be accomplished with the minimal tools chosen. Phase 1 focused on adding, cleaning, completing, verifying, and organizing the bibliographic metadata for the secondary source materials (e.g., item type, title, author, publication information, DOI and/or URL, and abstract) to create a Zotero group library. Phase 2 focused on the primary source materials, determining the object types, the metadata fields for each object type, the relations among the objects, and the selected items for the prototype built with CollectionBuilder.

Entering the bibliographic data for the secondary materials proved more straightforward than for the primary. With 491 entries in the Zotero bibliography by the end of 2023, the secondary materials were organized in folders by publication period, resource type, or topic area: nineteenth-century editions; twentieth- and twenty-first-century editions; anthologies and collections; biographies, biographical sketches, anecdotes; biographies, memories, letters of others; fictional biographies and accounts; indexes; miscellaneous (a placeholder for items not fitting elsewhere); portraits and caricatures; reference; scholarship; and theater. Shared on December 26, 2023—the anniversary of Mary Robinson's passing—on a Romanticism studies discussion list, the Mary Robinson Bibliography is publicly available for use. The bibliography provides persistent links whenever possible to digital collections and/or Worldcat for books and book sections; DOIs and/or URLs for journal articles; and URLs for digital materials.

To determine CollectionBuilder's affordances for connecting the volumes of Robinson's work with the reviews and the portraits used as frontispieces, I selected specific works for the prototype to explore how the framework would accommodate these relations: 31 volumes, 65 reviews and publication notices, and 14 portraits. In addition to the bibliographic metadata (e.g., title, edition, signature, publisher, year, publication format, and price), each entry includes persistent links to the items available in digital collections (e.g., Worldcat, HathiTrust, and library digital collections)—at the page level for reviews. Materials in licensed collections presented the first challenge: Because links to these materials require an institutional proxy for access, these digital collections may only be only identified rather than linked (e.g., *Eighteenth Century Collections Online* [Gale] and *Nineteenth Century Collections Online* [Gale]). Similarly, the related paratextual materials (i.e., advertisements and puffs) only available through licensed digital collections are simply identified by newspaper and date.

The second challenge arose with recent cyberattacks on digital collection sites that beg questions about "persistent links." In October 2023, the British Library's site was disrupted, and it has been working since to restore access (Keating). As a result, the links collected for this project for both the British Library's digital collections and the *English Short Title Catalogue* (ESTC) will need to be updated when access is restored. On October 8, 2024, access to *Internet Archive* was similarly disrupted, but when services were restored days later, the links collected continued to connect to the materials (Kahle). The vulnerability of digital collections' infrastructure has forced reconsidering the archival intervention possible. Will changes to the infrastructure of digital collections—whether prompted by cyberattacks or by the adoption of new technologies in the future—render persistent links unreliable? At best, can digital bibliographies only identify the digital collections that hold specific items? Researchers want digital collections to be as enduring as physical collections; the fact that they are not yet, however, has implications for their use and for the archival interventions possible. In this case, the digital bibliography's reliability and long-term sustainability as a portal to digital surrogates of cultural heritage materials depends on the digital collections' reliability and long-term sustainability.

Working through the process of identifying, structuring, and contextualizing the primary and secondary materials during this "experiment"—and thinking through the unanticipated challenges—taught me a great deal. It demonstrated the affordances and limitations of digital bibliography as an archival intervention to support literary and textual studies by connecting—or at least identifying—the network of ever-increasing digital collections available to archival researchers. It bared the challenges that licensed collections present for access and the unreliability of persistent links to digital collections. Most important, it laid the groundwork for continuing the work as an iterative process, accounting for new digitized materials and new discoveries in existing digitized materials, and refining the data structure to realize the archival intervention possible.

Imagined as a form of archival intervention, digital bibliography could serve researchers, as print bibliographies always have but with the benefit of being extensible to account for new additions to digital collections. It could make visible the social, cultural, and historical records available to work toward the future Jerome McGann forecasted twenty-two years ago: "In the next 50 years, the entirety of our inherited archive of cultural works will have to be re-edited within a network of digital storage, access, and dissemination" ("Literary"). For writers like Mary Robinson, that future is much further from being realized. In the meantime, researchers can take advantage of the opportunities the network of digital collections and sustainable tools afford us—even if the work ultimately ends as a spreadsheet.

Works Cited

Bass, Robert D. *The Green Dragoon: The Lives of Banastre Tarleton and Mary Robinson.* Sandlapper Publishing, 1973.

Bibliographical Society of America. "Bibliography Defined: Further Reading." *The Bibliographical Society of America,* 2024, https://bibsocamer.org/about/what-is-bibliography/further-reading#terry-belanger-on-types-of-bibliographical-practice-1977.

Bonds, E. Leigh. *Mary Robinson Bibliography.* Zotero, https://www.zotero.org/groups/4926038/mary_robinson_bibliography/library.

Bonds, E. Leigh, et al., editors. "Mary Robinson Née Darby (1757–1800)." *The Routledge Companion to Romantic Women Writers,* Routledge, 2023, pp. 412–29, https://doi.org/10.4324/9781315613536-45.

Byrne, Paula. *Perdita: The Literary, Theatrical, Scandalous Life of Mary Robinson.* Random House, 2004.

Cavanaugh, Erica, and Alix Shield. "Drupal for Digital Humanities Projects." Digital Humanities Summer Institute, June 2018.

Coker, Cait, and Kate Ozment. "Building the *Women in Book History Bibliography,* or Digital Enumerative Bibliography as Preservation of Feminist Labor." *DHQ: Digital Humanities Quarterly,* vol. 13, no. 3, 2019, https://www.digitalhumanities.org/dhq/vol/13/3/000428/000428.html.

Coker, Cait, and Spencer D. C. Keralis, editors. "Where's Mary?" *DH+BH: An Interdisciplinary Collection of Digital Humanities and Book History,* Illinois Open Publishing Network, 2024, https://doi.org/10.21900/pww.25.

CollectionBuilder. https://collectionbuilder.github.io.

Cordell, Ryan. *Machine Learning + Libraries: A Report on the State of the Field.* LC Labs, Library of Congress, 14 July 2020, https://labs.loc.gov/static/labs/work/reports/Cordell-LOC-ML-report.pdf?loclr=blogsig.

Darnton, Robert. "What Is the History of Books?" *Reading in America: Literature & Social History,* edited by Cathy N. Davidson, Johns Hopkins University Press, 1989, pp. 27–52, https://doi.org/10.56021/9780801837999.

Davenport, Hester. *The Prince's Mistress: A Life of Mary Robinson.* Sutton Publishing, 2004.

Dombrowski, Quinn. "Sorry for All the Drupal: Reflections on the 3rd Anniversary of 'Drupal for Humanists.'" 8 Nov. 2019, https://quinndombrowski.com/blog/2019/11/08/sorry-all-drupal-reflections-3rd-anniversary-drupal-humanists/.

Earhart, Amy E. *Traces of the Old, Uses of the New: The Emergence of Digital Literary Studies.* University of Michigan Press, 2015, https://doi.org/10.2307/j.ctv65swvf.

The Endings Project. Building Sustainable Digital Humanities Projects, https://endings.uvic.ca.

Forster, Antonia. *Index to Book Reviews in England, 1775–1800.* British Library, 1997.

Genette, Gérard. *Paratexts: Thresholds of Interpretation.* Cambridge University Press, 1997.

Gil, Alex. "The User, the Learner and the Machines We Make." *Minimal Computing: A Working Group of GO::DH,* 21 May 2015, https://go-dh.github.io/mincomp/thoughts/2015/05/21/user-vs-learner/.

Greetham, D. C. *Textual Scholarship: An Introduction.* Garland, 2005.

Gristwood, Sarah. *Perdita: Royal Mistress, Writer, Romantic.* Bantam Press, 2005.

HathiTrust. *HathiTrust Strategic Vision. HathiTrust,* May 2024, https://www.hathitrust.org/about/mission-history/strategic-vision.

Hawkins, Ann R. "General Introduction." *Romantic Women Writers Reviewed,* vol. 1, edited by Ann R. Hawkins and Stephanie Eckroth, Pickering and Chatto, 2011, pp. ix–xxxi.

Hawkins, Ann R., and Stephanie Eckroth, editors. *Romantic Women Writers Reviewed.* Pickering and Chatto, 2011–13. 9 vols.

Highfill, Philip H., Jr., et al. *A Biographical Dictionary of Actors, Actresses, Musicians, Dancers, Managers & Other Stage Personnel in London, 1660–1800,* vol. 13. Southern Illinois University Press, 1991.

Hill, M. J., and S. Hengchen. "Quantifying the Impact of Dirty OCR on Historical Text Analysis: Eighteenth Century Collections Online as a Case Study." *Digital Scholarship in the Humanities,* vol. 34, no. 4, 2019, pp. 825–43.

Hume, Robert D. "The Aims and Uses of 'Textual Studies.'" *Papers of the Bibliographical Society of America,* vol. 99, no. 2, 2005, pp. 197–230, https://www.jstor.org/stable/24295916.

Kahle, Brewster. "Internet Archive Services Update: 2024-10-17." *Internet Archive Blogs,* 18 Oct. 2024. https://blog.archive.org/2024/10/18/internet-archive-services-update-2024-10-17/.

Keating, Roly. "Learning Lessons from the Cyber-Attack." *Knowledge Matters Blog,* British Library, 8 Mar. 2024, https://blogs.bl.uk/living-knowledge/2024/03/learning-lessons-from-the-cyber-attack.html.

Kenfield, Ayla Stein, et al. "Toward a Definition of Digital Object Reuse." *Digital Library Perspectives,* vol. 38, no. 3, 2022, pp. 378–94, https://doi.org/10.1108/DLP-06-2021-0044.

Lorang, Elizabeth, et al. *Digital Libraries, Intelligent Data Analytics, and Augmented Description: A Demonstration Project.* University of Nebraska-Lincoln Libraries, 10 Jan. 2020, https://digitalcommons.unl.edu/libraryscience/396.

Mandell, Laura. "Gendering Digital Literary History: What Counts for Digital Humanities." *A New Companion to Digital Humanities,* edited by Susan Schreibman et al., Wiley Blackwell, 2016, https://doi.org/10.1002/9781118680605.ch35.

McGann, Jerome J. "Literary Scholarship in the Digital Future." *Chronicle of Higher Education,* vol. 49, no. 16, 2002, p. B7.

McGann, Jerome J. *A New Republic of Letters: Memory and Scholarship in the Age of Digital Reproduction.* Harvard University Press, 2014.

McGann, Jerome J. *The Textual Condition.* Princeton University Press, 1991, https://muse.jhu.edu/book/77448.

McKenzie, D. F. *Bibliography and the Sociology of Texts.* Cambridge University Press, 1999.

Ortega, Élika. "There Is Nothing More Ephemeral Than a Website." *Skeuomorph Press* (blog), 14 Jan. 2025, https://elikaortega.net/blog/2025/theres-nothing-more-epehemeral/.

Otis, Jessica. "Managing the Digital Backlist: Sustaining, Preserving, and Deleting Old Projects." *Jessica Otis,* 13 Mar. 2023, https://jessicaotis.com/digital-humanities/managing-the-digital-backlist.

Ozment, Kate. "From Recovery to Restoration: Aphra Behn and Feminist Bibliography." *Early Modern Women: An Interdisciplinary Journal,* vol. 13, no. 1, 2018, pp. 106–17, https://doi.org/10.1353/emw.2018.0054.

Padilla, Thomas. *Responsible Operations: Data Science, Machine Learning, and AI in Libraries.* OCLC Research, Dec. 2019, https://doi.org/10.25333/xk7z-9g97.

Pascoe, Judith, editor. *Mary Robinson: Selected Poems.* Broadview Press, 2000.

Prescott, Andrew. "Searching for Dr. Johnson: The Digitisation of the Burney Newspaper Collection." *Travelling Chronicles: News and Newspapers from the Early Modern Period to the Eighteenth Century,* edited by Siv Gøril Brandtzæg et al., Brill, 22 Mar. 2018, pp. 51–71, https://doi.org/10.1163/9789004362871_004.

Risam, Roopika, and Alex Gil. "Introduction: The Questions of Minimal Computing." *DHQ: Digital Humanities Quarterly,* vol. 16, no. 2, 2022.

Robinson, Daniel, editor. *Poems. Works of Mary Robinson,* vols. 1–2. General editor, William D. Brewer, Pickering and Chatto, 2009–10.

Smith, Martha Nell. "The Human Touch Software of the Highest Order: Revisiting Editing as Interpretation." *Textual Cultures: Texts, Contexts, Interpretation,* vol. 2, no. 1, 2007, pp. 1–15, https://muse.jhu.edu/article/251864.

The Socio-Technical Sustainability Roadmap. https://sites.haa.pitt.edu/sustainabilityroadmap.

Tanner, Simon, et al. "Measuring Mass Text Digitization Quality and Usefulness: Lessons Learned from Assessing the OCR Accuracy of the British Library's 19th Century Online Newspaper Archive." *D-Lib Magazine,* vol. 15, no. 7–8, 2009, https://doi.org/10.1045/july2009-munoz.

Visual Media Workshop at the University of Pittsburgh. *The Socio-Technical Sustainability Roadmap,* http://sustainingdh.net.

Ward, William. *Literary Reviews in British Periodicals, 1789–1797.* Garland, 1972.

Ward, William. *Literary Reviews in British Periodicals, 1798–1820.* 2 vols. Garland, 1972.

Zotero. https://www.zotero.org.

Ziegler, S. L. "Digitization Selection Criteria as Anti-Racist Action." *code{4}lib,* vol. 45, 9 Aug. 2019, https://journal.code4lib.org/articles/14667.

PART 3

ANCESTRAL PRACTICES AND OTHERWISE ARCHIVES

PART 3 INTRODUCTION

PUJA BATRA-WELLS AND HARMONY BENCH

The final section of this book, Ancestral Practices and Otherwise Archives, returns us to the question of the archive, of what can be archived and what can be an archive, and its limitations for holding complex histories or lifeways outside of dominant Western frameworks. The contributions in this section invite us to consider memory practices in relation to lively objects as well as the bodies and practices they are entangled with. Authors consider how archives reproduce cultural authority (Wibbelsman, Banerji), especially the regulatory function of archives in relation to documentary residues of bodily experience and the laboring body (Banerji, Schneider, Barchiesi). They trouble the normative power of archival thought and make space for sensory engagement as we also saw in the Networked Memories and Minor Histories section, but they do not necessarily propose artistic or bodily engagement as an escape from the power of the archive. Indeed, even otherwise archives may present themselves as disciplinary vectors. Many contributors in this section prioritize Indigenous memory practices, decentering dominant Western modes of organizing knowledge (Schneider, Lukin Linklater, Bird) or even rejecting them outright (Wibbelsman). They question the conceptual efficacy of linear temporality for capturing the complexity of memory and the ways that histories reverberate across generations. If an archive is traditionally understood as a carefully managed temperature-controlled warehouse where artifacts can be consulted by the privileged few, in this section, bodies and objects are also archives; in a very real sense, they are living archives where memory is both stored and activated.

This section is bookended with contributions centering Indigenous practices that directly grapple with inheritances from archival thinking. After introducing readers to her own teaching collection of physical Andean objects that have been digitized for online access, Michelle Wibbelsman confronts readers with the provocation that even "inclusive" archival collection and display do not go far enough toward dismantling the coloniality of archival structures. Instead of collection, she proposes "participation in living traditions"—"if/when invited," she qualifies, rather than confusing acquisition for understanding. The book's closing entries of sharing alongside and with artist Tanya Lukin Linklater demonstrate one possible approach to engagement from a place of witnessing and reciprocity. Kelly Kivland curated Lukin Linklater's work at the Wexner Center for the Arts in 2024 and offers a prelude informed by the exhibition, to which Johannah Bird also responds in a series of poems. Lukin Linklater's Event Scores are instructions for action, but they may or may not be performed as such. Some scores connote danger in the public display of sacred knowledge, and others assert the unassimilability of Indigenous thought, people, and practices to the Western containers intended to box them in. Lukin Linklater and Bird both play with multivocality and untranslatability. Must audiences know what the artists know? What is understanding without grasping? What is listening without answering? What are the lessons here, in Bird's words, for "how to gather / how to harvest," that could shape emergent archives of relation?

Just as Lukin Linklater and Bird challenge the terms of legibility and containment, other traditions reveal how aesthetic forms have long encoded hierarchies such as in Anurima Banerji's study of how the *Natyashastra* is bound to the Hindu caste system. As an ancient repository of aesthetic knowledge for performance traditions that reach across India and the Hindu diaspora, the text functions as an archive for bodily practices. The *Natyashastra* preserves depictions of caste differences from the past, but as a canonical text, how characters *were* portrayed asserts regulatory pressure on how characters *should* be portrayed—even in contemporary performance. Its codified system of representation "lifts the aesthetic treatise into the space of authoritative sanction and command" that "constructs an identitarian politics of difference on the grounds of caste." Brahmin social codes are transformed into a form of aesthetic law through stage directions and guidelines for bodily comportment that reproduce caste difference as they make it legible. Banerji notes that this is all the more remarkable because the performers of ancient India were by and large caste-oppressed and were thus enlisted to perform stereotypes of themselves. Franco Barchiesi likewise considers the role of the archive in producing difference through the laboring body, focusing on the entanglement of global antiblackness and global capitalism in colonial Africa. Governability within this frame required conformity to European systems "equating freedom with the labor contract" in a "work-centered personhood" both required of and withheld from Black laborers in colonial archives. In this slippery logic, proof of freedom resided in one's acquiescence to economic exploitation and natural resource extraction (sugar, minerals), as though these were not extensions of the conditions of slavery. Barchiesi investigates colonial archives to reveal how administrators leveraged racialized oppression in the name of liberal democratization, even as they erased the blackness of the workers they were trying to forge by force.

This history of forced labor persists throughout Rebecca Schneider's contribution, which analyzes work by Barbadian-born multimedia artist Alberta Whittle. In particular, Schneider focuses on a glitch she witnessed during a webinar screening of Whittle's film "What is a better life (exorcised in the middle)." Rather than ignore a hiccup in digital transmission, this glitch becomes central to Schneider's understanding as it reverberates beyond the scene onscreen. She had no way of knowing that it was an artifact of mediality and pandemic-era online gatherings rather than artistic intention. This cut cracks open Schneider's experience in a productive way. It destabilizes her own memory and assessment of what she saw, and it has the potential to "confuse the consolidation of such a work into any imperial archive." The glitch writes its way into the affective fragments of Schneider's writing, disrupting scholarly capture while sitting with rupture as also a form of knowledge.

Troubling the history of the archive as practice and site, questions that come into the foreground in Ancestral Practices and Otherwise Archives include: What modes of thought and memory-keeping are and are not accommodated by the archive as traditionally understood? To what extent is the archive an imperial-colonial technology of memory, and are decolonial archives actually possible? In what ways can archives accommodate experiences of grief at the magnitudes of loss they both index and hide? What implications do embodied archives and nonlinear approaches to memory and history have for conceptualizing alternate archival possibilities? What otherwise archives can be imagined without constructing knowledge as a form of domination? Are there modes of scholarly engagement that can foster repair? And simply, can archives heal?

CHAPTER 12

Indigenous Meaning-Making, the Limits of Archives, and the Promise of Practice

MICHELLE WIBBELSMAN

In 2022–23 a Global Arts and Humanities Discovery Theme Society of Fellows formed around the topic "Archival Imaginations," which challenged our cohort of faculty, graduate, and undergraduate students to reimagine our knowledge repositories, reflect on its inclusions and exclusions, consider its limitations, and even rethink Western notions of what constitutes knowledge and the processes by which it is made. Reimagining archives, museums, and libraries in the context of academic institutions has proven particularly challenging in relation to Indigenous epistemologies and Indigenous politics of representation. On the one hand, institutions face the urgency of diversifying Western conceptualizations of archives and working for broader inclusivity to redress historical exclusions and misrepresentations of non-Western knowledges and meaning-making practices. On the other hand, Indigenous epistemologies test the limits of Western archival traditions and compel reflections on whether Western institutional frameworks are valid at all, regardless of diversification efforts, for engaging non-Western cultures in any meaningful way.

The first proposition focuses on the need for interventions within existing archival structures to make space for non-Western knowledges. It necessarily holds tension between pursuing Indigenous inclusion and representation within existing knowledge-producing systems and at the same time recognizing that these institutional structures are dominated by non-Indigenous agendas and in many ways rigged against Indigenous interests (Kovach 90). Archives and museums as mechanisms of colonialist and nationalist hegemony have, after all, played a defining role in dispossessing and misrepresenting

Indigenous peoples (Lonetree, *Decolonizing Museums* 9). Nonetheless, as Māori scholar Graham Hingangaroa Smith warns in an interview with Margaret Kovach, Indigenous people walk away from and disengage from these sites of struggle at their own peril given the central role these institutions play in producing knowledge in society (Kovach 88). Archival and historical systems are, after all, about power in the present, as Joanne Rappaport writes, and as such "can serve to maintain power, or can become a vehicle for empowerment" (*Politics of Memory* 16). Navigating this ambiguous terrain, Indigenous scholars like Hingangaroa Smith, Kovach, and others advocate for exploring "the limits and capacities of what can be achieved" within Western institutions and making "strategic concessions" to win what is possible, with the critical hope of transforming sites like archives and museums to create spaces of intervention, critical reflection, broader inclusion, diversification, and Indigenous participation (Kovach 90). The difficult question, though, as Lonetree posits, is whether, how, and to what extent historical "sites of oppression" such as archives and museums "have the potential to transform into sites of revitalization" (*Decolonizing Museums* 173).

The second consideration presents a more sobering outlook. Namely, it asserts that archives and museums remain unequivocally grounded in colonial hegemonic practices and epistemic frameworks that are not only incompatible with, but antithetical to Indigenous meaning-making, and that as such they are incapable of truly engaging with Indigenous epistemologies. As Lawrence Sullivan writes in the case of South America, the labor of understanding indigeneity is not a quick fix that requires changing only a few ideas about "the other" or simply tweaking our existing structures (2–3). According to Sullivan, it requires dismantling the very foundations of Western interpretive constructs and re-examining Western classificatory systems along with the power inequalities that sustain them. In his nearly 1,000-page book *Icanchu's Drum,* Sullivan guides readers through critical processes of unlearning which are integral to decolonial acts of undoing ethnocentric and provincial outlooks in order to glimpse "the broader horizons of human creativity." "Terrifying or liberating," he goes on to write, the task is urgent not only in terms of acknowledging the agency of Indigenous others, but because this work of understanding ultimately reflects back on us and our ability to assess the limitations of Western perspectives and interact with the world in more deliberate ways (Sullivan 2).

In this chapter I reflect on these two predicaments for archival and museum practices as they unfold in the experiences of the Kawsay Ukhunchay Andean and Amazonian Indigenous Art and Cultural Artifacts Research Collection at The Ohio State University, where the quandary of collecting, exhibiting, representing, and engaging Indigenous meaning-making continuously challenges student and faculty researchers who look after the collection.

Kawsay Ukhunchay—Holding Space for Productive Tensions

The Kawsay Ukhunchay Andean and Amazonian Indigenous Art and Cultural Artifacts Research Collection,[1] established in 2015 with Title VI National Research Center federal funds and private donations, is a research, teaching, and outreach resource at Ohio State.[2] Managed and maintained by an interdisciplinary team of undergraduate and graduate student researchers/curators under my supervision,[3] the Kawsay Ukhunchay Collection promotes an appreciation of Indigenous art, oral traditions, and performance as meaning-making practices and forms of Indigenous expression, knowledge, power, resistance, representation, and self-determination. Collection holdings include contemporary Indigenous art including Canelos Quichua ceramics from Amazonia, textiles made by master weavers from Peru and Bolivia, "Slice-of-life" Tigua paintings from highland Ecuador, etched story gourds, festival masks, feather art from Brazil, and more.

Kawsay Ukhunchay curators/researchers present this cultural heritage as "narratives" in their own right, "organizing strategies" with their own grammar and conventions for meaning-making (see Allen "Pebbles" and *Foxboy*; Harrison 83; Boone 15, 17). We navigate this allusion to "texts," "narratives," "grammars," and "writing without words" (Boone and Mignolo) not to suggest or double down on the authority of writing per se, but to attempt to bridge an appreciation of embodied and enacted forms of expression in terms that are familiar within contexts that privilege linguistic communication. Ultimately, and perhaps more precisely, what we maintain is that, beyond their aesthetic value, Indigenous art and performance present complex semiotic systems wherein not only their design but also their form and structure convey meaning (Conklin cited in Heckman 321).

---

1. See the Kawsay Ukhunchay Andean and Amazonian Collection here: https://u.osu.edu/aaac/.

2. *Kawsay* in Quechua connotes life, experience, or culture. *Ukhu* translates as deep or inside. The name of our collection translates roughly as "delving deeply into cultures and experiences."

3. Kawsay Ukhunchay Andean and Amazonian Collection, "Our Kawsay Waqaychaqkuna," https://u.osu.edu/aaac/our-people/student-curators/.

FIGURE 12.1. Tigua painting from highland Ecuador by César Ugsha. Photo courtesy of Kawsay Ukhunchay Andean and Amazonian Indigenous Art Research Collection.

Beneath their vibrant colors and depictions of bucolic Andean landscapes and daily life, Tigua paintings (see figure 12.1), for instance, encode at least three distinct spatial-temporal layers, placing activities simultaneously in mythic, historical, and present time as well as imagined futures (Weismantel). Tigua artists, in effect, break with linear progressive time and depict subjects from time in all of its dimensions as contemporaries (see also Rappaport, *Politics of Memory*), offering a glimpse at Indigenous temporalities of quantumlike entanglement where things are connected and interdependent despite temporal or spatial distance. Within this complex configuration of nonlinear and nonprogressive time and space, there is conceivably no past to remember and no future to look forward to, as it is all one simultaneous, overlapping, contemporaneous, and present moment. I venture to suggest that this view potentially brings the very notion of social memory and archival memory into question. Techniques of depth perspective, sense of motion, and great detail in these paintings, moreover, allow discerning viewers to pinpoint locations, historical moments, and even specific individuals portrayed (Whitten 246–47). The staggering detail in these paintings has led Dorothea Whitten to describe them, in fact, as ethnographic, hinting at their capacity as compelling alternatives to alphabetic writing for cultural documentation and representation.

Similarly, while the tiny etchings on story gourds capture daily and mythic Andean scenes on the surface, their spherical shape which invites turning the gourd in any direction to view the "story" hints at nonlinear narratives—stories with no beginning, middle, or end (see figure 12.2). Miniaturization and the globelike appearance of gourds, furthermore, allude to a microcosm that, according to Lévi-Strauss, facilitates an "instant apprehension of the whole,"

FIGURE 12.2. Etched story gourd (*calabaza tallada*). Photo courtesy of Kawsay Ukhunchay Andean and Amazonian Indigenous Art Research Collection.

thus reversing conventional analytical models that typically progress from the analysis of parts to conclusions about the whole (cited in Allen, "Pebbles" 81).

Another example that alludes to theoretical and methodological considerations deriving from Indigenous epistemologies is the highland Andean Aya Uma double-sided festival mask with one countenance looking forward to the past in all of its dimensions while the other faces backward to the future (see figure 12.3). The Aya Uma mask embodies unique conceptualizations of time-space wherein forward movement in space is concurrently backward movement in time. A single word in Kichwa/Quechua, *ñawpa,* denotes both movements. Similarly, *quipa* indicates backward in space as well as forward in time. This mask and the concepts that undergird its significance interrupt Western perspectives on the correlation between time and space, and, moreover, the presumption that linear time with the past behind us and the future in front of us is somehow universal. It further introduces the curious prospect, as Rappaport writes, of potentially "remember(ing) the future; imagin(ing) the past" (*Politics of Memory* 17).

FIGURE 12.3. Aya Uma festival mask with two faces. Photo courtesy of Kawsay Ukhunchay Andean and Amazonian Indigenous Art Research Collection.

FIGURE 12.4. Textile from Chinchero, Peru. Photo courtesy of Kawsay Ukhunchay Andean and Amazonian Indigenous Art Research Collection.

Other items in the collection touch upon symbolism, coded content, and patterns that reiterate at different scales and across different mediums of expression, all referred to as "pathways of knowledge" (Arnold and Yapita 275) (see figure 12.4). So too, we delve into ontological concepts regarding the agency and personhood of certain objects in our care (see Wibbelsman, *Ritual Encounters* for more).

As caretakers of the collection, we go beyond using items to simply talk about Indigenous cultures. Instead, and most importantly, we insist on engaging with Indigenous epistemologies. What this means is that aside from remarking on the significance of designs, forms, and structures as meaningful and meaning-making, we endeavor to dialogue with the unique theoretical perspectives they present, integrate the methodologies they proffer, and challenge ourselves to apply some of the concepts in critical reflections of our own work as attempts to learn how to "think otherwise" and imagine new paradigms (Santos). We pursue this further through sustained dialogue with Indigenous artists, project-based collaborations, and applied learning, all of which guide our approaches to inquiry. One inevitable question that arises revolves around the profound and possibly radical implications that Indigenous epistemologies, their models, and unique methods for the production of knowledge and meaning might have for archives and archival studies. As we probe this idea, the strategic presence of the collection in a department of Spanish and Portuguese and more broadly in an academic building dedicated to the study of world languages, literatures, and cultures, allows us to continuously decenter the prevalence of alphabetic writing and challenge assumptions about "canonical" corpuses of Western knowledge in an effort to provoke critical reflection about the omission of certain voices, languages, perspectives, forms of expression, and cultural practices.

Inviting diverse publics to interact with items in the collection and to glimpse other meaning-making possibilities and unusual perspectives of history and historiography, literacy, memory, and even time itself begins the process of raising awareness around relations of power and gaps, silencings, omissions, exclusions, and erasures in Western archives. Our collection tours begin not with a celebratory "rainbow narrative" (Rassool 108) of diversity and inclusivity or the "joyous, de-politicized celebration of reconciliation" that Amy Lonetree ("Museums" 324) criticizes, but with an acknowledgment (attentively curated for different publics) of the hard truths behind colonial suppression of Indigenous peoples and practices as a path conducive to transforming museums into the "sites of conscience" and "places that matter" that Lonetree (*Decolonizing Museums* 27) calls for.

We address the historical marginalization of Indigenous knowledge production beginning with the violence of the European conquest which took a human toll of unimaginable proportion, reducing a population of an estimated 90–112 million inhabitants on the American continent prior to the arrival of the Europeans by more than 93 percent in the 100 years that followed. We then point out the epistemic devastation brought on by the Spanish Inquisition as it reached the New World in 1569 with dire consequences for Indigenous knowledge-bearers, the targeted destruction of knowledge systems, and the suppression of Indigenous practices. Colonial frameworks of power and understanding with "harmfully narrow views" of what constituted knowledge and its expression subsequently came to determine which histories were acknowledged and what type of knowledge was preserved (Boone 9). Together with our audiences, we consider how these hegemonic formulas of historical erasure and banalization, as Michel-Rolph Trouillot designates them in *Silencing the Past,* guaranteed the systematic omission of Indigenous experiences, expertise, memories, and knowledge in official archives (96).

Non-European languages remain noticeably underrepresented or altogether absent in academic publications today. Enduring colonial legacies of knowledge tied almost exclusively to alphabetic literacy in Western institutions, moreover, continue to overlook semasiographic and supralinguistic meaning-making practices (sign systems decoupled from speech, including

FIGURE 12.5. Canelos Quichua ceramic made by Marta Vargas from Puyo, Ecuador. Photo courtesy of Kawsay Ukhunchay Andean and Amazonian Indigenous Art Research Collection.

such things as textile and ceramic art, music, performance; see figure 12.5 as an example) as knowledge repositories (Mignolo 309).

Archival power, as Trouillot reminds us, is an instrument of colonialism that promotes through its institutional gatekeeping practices a preferred and pervasive version of events, stipulates a particular structure, and sustains a hegemonic narrative of the unquestionable order of things. Its legacy is an "enduring matrix of power" (Walsh cited in Howard-Malverde 13) that, in Walter Mignolo's (309) view, aims to suppress diversity, orality, and performativity as part of a violent European agenda of "taming" native voices and "erasing the past as indigenous people had remembered it," effectively dispossessing people not only of their past but of their future as well (Rappaport, "Object and Alphabet" 217). Recognizing this manifold negation of

Indigenous meaning-making seems essential for understanding museums and archives as contact zones that, as Robin Boast observes, mask fundamental asymmetries, appropriations, and biases (cited in Lonetree, *Decolonizing Museums* 24).

Confronting these hard truths as a first step in developing awareness around epistemic plurality among our publics and fostering critical reflection on archives as well as more discerning outlooks regarding the potential and limitations of our own prevailing systems is delicate business. It requires curating contexts that foster trust as a foundation for enabling diverse publics to venture into difficult subject matter and unfamiliar concepts with intellectual curiosity and a disposition of openness to embracing the daunting process of unlearning and learning. Elsewhere, my colleague and I draw inspiration from the centrality of relationship-building in Indigenous scholarship and write about how attending to relations of care and trust as a priority in the context of Kawsay Ukhunchay Collection sustains the decolonial work we do (Wibbelsman and Fernandez Castro). As Marilyn Strathern observes, kinship and relations take priority over all else in Indigenous contexts where knowledge is not an end in and of itself but rather "the substance that links people in close relations" and serves as a means for those relations to come into being (33). Relating to one another in conversation around the items in the collection and the conviviality that emerges from it are, after all, integral to Indigenous epistemologies and the biggest takeaway for our audiences. In every aspect of our work we practice collegial and intellectual sociability, as Regina Bendix et al. discuss in their book *Sustaining Interdisciplinary Collaboration* (59–62). This includes conducting interdisciplinary and community-engaged research; hosting tours, open houses, workshops, and public talks; inviting and properly hosting Indigenous guest speakers and performers on campus; or conducting other forms of public outreach. It has become progressively clear to us that what we do primarily is to curate contexts for interactions, not holdings and acquisitions. The main purpose of the collection, in essence, is to create opportunities for encounters, conversations, and collaborations, and for tending to mutual relationships.

We are cognizant, nevertheless, of the latent collusion with Western museum practices of exhibiting objects and the possibility this has, on the one hand, to give visibility to forms of Indigenous expression and foster critical dialogue but, on the other, to decontextualize and potentially essentialize the cultures they represent (Lloyd New cited in McMullen 85). As we tend to our displays, we thus remain vigilant about problematizing colonial habits of collecting, categorizing, and displaying from a critical decolonial perspective. The tension we straddle is that the collection display as a vehicle for institutional inclusion, dissemination, and public engagement may simultaneously be the greatest impediment to genuine engagement with Indigenous cultural knowledges and practices. Let me explain further.

While we certainly learn from delving deeply into research on individual items in our collection as described in the examples of the Tigua paintings, story gourds, and masks, ultimately, as Rappaport contends, cultural articles such as these "cannot be understood as isolated texts, but only in conjunction with a whole range of activities, including ritual, pilgrimage and dance which clarify, elaborate upon and provide keys" to their interpretation (*Politics of Memory* 11). What is an Aya Uma mask, after all, without its dancer, without movement, without the music and sound that surround it in festival context? Pierre Nora traces a marked difference between "sites of memory"—fixed or externalized referents like commemorative markers (or cultural objects on display), static, frozen in time, inactive and cut off from their milieu—versus "contexts of memory"—dynamic environments of living traditions that set things in complex motion and interaction (cited in Wibbelsman, *Ritual Encounters* 131). In the case of the Andes, Rosaleen Howard-Malverde similarly underscores the precedence of context. Citing Geertz's metaphor of culture as "webs of significance," she highlights the ways in which individual expression is understood to be constituted by and constitutive of broader contexts (7). Isolating cultural objects from their constellation of activities and mutually defining contexts in Western traditions of archival conservation and preservation, in Ann McMullen's words, amounts to a sort of "cultural embalming process wherein obsolete cultural ways are kept going beyond their time" and current objects are cut off from living traditions before their time (84).

Indigenous art, performance, oral traditions, ritual, and other forms of expression are not intended to "represent" culture or to "preserve" things as "evidence of what went before" (Schwartz and Cook 18) or "as images of the frozen past, sources of nostalgia, or resources for the future" (McMullen 82). Rather, as Indigenous artists from across the continent insist, they are intended to bring things into being and to render things present in experiential ways. In other words, these forms of expression do not function metonymically to exemplify or explicate culture or mnemonically as a memory aid. Many Indigenous scholars, both Latin American and North American, stress that in their respective communities, knowledge and meaning-making are not so much about remembering or preserving commemorative objects as they are about practice. Ancestors, for instance, who in Indigenous conceptions reside not in the past but as regular members of contemporary society, are kept alive through sustained practices of dialogue and frequent visits. The moment that honoring the ancestors passes from a context of shared conviviality to commemoration, their souls die.[4] Similarly, objects preserved, knowledges archivally conserved, or weaving patterns and melodies repeated year after year are considered to become stale and inert, incapable of acting upon and affecting the world (Stobart). What Indigenous communities throughout the continent value and maintain above all else are practices of regular convergence around embodied and collective lived experiences (in Spanish, *convivencia*).

The End of Archives? Toward Paradigms of Practice

Indigenous meaning-making approaches, insistent on generative and regenerative practice, participation, embodied experience, and regularly coming together, conceivably bring us to the brink of archival possibilities. While acknowledging the difficult and important work of colleagues like Michelle Caswell ("Archival Pluralism"; *Urgent Archives*) and others in decentering singular archival designs and advocating for the plurality and diversification of archives (which is absolutely urgent and essential), it bears pointing out that archival pluralism, conceptualizations of an archival multiverse, efforts to activate and perform archives, and even proposals for autonomous archives in the hands of communities themselves continue to revolve around archival collecting, preservation, and documentation in one form or another as "the foundation for historical understanding" (Schwartz and Cook 18). Robin Boast contends that this conception of archives and museums as sites of accumulation, gatekeepers of authority, and ultimate caretakers of objects "has to be completely redrafted" (cited in Lonetree, *Decolonizing Museums* 24).

We are, after all, hard-pressed to reconcile coming to appreciate the methodological and theoretical breadth of Indigenous epistemologies and to engage with their extraordinary propositions of alternative meaning-making only to coerce these expressions back into analytical and conceptual frameworks that do not correspond to them and cannot apprehend or accommodate their complexity. As Rappaport writes, attempts at integrating Indigenous thoughts, processes, and understandings within Western-style discourse inevitably yield what Frank Salomon calls "chronicles of the impossible," an end result where both perspectives are hopelessly compromised because they contradict each other (*Politics of Memory* 2). The formula "add Indigenous and stir," even if carried out in creative ways that potentially inform and attempt to expand and diversify existing archives, as Kovach insists, is simply not enough (156).

4. See Wibbelsman, *Ritual Encounters* ch. 5.

Acknowledging and responding to Indigenous epistemologies requires "new mental architectures," and more specifically models centered around practice and lived experience (Arnold and Yapita 287–88).

Rather than archival imaginations, this proposition may well imply imagining beyond archives and, in fact, contemplating the end of archives as holdings. Indigenous artists, scholars, and activists from communities in Ecuador, Peru, Bolivia, Colombia, Chile, Brazil, and North America involved with the Kawsay Ukhunchay Collection have consistently expressed their uneasiness with archival habits of conservation and preservation along with the fixity, interpretive finality, analytical dissection, and incomplete understanding these imply. They have repeatedly conveyed the value and primacy of practice and experience in Indigenous meaning-making, particularly the practice of gathering regularly in a spirit of *convivencia,* shared lived experience and convivial interaction.

If we are to respond honestly to Indigenous propositions for meaning-making, would our energies and resources not be better invested in supporting recurring Indigenous community gatherings independent of institutional teleological ends and away from the "hungry" eye or ear of archival endeavors (Robinson)? Can we embrace the ephemeral nature of lived experiences so central to Indigenous epistemologies and temporalities and come to terms with the fact that these may or may not leave a collectable trace? In what ways would a convergence around experience affect Western approaches to understanding and institutional priorities? If it is only by being present (if/when invited) and by participating in convivial encounters that we might hope to glimpse beyond isolated cultural fragments and truly appreciate the dynamic contexts of lived experience that give them meaning, are we also prepared to come to grips with the implications of not being there? Contemplating the end of archives ostensibly requires not just decentering (which is a model for diversity and broader inclusion) but conceivably dismantling some of the mainstays of Western institutions and their colonial legacies. This might begin with a move toward privileging contexts of interaction and obligations to tend to relationships rather than a preoccupation with cultural objects; toward endorsing practices of participation in living traditions rather than archival collection as pathways to understanding.

Acknowledgments

An enormous debt of gratitude to the *kawsay waqaychaqkuna* student researchers/curators of the Kawsay Ukhunchay Andean and Amazonian Indigenous Art and Cultural Artifacts Research Collection at The Ohio State

University and to the cohort of faculty and student fellows for the Global Arts and Humanities Discovery Theme "Archival Imaginations." I extend my many thanks to the editors of the volume as well for their guidance and their patience.

Works Cited

Abercrombie, Thomas A. *Pathways of Memory and Power: Ethnography and History Among an Andean People.* University of Wisconsin Press, 1998.

Allen, Catherine J. *Foxboy: Intimacy and Aesthetics in Andean Stories.* University of Texas Press, 2011.

Allen, Catherine J. "When Pebbles Move Mountains: Iconicity and Symbolism in Quechua Ritual." *Creating Context in Andean Cultures,* edited by Rosaleen Howard-Malverde, Oxford University Press, 1997, pp. 73–84.

Arnold, Denise Y., with Juan de Dios Yapita. *The Metamorphosis of Heads: Textual Struggles, Education and Land in the Andes.* University of Pittsburgh Press, 2006.

Bendix, Regina, et al., editors. *Sustaining Interdisciplinary Collaboration: A Guide for the Academy.* University of Illinois Press, 2017.

Boone, Elizabeth. "Introduction: Writing and Recording Knowledge." Boone and Mignolo, pp. 3–26.

Boone, Elizabeth Hill, and Walter D. Mignolo, editors. *Writing Without Words: Alternative Literacies in Mesoamerica and the Andes.* Duke University Press, 1994.

Caswell, Michelle. "On Archival Pluralism: What Religious Pluralism (and Its Critics) Can Teach Us About Archives." *Archival Science,* vol. 13, 2013, pp. 273–92.

Caswell, Michelle. *Urgent Archives: Enacting Liberatory Memory Work.* Routledge, 2021.

Conklin, William J. "A Khipu Information String Theory." *Narrative Threads: Accounting and Recounting in Andean Khipu,* edited by Jeffrey Quilter and Gary Urton, University of Texas Press, 2002, pp. 53–86.

Eliade, Mircea. *Myth and Reality.* Harper & Row, 1963.

Geertz, Clifford. *The Interpretation of Cultures: Selected Essays by Clifford Geertz.* Basic Books, 1973.

Harrison, Regina. *Signos, cantos y memoria en los Andes: Traduciendo la lengua y la cultura quechua.* Ediciones Abya-Yala, 1994.

Heckman, Andrea. *Woven Stories: Andean Textiles and Rituals.* University of New Mexico Press, 2003.

Howard-Malverde, Rosaleen. "Introduction: Between Text and Context in the Evocation of Culture." *Creating Context in Andean Cultures,* edited by Rosaleen Howard-Malverde, Oxford University Press, 1997, pp. 3–20.

Kovach, Margaret. *Indigenous Methodologies: Characteristics, Conversations, and Contexts.* University of Toronto Press, 2009.

Lawrence, David Todd. "Failing to See: A Meditation on Ethnography." Invited Humanities Institute / Mershon Center Lecture, The Ohio State University, Feb. 2023.

Lonetree, Amy. *Decolonizing Museums: Representing Native America in National and Tribal Museums.* University of North Carolina Press, 2012.

Lonetree, Amy. "Museums as Sites of Decolonization: Truth Telling in National Tribal Museums." Sleeper-Smith, pp. 322–38.

McMullen, Ann. "Reinventing George Heye: Nationalizing the Museum of the American Indian and Its Collections." Sleeper-Smith, pp. 65–105.

Mignolo, Walter. "Afterword: Writing and Recorded Knowledge in Colonial and Postcolonial Situations." Boone and Mignolo, pp. 292–312.

Rappaport, Joanne. "Object and Alphabet: Andean Indians and Documents in the Colonial Period." Boone and Mignolo, pp. 271–91.

Rappaport, Joanne. *The Politics of Memory: Native Historical Interpretation in the Colombian Andes.* Duke University Press, 1990.

Rassool, Ciraj. "Ethnographic Ela Orations, Indigenous Contestations, and the Cultural Politics of Imagining Community: A View from the District Six Museum in South Africa." Sleeper-Smith, pp. 106–28.

Robinson, Dylan. *Hungry Listening: Resonant Theory for Indigenous Sound Studies.* University of Minnesota Press, 2020.

Santos, Boaventura de Souza. *Epistemologies of the South: Justice Against Epistemicide.* Taylor & Francis, 2014.

Schwartz, Joan M., and Terry Cook. "Archives, Records, and Power: The Making of Modern Memory." *Archival Science,* vol. 2, 2002, pp. 1–19.

Sleeper-Smith, Susan, editor. *Contesting Knowledge: Museums and Indigenous Perspectives.* University of Nebraska Press, 2009.

Sleeper-Smith, Susan. Introduction. Sleeper-Smith, pp. 1–5.

Strathern, Marilyn. "Opening Up Relations." *A World of Many Worlds,* edited by Marisol de la Cadena and Mario Blazer, Duke University Press, 2018, pp. 23–52.

Stobart, Henry. "Flourishing Horns and Enchanted Tubers: Music and Potatoes in Highland Bolivia." *British Journal of Ethnomusicology,* vol. 3, 1994, pp. 35–48.

Sullivan, Lawrence. *Icanchu's Drum: An Orientation to Meaning in South American Religions.* Macmillan, New York, 1988.

Trouillot, Michel-Rolph. *Silencing the Past: Power and the Production of History.* Beacon Press, 1995.

Weismantel, Mary J. *Food, Gender, and Poverty in the Ecuadorian Andes.* Waveland Press, 1998.

Whitten, Dorothea Scott. "Actors and Artists from Amazonia and the Andes." *Millennial Ecuador: Critical Essays on Cultural Transformations and Social Dynamics,* edited by Norman E. Whitten Jr., University of Iowa Press, 2003, pp. 242–74.

Wibbelsman, Michelle. "Andean and Amazonian Material Culture and Performance Traditions as Sites of Indigenous Knowledges and Memory." *TRANSMODERNITY: Journal of Peripheral Cultural Production of the Luso-Hispanic World Special Issue: Indigenous Knowledges and Sites of Indigenous Memory,* edited by Arturo Arias, vol. 7, no. 1, 2017, https://escholarship.org/uc/item/5223g28c.

Wibbelsman, Michelle. *Ritual Encounters: Otavalan Modern and Mythic Community.* Ethnographic Series: Interpretations of Culture in the New Millennium. University of Illinois Press, 2009.

Wibbelsman, Michelle, and Anaís Fernandez Castro. "*Pukllay Pampa*: Andean-Inspired Time-Spaces for Learning and Unlearning." *Journal of Curriculum and Pedagogy,* 26 Oct. 2023, https://www.tandfonline.com/doi/full/10.1080/15505170.2023.2273538.

CHAPTER 13

The Laws of Movement

The *Natyashastra*, Caste, and Archives of Indian Classical Dance

ANURIMA BANERJI

The *Natyashastra* is considered a master archive for Indian performance. Its principles and tenets organize much of the movement patterns and expressive codes of the canon of Indian classical dance.[1] This Hindu treatise, dating to the ancient period (ca. second century BCE–second century CE) is presented as a compendium of performance knowledge in the Indian subcontinent at its temporal juncture. It offers a valuable taxonomy of drama, dance, and music as integrated fields, coalescing in the *natya* concept, which is often translated into English as "performance."[2] As a multiply layered text of uncommon significance, its historical, philosophical, and aesthetic dimensions have been widely explored by a constellation of critics and commentators, its vitality continually affirmed and challenged in the world of artistic practice.

1. This chapter has been adapted from "The Laws of Movement: The *Natyashastra* as Archive for Indian Classical Dance," *Contemporary Theatre Review*, vol. 31, no. 1, Outing Archives, Archives Outing, pp. 132–52.

2. In the preface to his translation, Rangacharya states that the *Natyasastra* "remains the origin of our dramatic tradition" (xxi). *Natya* is denoted in the text as the synthesis of multiple mediums, like music, acting, movement, and in a staged concert; this confluence is often described as "total theater" or cited as "performance" in English. It should be noted that none of the disciplines incorporated in natya was understood to exist autonomously, since in practice they folded into each other; however, they are sometimes analytically separated as specific points of discussion in the *Natyashastra*. (See also Bharatmuni/Ghosh; Tarlekar; Vatsyayan, "Technique" and *Bharata*). Most scholars agree the original Sanskrit treatise was likely composed sometime between the second century BCE and second century CE, although its exact date is still unknown. Bharat Gupt speculates it may have emerged even earlier, in the fifth century BCE, in "The Date of the *Natyashastra*."

Inhabiting a rarefied discursive space, and positioned authoritatively as the "fifth Veda," the *Natyashastra* inaugurated a profound series of philosophical debates and interpretations about performance, and in parallel anchored a host of creative applications, theories, and techniques in myriad art genres.[3] The *Natyashastra*'s formidable hold on Indian/diasporic artistic imaginaries and scholarship into the present can be attributed partly to its intrinsic complexity, its deep and comprehensive coverage of a whole performance process, and partly to external reasons—a broad social consensus that emerged over the centuries elevating it to a position of veneration and renown, and also revealing it as a hegemonic object of contestation.[4]

Kapila Vatsyayan, the late distinguished scholar of Indian aesthetics, declares in "The Theory and Technique of Indian Classical Dancing" that the *Natyashastra* and related aesthetic philosophies, in their eminence and reach, represent "the laws of movement."[5] Additionally, she suggests "if these principles and conventions are witnessed to this day in their unpolluted form anywhere, it is in the stage presentation of some of these compositions of classical dance in India" (230). I wish to consider that Vatsyayan deliberately uses the framing of "law" in relation to dance—not recommendations, not guidelines, not proposals. This construct lifts the aesthetic treatise into the space of authoritative sanction and command, regulation and restraint, enforcement and control. Vatsyayan's pronouncement is important because it reflects a widely held view in the mainstream Indian classical dance scene about the *Natyashastra* as the quintessential source of directives for performance. Taking Vatsyayan's proposition seriously, in what follows I engage in a thought experiment about how we might think about the *Natyashastra* as an archive joining social and aesthetic laws for Indian classical dance. I first situate the

---

3. The four ancient Vedas are regarded as the foundational sacred texts in mainstream Hinduism. Brahmin patriarchal authorities served as custodians of this esoteric Sanskrit opus, according to orthodox caste hierarchies. The *Natyashastra* drew elements from the quartet of texts and was documented in the simpler Prakrit language, making it the "fifth Veda" available to the masses—apparently superseding caste, class, gender, and other social restrictions of the time determining access to elite knowledge (Vatsyayan, *Bharata* 21).

4. See Tripathi, *Lectures* and *Natyasastra*; Vatsyayan, *Bharata*; Bose; Srinivasan, *Knowledge*; Nair.

5. "The Theory and Technique of Indian Classical Dancing" is Vatsyayan's succinct and erudite summary of movement principles outlined in major aesthetic texts, including the *Natyashastra* (henceforth *NS* in the notes), the *Sangitaratnakara*, and *Abhinaya Darpanam*: "The *nrtta* technique of the Indian dance as discussed in the treatises has to be understood as the laws and methodology of human movement" (232). The *NS* divides stylized movement into two types: nrtta, or formalist explorations of "pure dance," and *abhinaya*, or affective enactments of poetry or narrative. Vatsyayan, a towering figure in the world of arts and letters, left this world on September 16, 2020.

trajectory which led to the *Natyashastra*'s modern recognition as a "law of movement," address its relationship to the concepts of archive and governmentality, and then examine how the text constructs an identitarian politics of difference on the grounds of caste.

An exclusive focus on the *Natyashastra* as an elite repository and "precious legacy" of aesthetic techniques obscures the necessary analysis of the ways it reflects and reproduces social inequalities through its "laws of movement" (Roberge). Surprisingly, these social dimensions of the *Natyashastra* are rarely engaged by classical dance scholars and practitioners; sometimes, they are duly reported as facts but glossed over without critical scrutiny or discussion of their import.[6] It might be argued in protest that the text contains an inherent flexibility, and that it should not be viewed monolithically as an instrument of power on the grounds that its tenets are never absolute but contingent, that it encourages adaptation of its principles according to the temporal and spatial circumstance, with the effect that its normative tendencies might be curtailed or undermined, perhaps even made irrelevant, through subversive interventions.[7] Christine Garlough observes, "it long has been recognized that traditional texts are inexhaustible; they are always in the process of being defined as the course of history reveals new meaning" (170). It is also true that the *Natyashastra* proposes a dialectical interface between theory and practice, *sastra* and *prayoga,* and that many dance specialists have engaged the text in innovative ways, mobilizing its precepts to construct differential interpretations from what is prescribed on the surface.[8] Others have rejected it entirely as a biased product of a patriarchal Brahmin worldview and thus

6. Anupa Pande is an exception and offers a sociological description of the world in which the text is situated, in *Historical and Cultural Study of the "Natyasastra"* and *The "Natyashastra" Tradition and Ancient Indian Society.* See especially ch. 5, "Aspects of Social Life: Institutions, Structure, and Value" in the former, and ch. 10, "Some Socially Depressed Classes—The Candalas," in the latter. Kapila Vatsyayan does briefly address the question of social stratification in *Bharata* (21–24). Urmimala Sarkar Munsi and Brahma Prakash, whose work I discuss later, provide the deepest analyses of inequities in the text. See Sarkar Munsi and Dutt; Prakash.

7. See Tripathi, *Lectures*; Srinivasan, *Knowledge*; Gupt, *Revisited.*

8. Artists have long negotiated the principles embedded in the text in complex ways. Some validate it as the originary source for classical dance and attempt to faithfully mimic its contents; see, for instance, Padma Subrahmanyam's work in the area of Bharata Nritya, modeled on the *NS,* in *Bharatiya Natyashastra.* Some see the *NS* as an intriguing source of movement information and play with select ideas while repudiating others they find objectionable—like the Odissi dancer Bijayini Satpathy, who has fruitfully expanded the repertoire of the form by building on *nritta* elements from the text. See also Chatterjee and Lee. Some have explicitly discarded it as a source after initially training according to its tenets, like the late Chandralekha, who was a classical exponent of Bharatanatyam before delving into contemporary choreography (see Chatterjea). Unlike Vatsyayan and related thinkers, Chandralekha saw the historical source of Indian dance residing in the movement and martial arts traditions of village-based communities. See also the late choreographer Ranjabati Sircar's critique of classical dance.

repudiated its paradigms in favor of producing new lexicons.[9] It is clear that the capacity for innovation that resides in the text coexists with its capacity for hegemonic consolidation. Here, I am particularly interested in the dominative ideological matrix that the text both inhabits and reproduces, how it arrived at its honorific position as master archive for classical dance, and the norms of social and aesthetic discriminations it upholds through its inscribed "laws of movement."[10]

Specifically, I examine how the *Natyashastra* acts as a purveyor of social and aesthetic laws and illustrates its ideological encodings through the mechanisms of *prohibition* with caste. This is not the only form of social stratification reified by the text; gender, class, disability, and regional difference figure in it as well. Since these social aspects of the *Natyashastra* are marginally considered, highlighting their operations remains an imperative critical task, as Urmimala Sarkar Munsi and Brahma Prakash have shown in their comprehensive analyses of how the injustices of gender and caste surface in the text. Sarkar Munsi delivered an earlier sustained critique of the these two identity markers and their interlocking in *Engendering Performance*, where she frames the *Natyashastra* "as *almost* a universal rule book of control, and a source of authority" that guides present-day dancers in the tenets of performance, training them both on and off stage to rehearse restrictive identity scripts under the guise of perpetuating a "great tradition" (183). As she rightfully shows, while rooted in the worldviews and values of ancient India, these discourses of caste/gender difference and discrimination linger palpably into the present, and thus brim with contemporary relevance. I extend her argument about the social-aesthetic continuum registered in the *Natyashastra* by suggesting that the book is not "almost" a rule book of control but functionally represents, in Vatsyayan's terms, the elevated "laws of movement." I focus on caste because of the ways it uniquely shapes and pervades the text.

The *Natyashastra* and Indian Classical Dance

Historically hailed as a cardinal source for Indian performance, the *Natyashastra* assumed renewed significance in the time of colonial modernity,

9. See Tarlekar; Allen; Vatsyayan, *Classical*; Meduri; Nair.

10. Methodologically, I am indebted to the insights of Raymond Williams, Edward Said (*Orientalism* and *The World, the Text, and the Critic*), Romila Thapar ("Epic and History"), and Susan Foster (*Choreographing Empathy*), who have studied how aesthetic practices like writing and dance are part of a whole social, cultural, and historical process, and circulate as bearers of ideology—far from the fantasy that they might exist in some sequestered sphere of neutrality where art is governed entirely by formalist concerns, devoid of political consideration.

since the time of its rediscovery and reassemblage into a unified text generated from diverse, partial manuscripts, under the auspices of Orientalist scholarship and Indian expertise from the late nineteenth into the early twentieth century.[11] While its authorship is attributed to the sage Bharatmuni, most scholars agree that the text as we know it today is likely a product of multiple rescensions and interpolations over time and represents the collective labor of a host of contributors (Vatsyayan, *Bharata*).

The *Natyashastra* presents a comprehensive organization of the purposes, principles, conventions, and methodologies associated with performance. It carefully addresses topics such as the preparation and consecration of the stage, the training of the performing body, and audience relations. Speaking to the significance of this corpus of knowledge, Sheldon Pollock indicates that the *Natyashastra* is "the closest thing we have to a foundational text of the discipline of aesthetics" (7). The treatise systematically outlines the qualities of movement and their manner of expression (*vritti*), the modes of presentation (*lokadharmi*, realism and *natyadharmi*, stylization), the predominant patterns of movement according to region, the formalist explorations of dance (*nritta*) and the different communicative forms attached to *abhinaya*, or acting: *angika* (bodily expressions), *vacika* (speech), *aharya* (costumes, jewelry, makeup, and other accoutrements), and *sattvika* (the spontaneous display of emotion). One of its main features is the articulation of *rasa*, the "taste" of performance—a sophisticated theory of aesthetic pleasure and perception that has been characterized by Pollock as "among India's most luminous contributions to humanist knowledge" (xi). The text codifies how the performer should express *bhava*, the affective states intended to generate corresponding rasa for the onlookers, as well as delineating the conditions of ideal spectatorship.

The resurrection of the *Natyashastra* as a significant text during imperial India coincided with the emergence of a complex political period, which ironically witnessed the rise of a powerful "anti-nautch" (anti-dance) movement initiated by colonial and Indian elites and saw the concomitant appearance of a counterdiscourse of cultural nationalism promoting the value of dance as a heritage practice.[12] The tensions between these camps led to major public

11. Various scholars chanced upon parts of the *NS* manuscript and published them—Fitzedward Hall in 1861–65; Heymann in 1874; Paul Regnaud in 1884. And J. Grosset in 1898. Pandit Sivadatta and Kashinaath Pandurang Parab issued the complete Sanskrit text in 1894. Manavalli Ramakrishna Kavi made available a critical edition from Gaekwad in 1926. A 1929 publication edited by Batuknath Sharma and Baladev Upadhyaya provided the basis for the 1956 English translation prepared by Manmohan Ghosh. For details of the manuscript history, see Bharatmuni/Rangacharya and Bharatmuni/Ghosh.

12. The anti-nautch campaigns began in the 1880s and extended into the 1930s, culminating in a total ban on the dedication of dancers to temples in 1947. See Srinivasan, "Reform"; Soneji, *Unfinished Gestures*.

debates about the moral economy of Indian dance and placed in deep crisis its merit as a form of embodied cultural capital. However, the new prominence accorded to the *Natyashastra* and related texts in this crucial moment energized the proponents of traditional performance, who could now justify their modern artistic pursuits through recourse to ancient evidence, and realign the political narratives in their favor by pointing to the long-standing value and praxis of dance in the Indian landscape, as attested by an eminent philosophical archive moored in antiquity.

The idea of the *Natyashastra* as *the* privileged progenitor of dance pedagogy and performance acquired salience only with the efflorescence of "classical" discourse in modern India of the 1930s, with the growth of artistic enterprises that sought to establish their links to Hindu antiquity and looked to the text as a principal archival source for such corroboration, reflecting a new logocentric bias in the world of dance praxis. This was exampled in the consolidation of Bharatanatyam as a classical form, most prominently in Rukmini Arundale's version modeled at Kalakshetra, which installed the *Natyashastra* as its chief choreographic source (Meduri; Kothari). Such an approach was connected to the Brahminisation of Indian dance, its reconfiguration as a class-bound, caste-privileged pursuit of building the nation, and led to the pedestalization of the Sanskritized dancing body (Coorlawala). This dynamic reversed the reigning precolonial model that valorized corporeal knowledge over written epistemologies—a position also acknowledged in the *Natyashastra* itself. The critical move of marginalizing the modern body and exalting the ancient text occurred at a key historical juncture when the dance was being purified from its associations with stigmatized sexuality and reframed through respectability politics as a response to the anti-nautch campaign, dissociated from its diverse histories and the figure of the female public dancer, and transformed into an articulation of modern bourgeois identity instead.[13]

The *Natyashastra* and Theories of the Archive

The "will to archive" (Lepecki) is clearly a strong impulse in the space of Indian aesthetics, as exemplified by the philosophical tradition enfolding the *Natyashastra* and the debates that took place in the field between various interlocutors in the confines of the page and in person across the centuries.[14] In this regard it is useful to revisit ongoing discussions in dance

13. See O'Shea; Chakravorty, *Bells*; Soneji, *Bharatanatyam*; Banerji, *Odissi*.
14. See Bose; Ganser; Gupt, *Dramatic*.

and performance studies, revolving around the nature and question of the archive, its inadequacy for attending to dance as an unfixed and ungraspable art, and the relationship between corporeality and logocentric repositories. In *The Archive and the Repertoire,* Diana Taylor proposed the influential concepts of "archive" and "repertoire"—dividing the storehouse of artifacts from cultural labors of the human body—to name the different "acts of transfer" accomplished by each knowledge system; their segregation is never total, as they interact and mutually inform each other. In a political economic framework compatible with the archive/repertoire ideation, Susan Foster's *Valuing Dance* studies the contrast between dance posited as immaterial labor and the objectified commodity as a tangible thing, as she demonstrates the material value of the choreographic enterprise within capitalist and gift-based forms of exchange. Taylor and Foster show how a Cartesian bias has contributed to the impoverished status of dance and performance in the Global North by granting superior value to logocentric epistemologies. Jacqueline Shea Murphy and André Lepecki take an appositional view by regarding the body *as* archive, examining this conceit in Native American compositions in "Mobilizing (in) the Archive" and performance art premised on re-enactments of an original work in "The Body as Archive," respectively. Sally Ann Ness's "The Inscription of Gesture" holds a dovetailing position that movement is held and inscribed in the interior realms of the body as receptacle. Rebecca Schneider reconciles these diffuse approaches in *Performing Remains,* arguing that the body can be framed as simply a distinctive type of record, separate from the traditional relic in a repository, and pushes the analysis further by underscoring the archival institution and its contents as open, unfixed, and unstable—the archive itself as a performance.

As vital as these arguments are, I would argue that none of them wholly apply to the archival formations for Indian classical dance, in terms of the trajectory of aesthetic philosophy concerning the *Natyashastra* and its commentaries. Rather, an argument can be made that the dancing body is conceptually recognized as a special type of archive, *and* distinguished from it as a site of practice. Neither premise cancels out the other, but enfolds the other within its imaginary.[15] That is, the body cannot be located on one side of the archive/repertoire binary and may instead be envisioned as a continuum, since the theory-practice engagement in the *Natyashastra* suggests the body is a multilayered entity which exists as an anatomical object for recording and relaying prescribed aesthetic codes but also generates elusive dance epistemologies that are only partly graspable and partly unfathomable within the

15. See Menon et al.; Vatsyayan, *Bharata*; Bose.

confines of the text or other mediums of representation.[16] And going beyond the prior propositions of the body and/as archive, the *Natyashastra* introduces a new dimension to this relationship by theorizing the text metonymically *as a body* (Vatsyayan, *Bharata* 74–80), positioning this archive as "vibrant matter," in Jane Bennett's words, perpetually alive for activation in the dance world.[17]

So, it is not that archive/repertoire are invalid concepts for thinking through Indian performance but that their very contours can be reconceptualized in this context, given their deeply dialectical relationship and their rooting in a unique set of cultural assumptions and histories. Their ideations and interactions will also differ, depending on the dance genre in question. I also draw here from Anjali Arondekar's brilliant observation that the reigning (Western) model of the archive is structured primarily by the logic of loss.[18] Hence, it is the possibility of loss, and the melancholic view of past time as disappearing rather than durational, that mandates the frenzied collection of materials and their preservation in the present for recovery in the future.

Yet many archives of Indian performance, Arondekar argues, are marked not by the trope of scarcity but by abundance. Citing the example of the Gomantak Maratha Samaj, a devadasi institution in Maharashtra and Goa, Arondekar notes that the sheer volume and longevity of its collections makes that space a site of excess rather than sparsity, its contents virtually inexhaustible, with no sign of anxiety on part of its affiliates over the potential disappearance or degradation of the materials in question: "If the restoration of the devadasi has been tethered to forms of paucity, loss, and erasure, [the Samaj] offers a different possibility by denaturalizing any such presumptive understanding of the devadasi's customary forms, particularly under colonialism" ("Subject to Sex" 247). The Samaj is unique, Arondekar observes, in that the female ritual specialists who make up its membership self-consciously produce their own histories through the act of recordkeeping.

In this milieu, there is too much, rather than too little. This appears to be true also for specific archives of classical dance, with the caveat that a

16. See Vatsyayan, *Bharata* 80, 89; Bharatmuni/Ghosh, *Natyashastra*, vol. 1, ch. 21, nos. 120–24, ch. 26, nos. 124–25.

17. Vatsyayana reveals that in describing the dramatic structure, the *NS* pointedly draws on analogies with human anatomical structures, identifying different aspects of the plot and themes through bodily metaphors, like *purusa* (human figuration), *mukha* (mouth), *garbha* (womb), *sandhi* (joints), and *upanga* (limbs). The *NS* as text also develops along the lines of describing individuated movement units that build on each other and integrate into a complete and coherent 'body' of performance knowledge. The extraordinary preoccupation with the anatomy, senses, internal and externalized emotions, relationality, and mind-body links addressed in the *NS*, along with the liberal use of physical metaphors, suggest that the engagement with corporeality goes well beyond surface concerns of documenting aesthetic expression.

18. See Arondekar, "Subject to Sex."

surviving idea of archive and abundance sits rather uncomfortably with the modern twinning of archive and loss, in complicated ways. Nevertheless, Arondekar theorizes an alternative archival modality that is strikingly relevant here. For dance artifacts in India proliferate in the form of literature, philosophy, visual media, epigraphs, scores, sculpture, music, material culture, and many other cultural inventories (Vatsyayan, *Classical*) . . . so much so that capturing choreography in its staggering multiform traces and representations is practically impossible. These sources may be ambiguous, but seldom are they precarious. The availability of a profuse textual and artifactual archive, coupled with robust mnemonic traditions and forms of transmission that ensure that knowledge regularly and reliably emigrates from body to body, works against the general notion of performance haunted by the specter of absence and fuels the discourse of plenitude instead. So the question is not *is* there an archive for Indian dance? But what *kind* of an archive is it? In the case of the *Natyashastra,* it is an archive conjoining social and aesthetic laws.

While its status as an ancient source of Indian choreography is customarily accepted, the *Natyashastra* exceeds a position as historical artifact and symbolizes much more than a venerable manual of performance. Its value and significance thus lie beyond its general archival form. Thinking through its role in the reconstitution of classical dance in twentieth-century India, and its specific textual contents, we can posit the *Natyashastra* as an archive that identifies key "laws of movement" in social and aesthetic terms for its subjects and analyze its nomic value and disciplinary functions in that regard. That is, we can interpret its operations as a kind of legal apparatus that regulates the production of ideal bodies and intersubjective relations in the performance scenario.

Caste and the *Natyashastra*

Among other forms of social division, caste features as a prominent concern in the worldview of the text.[19] As Brahma Prakash notes in his study of Indian

19. Caste in ancient Hindu society, as described through the *varnashrama dharma* system, divided people into four categories by descending rank: Brahmin (priests), Kshatriya (aristocrats and warriors), Vaishya (merchants, traders, landowners) and Sudra (artisans, peasants, and laborers serving other castes). Depending on context, the Sudra group sometimes includes both workers within the caste system and so-called untouchables outside of it. Those acknowledged within the caste system are called Savarna while those outside of it, like the "untouchables" and "tribal" groups, are called Avarna. Besides organizing these groups hierarchically, caste was also a mode of monitoring social relations, with rules of purity and pollution regulating permitted or forbidden contact between caste communities and determining

folk traditions, the caste order "claims to have a divine origin and gets its sanction from religious and philosophical texts" (19). The *Natyashastra* firmly resides within such a network of writings that reflects, reproduces, and reifies caste ideologies, and does so transparently; Prakash observes that the treatise "divulges the whole gamut of the hegemonic politics of representation and counter-hegemony of the other" (23). He discusses an illustrative mythological episode in the *Natyashastra*'s opening chapter, involving a conflict around the performance of the originary play, *Samudramanthan,* which favors the deities and disparages the demons in its telling. When the demons in the audience object to their portrayal, the god Brahma tries to deflect their outrage by suggesting they are merely witnessing a dramatic depiction, arguing for the mitigating effects of theater. However, Prakash offers the important corrective that this was "not just a play, it was the politics of representation," alluding to performance's capacity to generate and channel discriminatory effects (24). Proceeding from an analysis of this tense and revealing fictional encounter—which sets up a general logic that makes it possible to read the text as a chronicle of asymmetrical social arrangements—Prakash analyzes how the *Natyashastra* further vilifies a variety of folk styles, concluding that "the classist canon is constructed after the erasure of certain kinds of bodily materiality," especially that of caste-oppressed groups (160).

Building on Prakash's intervention, I want to explore these very politics of effacement that mark the *Natyashastra.* There is no doubt that the text legislates the norms of caste in its descriptions of movement codes, storytelling conventions, characters, and dramatic situations. One stark example comes from the part describing walks, named "Gaits of Lowly Persons": "Persons of inferior birth are to walk with eyes looking around, protecting their limbs from the contact of other people" (Bharatmuni/Ghosh *Natyashastra* vol. I, ch. 13, no. 150). This choreographic instruction reflects the social code prohibiting physical proximity or direct eye contact between the caste-oppressed Sudra and caste-privileged subjects. Such directives are all the more problematic,

ritual privileges and exclusions. Yet caste also enabled the formation of group identifications, genealogies, occupations, and political organizing. The matter of whether caste was originally assigned by birth, hereditary profession, or character and comportment is a subject of much debate in the historical scholarship, as is the question of whether caste was a complex system that changed over time, or whether it was a crude social matrix consolidated in the modern colonial period. While a history of the nuances of caste formation is outside the scope of this discussion, it is clear that caste continues to function as a key signifier of social status and oppression in South Asian communities. Some Sudra and Avarna subjects have claimed a new identity as Bahujan or Dalit to indicate their politically subjugated condition and for activist mobilizations. For more on this topic, see the informative discussions by Chakravarti; Gupta; Ambedkar; Guru and Sarukkai.

given that persons placed lower on the caste rung also made up the majority of performers in ancient India, and thus ironically participated in reifying their own oppression by depicting unjust stereotypes and social relations on stage in order to exhibit their aesthetic virtuosity, in line with dominant *shastric* codes (Pande, *Historical* and *Natyashastra Tradition*). While Prakash focuses on the text's such contents, productively mining it for mentions and characterizations of folk idioms to highlight how these are negatively rendered, I am interested in the different question of form—specifically, the text's inaugural logic, which provides the rationale for its basic ideological organization in relation to caste. To consider this, I focus on a moment in the narrative about "The Origin of Natya" in the same first chapter.

The sage Bharata explains the impetus behind the development of the *Natyashastra* to a group of learned interlocutors. He indicates that although he wrote the great work, the god Brahma is the true source and inspiration for his endeavor. The world was in a state of chaos and disorder, populated by unruly elements. To restore a sense of harmony, Shiva and other deities approached Brahma, asking him to create a style of performance that might deliver proper moral instruction to their wayward subjects: "Please give us something which would not only teach us but be pleasing both to eyes and ears. (True) the Vedas are there but (some like) the Sudras are prohibited from listening to (learning from) them. Why not create for us a fifth Veda which would be accessible to all the varna-s (castes)?" (Bharatmuni/Rangacharya, *Natyasastra* ch. 1, nos. 1–20). Brahma assented, and after a period of intense meditation, he produced a composition made up of the elements of the four Vedas: language from the *Rigveda,* music from *Samaveda,* movements and adornments from *Yajurveda,* and acting from *Atharvanaveda.* Bharata reveals that he served mainly as a conduit of this performance knowledge delivered by Brahma, and recorded it in the form of the *Natyashastra.*

The moment where Shiva mentions the Sudra prohibition is arresting and deserves special contemplation. It reveals how the structuring exclusion of caste determines the *Natyashastra*'s very condition of possibility. Caste governs the formal framework of the text, given that the *Natyashastra*'s genesis depends on its breach of the dominant protocol, and its anomalous status as a "fifth Veda," democratically available to all, must be specially announced. At first glance, this appears to be an inclusive maneuver; Vatsyayan, for instance, argues that "this breaking of boundaries and hierarchies would make the author and the text radical, if not revolutionary" (*Bharata* 21). However, the position of the *Natyashastra* as the singular canonical text sanctioned for sharing with all castes only emphasizes the bodily erasure of the Sudra from the general realm of knowledge in the normative constitutions of community.

For the text is marked as an *exception* to the social law otherwise precluding Sudra subjects from accessing elite knowledge systems represented by the Vedic oeuvre, safeguarded by Brahmin gatekeepers. The fact of the Sudra's social segregation is ambivalently premised as a form of inclusion in this extraordinary circumstance. Here, the "law of movement" relates directly to the everyday world surrounding the text, where the Sudra body lacks free mobility, constrained by the inhibiting codes put in place on their movement by caste-privileged agents. It also refers to the world of the *shastras* themselves, which were usually prohibited from circulating outside preferential networks of exchange. The *Natyashastra* self-consciously constructs itself as distinct source of authority because it enacts what is otherwise deterred: It breaks the dominant "laws of movement" which apply to Sudra persons and shastras, and instates an alternative form, permitting the distribution of the text to the masses in the interest of promoting performance. However, Shiva's discourse indicates that the *Natyashastra* was not just intended for benign sharing; the text serves a didactic purpose and is clearly intended as a system of discipline and instruction imparted through the device of entertainment, a mode of dispersing elite norms and values to marginalized publics. These dynamics highlight the double function of *Natyashastra* as a sign of exclusion *and* inclusion, proscription *and* permission. Within its boundaries, where it qualifies performance as a mirror of social relations, the *Natyashastra* maintains the same identitarian hierarchies it seeks to overturn in the justifying moment of its constitution. Its authors bluntly write the social law of caste into the aesthetic frame of the text even as they claim to erase the barriers of caste difference that would otherwise impede access to its hallowed contents. The treatise thus reinforces the normative caste order simultaneous to its seeming disruption of it.

Conclusion

I have argued here that the *Natyashastra* as an archival source for Indian classical dance can be understood as a form of social and aesthetic law that enacts political hierarchies, as exemplified in the case of caste. While the social inequities the *Natyashastra* advances are apparent in the text, in the contexts of artistic training, performance, and much of the scholarly literature, there is scant discussion of its dominative values, political dimensions, or the structures of inequality it upholds. These aspects tend to be generally ignored, eclipsed, or selectively highlighted to ensure a positive reading of the text as a purely aesthetic philosophy suitable as a source for training current disciples of classical dance. And what are we performing when we dance in total fidelity to the *Natyashastra*? My answer, in solidarity with the stances of progressive observers, is that we are often dancing social power, often perpetuating retrograde stereotypes, and often advancing political prejudice—if we do not approach the text's choreographic mandates with a critical consciousness. Only a truly gifted interpreter of its directives might be capable of subverting or transcending the constricted social visions it contains, in the performance realm. Undeniably, the *Natyashastra* is a major symbolic and choreographic force in Indian dance, and attending to the modes through which it exercises inordinate power is thus an essential task. Understanding the *Natyashastra* as a body of social and aesthetic law, as what choreographer William Forsythe calls an "art of command," allows us to critically engage with its terms (qtd. in Franko 17). And if we accept this configuration of the *Natyashastra* as the "laws of movement," perhaps we can combine the goal of "justice" with "virtuosity," deploying transformative interpretations of the text to perform egalitarian social relations instead.

Works Cited

Allen, Matthew Harp. "Rewriting the Script for South Indian Dance." *The Drama Review,*= vol. 41, no. 3, 1997, pp. 63–100.

Ambedkar, Bhimrao Ramji. *The Annihilation of Caste.* Verso, 2016.

Anker, Elizabeth, and Bernadette Meyler, editors. *New Directions in Law and Literature.* Oxford University Press, 2017.

Arondekar, Anjali. *Abundance: Sexuality's History.* Duke University Press, 2023.

Arondekar, Anjali. "In the Absence of Reliable Ghosts: Sexuality, Historiography, South Asia." *Differences: A Journal of Feminist Cultural Studies,* vol. 25, no. 3, 2015, pp. 98–121.

Arondekar, Anjali. "Subject to Sex: A Small History of the Gomantak Maratha Samaj." *South Asian Feminisms,* edited by Ania Loomba and Ritty A. Lukose, Duke University Press, 2012, pp. 244–63.

Banerji, Anurima. *Dancing Odissi: Paratopic Performances of Gender and State.* Seagull Books / University of Chicago Press, 2019.

Banerji, Anurima. "Laws of Movement: The Natyashastra as Archive for Indian Classical Dance." *Contemporary Theatre Review,* vol. 31, no. 1, 2021, Outing Archives, Archives Outing, pp. 132–52.

Banerji, Anurima. "Nrityagram: Tradition and the Aesthetics of Transgression." *How to Do Politics with Art,* edited by Violaine Roussel and Anurima Banerji, Routledge, 2017, pp. 88–114.

Bennett, Jane. *Vibrant Matter: A Political Ecology of Things.* Duke University Press, 2010.

Bharatmuni. *Natyasastra.* Translated by Adya Rangacharya, Munshiram Manoharlal Publishers, 1996.

Bharatmuni. *Natyashastra, Ascribed to Bharata-Muni (A Treatise on Ancient India Dramaturgy and Histrionics),* vol. 1–4. Translated by Manmohan Ghosh, Chowkhamba Sanskrit Series Office, 2007.

Bose, Mandakranta. *Speaking of Dance: The Indian Critique.* D. K. Printworld, 2001.

Chakravarti, Uma. *Everyday Lives, Everyday Histories: Beyond the Kings and Brahmanas of 'Ancient' India.* 3rd ed., Tulika Books, 2012.

Chakravorty, Pallabi. *Bells of Change: Kathak Dance, Women and Modernity in India.* Seagull Books, 2008.

Chakravorty, Pallabi. "From Interculturalism to Historicism: Reflections on Classical Indian Dance." *Dance Research Journal,* vol. 32, no. 2, 2000–2001, pp. 100–111.

Chandralekha. "The Militant Origins of Indian Dance." *Social Scientist,* vol. 9, nos. 2–3, Sept.–Oct. 1980, pp. 80–85.

Chatterjea, Ananya. *Butting Out: Reading Resistive Choreographies Through Works by Jawole Willa Jo Zollar and Chandralekha.* Wesleyan University Press, 2004.

Chatterjee, Sandra, and Cynthia Ling Lee. "Remixing Natya: Revanta Sarabhai's *LDR* and Post *Natyam* Collective's *Super Ruwaxi: Origins.*" *Dance Matters Too: Markets, Memories, Identities,* edited by Pallabi Chakravorty and Nilanjana Gupta, Routledge, 2018, pp. 202–24.

Coorlawala, Uttara Asha. "The Birth of Bharatanatyam and the Sanskritized Body." *Rukmini Devi Arundale (1904–1986): A Visionary Architect of Indian Culture and the Performing Arts,* edited by Avanthi Meduri, Motilal Banarsidass, 2005, pp. 173–94.

Foster, Susan. *Choreographing Empathy.* Routledge, 2011.

Foster, Susan. *Valuing Dance: Commodities and Gifts in Motion.* Oxford University Press, 2019.

Franko, Mark. "Dance and the Political: States of Exception." *Dance Discourses: Keywords in Dance Research,* edited by Susanne Franco and Marina Nordera, Routledge, 2007.

Garlough, Christine Lynn. "On the Political Uses of Folklore: Performance and Grassroots Feminist Activism in India." *Journal of American Folklore,* vol. 121, no. 480, 2008, pp. 167–91.

Ganser, Elisa. "Thinking Dance Literature from Bharata to Bharatanatyam." *Rivista Degli Studi Orientali,* vol. 84, no. 1/4, 2011, pp. 145–61.

Gupt, Bharat. "The Date of the *Natyashastra.*" *Natyasastra—Revisited,* edited by Bharat Gupt, Bharatiya Vidya Bhavan, 2016, pp. 25–26.

Gupt, Bharat. *Dramatic Concepts Greek & Indian: A Study of the Poetics and the Natyasastra.* D. K. Printworld, 1994.

Gupt, Bharat, editor. *Natyasastra—Revisited.* Bharatiya Vidya Bhavan, 2016.

Gupta, Dipankar, editor. *Caste in Question: Identity or Hierarchy?* Sage Publications, 2007.

Guru, Gopal, and Sundar Sarukkai. *Experience, Caste, and the Everyday Social.* Oxford University Press, 2019.

Kothari, Sunil. "A Dance Historian's Note on How the Natyashastra Was Mastered." *Asian Age,* 9 May 2019, https://www.asianage.com/india/all-india/090519/a-dance-historians-notes-on-how-the-natyashastra-was-mastered.html.

Lepecki, André. "The Body as Archive: Will to Re-Enact and the Afterlives of Dances." *Dance Research Journal,* vol. 42, no. 2, 2010, pp. 28–48.

Meduri, Avanthi, editor. *Rukmini Devi Arundale (1904–1986): A Visionary Architect of Indian Culture and the Performing Arts.* Motilal Banarsidass, 2005.

Menon, Narayanan, et al. *Guru-Shishya Parampara: The Master-Disciple Tradition in Classical Indian Dance and Music.* Arts Council of Great Britain, 1982.

Nair, Sreenath, editor. *The Natyasastra and the Body in Performance: Essays on Indian Theories of Dance and Drama.* McFarland, 2015.

Ness, Sally Ann. "The Inscription of Gesture: Inward Migrations in Dance." *Migrations of Gesture,* edited by Sally Ann Ness and Carrie Noland, University of Minnesota Press, 2008, pp. 1–30.

O'Shea, Janet. *At Home in the World: Bharata Natyam on the Global Stage.* Wesleyan University Press, 2007.

Pande, Anupa. *Historical and Cultural Study of the Natyasastra.* Kusumanjali Prakashan, 1992.

Pande, Anupa. *The Natyashastra Tradition and Ancient Indian Society.* Kusumanjali Prakashan, 1993.

Pollock, Sheldon. *A Rasa Reader: Classical Indian Aesthetics.* Columbia University Press, 2018.

Prakash, Brahma. *Cultural Labour: Conceptualizing the "Folk Performance" in India.* Oxford University Press, 2019.

Roberge, Gaston. "Natyasastra—A Precious Legacy." *Natyasastra—Revisited,* edited by Bharat Gupt, Bharatiya Vidya Bhavan, 2016, pp. 215–24.

Said, Edward. *Orientalism.* Vintage, 1979.

Said, Edward. *The World, the Text, and the Critic.* Harvard University Press, 1983.

Sarkar Munsi, Urmimala. "A Century of Negotiations: The Changing Sphere of the Woman Dancer in India." *Beyond the Private World: Indian Women in the Public Sphere,* edited by Subrata Bagchi, Primus Books, 2014, pp. 293–312.

Sarkar Munsi, Urmimala, and Bishnupriya Dutt, *Engendering Performance: Indian Women Performers in Search of an Identity.* Sage Publications, 2010.

Schneider, Rebecca. *Performing Remains: Art and War in Times of Theatrical Reenactment.* Routledge, 2011.

Shea Murphy, Jacqueline. "Mobilizing (in) the Archive: Santee Smith's Kaha: wi." *Worlding Dance,* edited by Susan Leigh Foster, Palgrave Macmillan, 2009, pp. 32–52.

Sircar, Ranjabati. "Contemporary Indian Dance." *Rasa: The Indian Performing Arts in the Last Twenty-Five Years, Vol. I—Music and Dance,* edited by Bimal Mukherjee and Sunil Kothari, Anamika Kala Sangam, 1995, pp. 255–60.

Soneji, Davesh. *Bharatanatyam: A Reader.* Oxford University Press, 2010.

Soneji, Davesh. *Unfinished Gestures: Devadasis, Memory, and Modernity in South India.* University of Chicago Press, 2012.

Srinivasan, Amrit. "Reform or Conformity? Temple 'Prostitution' and the Community in the Madras Presidency." *Structures of Patriarchy,* edited by Bina Agarwal, Kali for Women, 1988, pp. 175–98.

Srinivasan, Amrit, editor. *Knowledge Tradition Text: Approaches to Bharata's Natyasastra.* Sangeet Natak Akademi, 2007.

Subrahmanyam, Padma. *Bharatiya Natyashastra,* vols. 1–2, Doordarshan archives, 2010. DVD. https://archive.org/details/dli.pb.natyashastra.1. Accessed 25 Jan. 2020.

Tarlekar, G. H. *The Natyasastra, with Special Reference to the Sanskrit Drama in Performance.* Revised 2nd ed., Motilal Banarsidass, 1991.

Taylor, Diana. *The Archive and the Repertoire: Performing Cultural Memory in the Americas.* Duke University Press, 2003.

Thapar, Romila. *Cultural Pasts: Essays in Early Indian History.* Oxford University Press, 2000.

Thapar, Romila. "Epic and History: Tradition, Dissent and Politics in India." *Past and Present,* vol. 125, Nov. 1989, pp. 3–26.

Thapar, Romila. *Sakuntala: Texts, Readings, Histories.* Columbia University Press, 2011.

Tripathi, K. D. "Natyashastra—Two Divergent Views of the Text." *Natyasastra—Revisited,* edited by Bharat Gupt, Bharatiya Vidya Bhavan, 2016, pp. 75–86.

Tripathi, Radha Vallabh. *Lectures on the "Natyasastra"* Center of Advanced Study in Sanskrit, University of Poona, 1991.

Tripathi, Radha Vallabh, editor. *"Natyasastra" in the Modern World.* D. K. Printworld, 2014.

Vatsyayan, Kapila. *Bharata: The Natyasastra.* Sahitya Akademi, 1996.

Vatsyayan, Kapila. *Indian Classical Dance.* 3rd ed., Publications Division, Ministry of Information and Broadcasting, Government of India, 1997.

Vatsyayan, Kapila. "The Theory and Technique of Classical Indian Dancing." *Artibus Asiae,* vol. 29, nos. 2–3, 1967, pp. 229–38.

Williams, Raymond. *Marxism and Literature.* Oxford University Press, 1997.

CHAPTER 14

Labor History, Social Death, and the Birth of the Black Worker

FRANCO BARCHIESI

The Antiblackness of Labor's Archive

The legal abolition of racial slavery in the Western hemisphere gave way, by the mid-nineteenth century, to a dilemma that haunted white rulers, capitalists, and social reformers: Will Blacks work without coercion (Holt, *Freedom*; Eudell; Hall)? Governing blackness was emerging as a global priority, while antislavery ideas informed the colonization of Africa in the name of "free labor." White rule did not relinquish its capacity for coercion—despite abolition's promise of a radical break with the slave past—but rather aimed to articulate racialized coercion with precepts of individual freedom and equality. By ideologically elaborating that articulation, liberalism would test its usefulness for white supremacy.

Making blackness productive within market relations and legalities that avowedly eschewed direct violence demanded new social categories capable of simultaneously securing capitalist political economy and the libidinal economy of white affects. The idea of the "Black worker" proved eminently suitable to these tasks. European rulers and their critics "*wanted* Africa to have a working class" (Cooper 14) as part of a broader colonial imagination casting natives working for wages as its "desired subjectivity" (Chakrabarty, *Rethinking* 223). The stability of capitalism as a value-creating machinery depended on how it could provide a terrain of contestation for actors with discernible motivations and negotiable agendas. If governability and predictability were the system's goals, its ultimate enemies were the messiness of local forms of life and their undecipherable cultural and spiritual values. In Africa, administrators and experts felt especially threatened by the potential for refusal of work and sabotage of capitalist work rhythms enabled by an agrarian world they deemed backward and stagnant (Atkins).

White desires for the Black worker as a legible, therefore governable, entity are heavily documented in postslavery and colonial archives, where one can also trace the passage of plantation economies in the Western hemisphere and extractivist capitalism in early colonial Africa to supposedly contractual arrangements. Contrary to the narrative shared by liberals and conservatives in the United States, abolition was neither an event in the linear march of freedom nor a clear-cut break with the "social death" of enslavement. It rather occurred within the paradigmatic time of Black captivity (Sharpe, *Monstrous*). The antiblack despotism of newly established African colonial states was concomitantly sanitized by their claims of carrying slave emancipation to conclusion (Blackburn). The persistence of slave labor itself was sometimes justified by European administrators on the continent as a temporary and practically expedient, if morally repugnant, way of gradually inducting Blacks into uncoerced labor relations (Lennihan; Deutsch). Liberalism promised ways of grafting bourgeois political economy onto assumptions on universal human nature while hierarchically organizing racial difference in the guise of free labor. By the early twentieth century, labor discipline and personal responsibility framed the expected conducts of nonwhite populations, but outside the horizon of full citizenship white workers started to access, in Europe as well as settler societies, as the payoff for the "social question" ignited by their struggles (Willoughby-Herard).

Equating freedom with the labor contract gradually overrode humanitarianism or the "civilizing mission" as justifications for imperial white rule. The structural violence upon which the colonial edifice rested was disavowed and secured by the association of insubordination and economic self-determination with unreasonable opposition to progress as an atavistic characteristic of blackness. Caribbean plantations and Southern African mining areas are exemplary, as the next section will show. Their racially despotic labor regimes produced a Black proletariat through various combinations of wage labor, small-scale subsistence agriculture, and household networks. Differences, in these two cases, of economic structures and historical connections to racial enslavement underscore the versatility of the apparatus intended to bring "free" Black workers to life.

The terms *labouring classes* or *native labourers* populate the late nineteenth- and early twentieth-century archive of sugar-producing Barbados or South Africa's Witwatersrand minerals-rich region, whose official records obliquely and often tacitly allude to the blackness of those workers. The erasure of "Black" performed by those very expressions speaks to a governance of racial difference in which culture was not admitted as a vehicle for legitimate claims and to be Black meant "to exist in exchange without being a party to exchange" (Wagner 2). "Labor" compressed and redacted Black existence and sentience, securing its "anagrammatic" dispersal and violent recombination along potentially endless modalities of use (Sharpe, *Wake*). By removing blackness from the subordinated categories of the citizen-worker or the culturally signifiable Indigenous, laboring status demanded the containment and annihilation of blackness itself.

The suppression of blackness by labor marks a drastic divergence between the colonized subaltern and the Black captive. Contrary to postcolonial critique, the colonizer's anxieties in confronting the Black did not derive from the culturally or spiritually unincorporated "history 2" of the colonized (Chakrabarty, *Provincializing*). Blackness did not represent precolonial forms of life whose "supplementary subversions" did not "add up" (Bhabha 232). In the process or in the aftermath of legalized racial enslavement, Blacks are not only fully incorporated into capitalist production but are in fact central to its rise, global projection, and ideological consolidation (Robinson; Sorentino). Since direct violence and terror, rather than social or cultural contestations, had structurally positioned racial blackness as enslavable, the slave's social life and resistive cultural practices do not presuppose autonomy (Hartman, *Subjection* 50–53, 51–62). The provisional and precarious spaces of freedom the enslaved wrests against gratuitous and nonnegotiable antiblack violence are not analogous to material and symbolic formations outside domination, which inspire Indigenous decolonial imagination. Indigenous studies scholars of a *Marxisant* tone have expanded the critique of capitalist political economy by centering land expropriation and cultural dispossession, which were not, however, the forces driving Black resubjugation in the wake of abolition (Coulthard). The inessentiality of culture to the structural positioning of blackness informed, if anything, persistent interdictions against the former slaves' access to landownership (Holt, *Contract*). Blackness remained a mark of untrustworthiness, and was thus confirmed as the essential antagonist of human conventions (Wynter; Wilderson 5).

It is not without a sense of irony that today's labor historians sifting colonial and postslavery archives find there precisely the entity—the Black worker—that the authorities assembling those archives had anxiously tried to fix in a legible frame. Not only does labor history sanction, albeit unwittingly, the ultimate success of that endeavor. It also dismisses the ways in which Black populations globally resisted, refused, or subverted their proletarianization.

For the expanding field of "global labor history" it is indeed essential to represent shifts from racial slavery to wage labor as the passage from one employment relation to another, in order to show how the slave expands the category of exploited workers beyond a Eurocentrically "respectable" formal proletariat, while confirming capitalism's tendency to formally equalize the conditions of exploitation (van der Linden 10, 60). Once blackness is removed, the slave as worker in the making stands as a figure of labor's historical differentiation and its ultimate commensurability across a range of exploitative experiences. The builders of the antiblack archive and its contemporary interpreters converge in a quest for productive subjectivity that finds in blackness its ultimate adversary.

Violence and the Transatlantic Desire for the Black Worker

South Africa and Barbados are examples of how fruitful liberal legalities were in consolidating antiblack labor regimes characterized by persistent despotism. Antiblackness also gave meaning to free labor for "poor whites" and settler working classes—numerous in both cases—in their confrontations with white capitalists, which could be managed and resolved around shared interests in racial domination. Black workers' status as producers and consumers precluded, instead, the citizenship rights that white workers claimed and obtained. Tasked with designing a postslavery arsenal of ideology and policies for putting Blacks to work, colonial states eschewed definitive positions on whether direct coercion had to be jettisoned. Old and opposing certainties—for example missionary humanitarian faith in the pedagogical capacities of waged work or assumptions on the inevitability of Black enslavement in conservative writers like Thomas Carlyle or James Anthony Froude—receded by the end of the nineteenth century (Hall 402–24). The archive rather traces the rise of more flexible and open-ended meditations. Black workers' discipline was expected to fit liberal views of individual rationality fostered by family-oriented respectability and ambition or the development of consumption habits requiring monetary incomes. Far from being clearly defined, however, such requirements were always open to new additions in an "including but not limited to . . ." format that ultimately deferred actual work-centered personhood, to which Black laborers were nonetheless always meant to aspire. The only alternative was the complete excommunication from social obligations that blackness metonymically signified as a term for unreason and chaos, embodied by colonized Africans' refusal of work, desertion of mining compounds, or fires set to plantations as well as the ways in which the formerly enslaved saw labor contracts backed by racial violence as a continuation of captivity itself.

In South Africa, "laborer" stood for the specifically precarious racial and productive status of Africans who were not deemed "employees," a term reserved to white workers well into the twentieth century. As I have argued elsewhere, "native" served to positively mark, for the European gaze, the African laborers' distance from their blackness, which was therefore doubly disavowed by the combination of "native" and "labor" (Barchiesi). As Native Affairs Commissioner in the Transvaal colony following the British victory in the 1899–1902 South African War, Godfrey Y. Lagden symbolized a new generation of white administrators steeped in political economy, ethnographic expertise, and an eminently practical orientation to governance.

Pursuing the goal of resuming African labor recruitment in the mines, upon which the postwar reconstruction of white rule depended, amid generalized Black desertion, Lagden maintained that restoring long-established practices of coercive control of native mobility and employment was undesirable on economic as well as moral grounds. Lagden's private papers and correspondence at Oxford's Bodleian Library document his hopes and worries in charting the "broadmindedness" of "liberal views" on the "labour question," in alternative to the "insular ideas" of an archaic and defeated Afrikaner colonialism (Lagden, August 21). Worrying that, without the resumption of African recruitment for the mineworks, the newly established British administration would go "bankrupt," Lagden rejected coercive "pressure," the earlier colonial modus operandi he symbolized with "the lash." Yet, he continued, "the native *ought* to work," in exchange for the protection and civilization the British purportedly brought to the newly unified South Africa. The solution he devised, in line with an overall shift from direct coercion to economic compulsion in British colonial thought (Eudell 101), consisted in developing an

> inducement to be born of a new sense of security coupled with a desire to be possessed with money for something that it will purchase. The ancient frame of mind of the aboriginal was contentment if he had some millet to feed upon, out of which too he made a merry making beer and a skin or other wherewithal to clothe himself. Where the masses reside they would cling to this ideal with all it came in barbarous pleasure and martial rivalry. There is I believe a tendency to dream that this ideal may yet be theirs again. It must be brushed away—roughly if needs be—so that they may realize that an enlightened Government requires of its people progress, and banishment of manners and customs repugnant to civilized thought. The Boers' policy was to keep the natives abased. It was easier then to coerce them into labour. Our

policy can only be to elevate them as gently as possible, cultivating in the process new tastes which require money to gratify. (Lagden, September 3)

The state's direct antiblack violence, of which legal restrictions on the Africans' movement and residence (the "pass laws") constituted the most oppressive expression in the eyes of nascent African political organizations, were not to be, however, entirely removed. They would rather be pragmatically updated within a new regulative framework positioning the African laborer as a decipherable economic agent, or an acquisitive consumer elevated from barbaric stagnation through market participation. The superiority of liberal ideas consisted, for Lagden, in their normative combination of abstract universalism and racially differentiated conduct. Flexible experimentations would allow white authorities to steer the ship of governance between the opposite hurdles of settler or Afrikaner opinion—still bound to racial control through physical coercion—and sections of the British public wary of measures resembling slavery (Lagden, August 27). In his 1904 testimony before the governmental Transvaal Labor Commission, Lagden would finally and publicly elaborate his vision of "regeneration" through labor of Africans into norm-abiding natives. Instead of being forced to "work as an animal," he opined, inducement through "wants"—crucially revolving around clothing and furnishing appropriate to domesticity gendered along British taste—would achieve the desired results (Transvaal).

Sites of intense racial despotism, like Africa's mining frontiers or Caribbean plantocratic monocultures, are not usually discussed as birthplaces of modern liberalism. The management of such locales by liberal-democratic Western powers is often dismissed as an aberration, an unsavory compromise with "evil," or a betrayal of liberal ideas. The foundational role of antiblack domination and violence in the making of modern liberalism comes nonetheless into clearer view by encompassing, beyond ideology, the dispositions of a social order bounded by private property, the market, and capitalist relations of production (Bell). The grounding of the political in the economic, its decoupling from social radicalism, its anchoring to prudent social reforms, and the negotiated subordination of labor's claims to productivity are quintessentially modern liberal principles. Liberalism's post-abolition ascent to global hegemony additionally necessitated its incorporation of racial domination.

Between the late nineteenth and the late twentieth century, Barbados transitioned from a brutally oppressive plantation system to independent nationhood committed to global competitiveness and political moderation. The island's archives abundantly document how the state's desire for the Black worker accompanied the refashioning of the slave plantation into liberal-democratic institutionality. Black challenges to centuries-old white landed monopoly spurred the planter elite and the colonial state toward reforming the Barbadian labor regime. Black workers did not fail to notice how work in sugar plantations reminisced enslavement, for example in the systematic recourse to corporal punishment. In the rare occasions when Black proletarian voices did resonate in the archive, as in the proceedings of the 1897 West Indian Royal Commission, one can read that "the Barbadian labourer had the fear of slavery in him, and he therefore disliked a contract" (Gaskin 182).

The routinized use, in the colonial archive, of expressions like "the Barbadian labourer," "the labouring classes," or simply "the masses" leaves their blackness generally unmentioned. Haunted by fears of insurrection, white passions and interests demanded from the formerly enslaved self-identification as workers, rather than Blacks. Archival redactions mirrored the ruling plantocracy's concerns with presenting the island's social system as consensual and underpinned by an assumed Black docility (Beckles; Browne; Carter). The archive suppressed blackness as it displaced it through laboring status. In a context of social reforms, of which the Royal Commission itself wanted to be an expression, Black people were notified that only analogizing their plight with the workers' toil would allow it to be, if not recognized as human suffering, at least heard as a simulacrum of it. Below that forced analogy lay figurations of blackness—the criminal, the loafer, those who set the canes on fire, the prostitute, the "single mother"—as humanity's menacing outside. Black laborers deserting work or raiding food supplies did not have their arguments heard in civil society's interlocutions, nor was it recorded in the colonial archive. They were, instead, mediated and ventriloquized by more "respectable" male members of the working class, rumors echoed in colonial dispatches, and police statistics.

In the liberal turn to plantation management, underway by the end of the nineteenth century, Black workers' representatives were invited, possibly for the first time, to make their case for improvements to the system, but on condition of virtually never mentioning racial oppression, focusing instead on contestation over productivity and valuation. A "joint committee of artisans and laborers," including future advocate of industrial education Washington Harper, presented workers' testimonies to the Royal Commission (Dowdridge 189). Despite stressing the basic fact that it is just "human nature" to refuse work in a sugar plantation for a week if the satisfaction of one's needs could be achieved by working only few days in an alternative occupation, the committee was more focused on vindicating the dignity of Black labor than voicing the totality of Black suffering. Black sentience and affect remained *inadmissible evidence* (Williams). By carefully eschewing any radical questioning of the plantation's gratuitous racial violence, the testimony of the Black workers' representatives implied that fairness and opportunity would pave the way to productivity and social consensus while steering the masses away from restive, unproductive, morally faulty blackness, which was therefore cast—in unison with the establishment's views—as a problematic object of intervention, rather than a subject of critique.

Reading the archive as a stage of contestation framed by liberal ideas allows for a global perspective on the conditions coercing Black speech within it. Institutionalized legalism as the only legitimate avenue for claim-making ended up abetting the state's virtually unlimited potential for antiblack violence (Farley). In South Africa, the insistence, by an unabashed racist like Godfrey Lagden, that the values of work were necessary for a liberal alternative to managing the "native" clearly resonated with the early leaders of what would then become the anticolonial and antiapartheid African National Congress (ANC), which, like colonial reformers, criticized white settlers' cruder methods. From social backgrounds that often combined Christianity, Western education, and literary or legal professions, those African activists found in liberal elements of the colonial register a platform for demanding dignity and fairness. The ANC's early president, John L. Dube, was an educationalist invested, like Harper and his main inspiration, Booker T. Washington, in social uplift through labor and political moderation. Convinced that "capitalists are the black man's best friends," Dube argued that proper wages, working conditions, and housing would correct a "lack of industrial habits" hampering African usefulness to the white economy (Limb 96, 290). In enabling socioeconomic interdependence between Blacks and whites, the hierarchical operations of which Dube did not fundamentally question, wage labor would redeem a "better class of natives" away from indolent and irresponsible rural masses and the urban *lumpenproletariat* (145–46).

In the postslavery archives of South Africa and Barbados, the Black worker aporetically fuses in the same expression presence (as worker) and absence (as Black), disturbing strategies of reimagining the archive as a site of reparative practice. How would restoring voice and visibility to the worker's body attend to the violence defining Black flesh as well as the ground of its possible "insurgency" (Spillers)? Lisa Lowe argued for the archive's redemptive potential through inclusivity and voice-giving, in opposition to liberalism's "intimacy" with colonialism and its attendant "economy of affirmation and forgetting" (2). For Lowe, it is the physical organization of the archive itself—for example shelving according to governmental agencies—that produces exclusion of subjugated knowledges by safeguarding the hypervisibility of specific economic or philosophical genres. Rearranging the archive would then liberate its unfulfilled potentialities (Lowe 41). It is a work of reclamation that relies on analogizing Black captivity with economic exploitation and land dispossession, reading indeed slavery as a subspecies of colonialism and blackness as an instantiation of subalternity. Rather than a graveyard of Black stories that, as Hartman writes, "could have been" but were violently and irredeemably curtailed ("Venus" 11), the archive is for Lowe a repository of stories waiting to be told and subjects to be restored through logistical and symbolic rearrangement.

In its humanistically life-affirming *élan*, anticolonial critique targets racial domination and violence as modes of "sociohistorical exclusion" and voice suppression, eschewing the positioning of blackness as the *non-being* against which being human defines itself (Ferreira da Silva). Blackness is then reduced to a figure of racial difference into which colonized and Indigenous are hierarchically ordered on account of sociocultural characteristics and experiences. Absence and erasure of culture and sociality, as the structural requirements defining both Black enslavement and its passage into "free" labor, have no place in critical discourses trying to resurrect the archive as a gathering of virtual subjects (including migrants, refugees, women, colonized subalterns, or Indigenous cultures) actualizing, symbolizing, or narrativizing their presence.

Radical Black Subversions of the Archive

Black critiques of labor have targeted not only its function in modes of domination and exploitation but also its articulation with political ontology, as a specific figuration of individual and collective human capacities standing in antagonism to blackness as assumed incapacity. The ongoing erasure and redaction of blackness in labor's archive is a violent work that, as Saidiya Hartman observed, the archive not only records but also strategically enacts ("Venus"). By centering the words of the perpetrators and beneficiaries of antiblackness, the archive domesticates and *familiarizes* an abyss of unspeakable violence into employment relations. Subverting such machinations, Hartman writes, is to *defamiliarize* the scenes of subjection arranged by the archive, which necessitates a refusal to romanticize productive blackness in the name of agency or subjectivity, even of a resistive kind (*Subjection* 54).

Kara Walker's 2014 installation, *A Subtlety*, is an example of subversion of the archive's claims to authority, either as a repository of knowledge or as a contested terrain for its possible diversification or pluralization. Walker's art rather operates as "critical fabulation," which Hartman theorized as a strategy of undermining the archive by thinking with the slave, whose enforced absence and coerced and travestied presence on the modern scene speak to the past as well as the present of antiblack violence ("Venus"). *A Subtlety* was arranged on the sprawling grounds of the Domino sugar factory in Brooklyn (New York), a site that, symbolizing the violence of plantation capitalism, was about to be effaced by the neighborhood's gentrification as a contemporary, financialized form of extraction eviscerating Black communities. The installation—made of sugar, molasses, and plastic materials—consisted of one giant "sphinx," an 80-feet long by 40-feet high completely white representation of a Black woman, in the pose of the eponymous Egyptian monument, with greatly pronounced anatomical features and wearing a headwrap. The figure was surrounded by fifteen "attendants," smaller dark sculptures modeled after the early modern figurines of subservient Black characters, which used to decorate affluent European homes. In an interview with Kara Rooney, Walker insisted on the importance to her project of the word "refined": The plantation is energized by white "desire for the refined," not only sugar from cane but also disciplined workers from unruly Blacks. Blackness is not productive as such but rather as "what is lost in the process of refining" as a "quest for whiteness, . . . this ideal of mastery over continents, people, bodies, ecology." Beyond the political economy of capital, the "sphinx" referred to a transhistorical, paradigmatic entity that, in its timelessness, renders the plantation a Black(ened) *nonplace,* rather than the laborer's work-place. Furthermore, Walker's strategic goals are explicitly defiant of disciplinarity authorized by the archive:

> I wasn't aiming to depict an accurate representation of labor. . . . I wanted to make something that would contain that sweat and labor in the histories of the totality of sugar production—the here and now and the past and present of it—but that would also elicit this terribly sad memory of all that's lost.

At stake is not a "decentering" of whiteness by pluralizing historical experiences and voices. Whiteness is rather placed at the center of a crime scene whose evidence is now archived. Yet tensions between Black presence and absence, nameable injuries and unnamable loss, historical and paradigmatic time cannot find resolution in labor's archives pitting the legibility of the Black worker against unthinkable blackness but rather decree the archive's irrelevance on grounds that are ethical as much as critical.

Works Cited

Atkins, Keletso E. *The Moon Is Dead! Give Us Our Money! The Cultural Origins of an African Work Ethic, Natal, South Africa, 1843–1900.* Heinemann, 1993.

Barchiesi, Franco. "The Problem with 'We': Affiliation, Political Economy, and the Counterhistory of Nonracialism." *Ties That Bind: Race and the Politics of Friendship in South Africa*, edited by Shannon Walsh and Jon Soske, Witwatersrand University Press, 2016, pp. 125–65.

Beckles, Hilary. *Great House Rules: Landless Emancipation and Workers' Protest in Barbados, 1838–1938*. Ian Randle, 2004.

Bell, Duncan. *Dreamworlds of Race: Empire and the Utopian Destiny of Anglo-America*. Princeton University Press, 2020.

Bhabha, Homi. *The Location of Culture*. Routledge, 1994.

Blackburn, Robin. *The American Crucible: Slavery, Emancipation and Human Rights*. Verso, 2011.

Browne, David V. C. *Race, Class, Politics and the Struggle for Empowerment in Barbados, 1914–1937*. Ian Randle, 2012.

Carter, Henderson. *Labour Pains: Resistance and Protest in Barbados, 1838–1904*. Ian Randle, 2012.

Chakrabarty, Dipesh. *Provincializing Europe: Postcolonial Thought and Historical Difference*. Princeton University Press, 2000.

Chakrabarty, Dipesh. *Rethinking Working-Class History: Bengal, 1890–1940*. Princeton University Press, 1988.

Cooper, Frederick. *Decolonization and African Society: The Labor Question in French and British Africa*. Cambridge University Press, 1996.

Coulthard, Glen. *Red Skin, White Masks: Rejecting the Colonial Politics of Recognition*. University of Minnesota Press, 2014.

Deutsch, Jan-Georg. *Emancipation Without Abolition in German East Africa, c. 1884–1914*. Ohio University Press, 2006.

Dowdridge, A., et al. *Report of the West Indian Royal Commission*, vol. 2. H. M. Stationery Office, 1897.

Dube, John L. "The Industrial Organisation of the Native People." *Report of the National European-Bantu Conference*, Cape Town, 6–9 Feb. 1929. Lovedale Institution Press, 1929, pp. 145–46.

Eudell, Demetrius L. *The Political Languages of Emancipation in the British Caribbean and the U.S. South*. University of North Carolina Press, 2002.

Farley, Anthony P. "Perfecting Slavery." *Loyola University of Chicago Law Journal*, vol. 36, no. 1, 2004, pp. 225–55.

Ferreira da Silva, Denise. *Toward a Global Idea of Race*. University of Minnesota Press, 2007.

Gaskin, J. Massiah. *Report of the West Indian Royal Commission* (WIRC), vol. 2. H. M. Stationery Office, 1897.

Hall, Catherine. *Civilising Subjects: Metropole and Colony in the English Imagination 1830–1867*. University of Chicago Press, 2002.

Hartman, Saidiya. *Scenes of Subjection: Terror Slavery and Self-Making in Nineteenth-Century America*. Oxford University Press, 1997.

Hartman, Saidiya. "Venus in Two Acts." *Small Axe*, vol. 12, no. 2, 2008, pp. 1–14.

Holt, Thomas C. "The Essence of Contract: The Articulation of Race, Gender, and Political Economy in British Emancipation Policy, 1838–1866." *Beyond Slavery: Explorations of Race, Labor, and Citizenship in Postemancipation Societies*, edited by Frederick Cooper et al., University of North Carolina Press, 2000, pp. 33–59.

Holt, Thomas C. *The Problem of Freedom: Race, Labor, and Politics in Jamaica and Britain, 1832–1938*. Johns Hopkins University Press, 1991.

Lagden, Godfrey. "Lagden to Spender, August 21, 1901." *Lagden Papers*. Bodleian Library, University of Oxford, Commonwealth and African Collections, LP, MSS Afr. S.174, box 6, no. 2, 1901.

Lagden, Godfrey. "Lagden to Spender, August 27, 1901." *Lagden Papers*. Bodleian Library, University of Oxford, Commonwealth and African Collections, LP, MSS Afr. S.174, box 6, no. 3, 1901.

Lagden, Godfrey. "Lagden to Spender, September 3, 1901." *Lagden Papers*. Bodleian Library, University of Oxford, Commonwealth and African Collections, LP, MSS Afr. S.174, box 6, no. 4, 1901.

Lennihan, Louise D. "Rights in Men and Rights in Land: Slavery, Wage Labor, and Smallholder Agriculture in Northern Nigeria." *Slavery & Abolition*, vol. 3, no. 2, 1982, pp. 111–39.

Limb, Peter. *The ANC's Early Years: Nation, Class, and Place in South Africa Before 1940*. UNISA Press, 2010.

Lowe, Lisa. *The Intimacies of Four Continents*. Duke University Press, 2015.

Robinson, Cedric J. *Black Marxism: The Making of the Black Radical Tradition*. Zed Books, 1984.

Sharpe, Christina. *In the Wake: On Blackness and Being*. Duke University Press, 2016.

Sharpe, Christina. *Monstrous Intimacies: Making Post-Slavery Subjects*. Duke University Press, 2010.

Sorentino, Sara-Maria. "The Abstract Slave: Anti-Blackness and Marx's Method." *International Labor and Working-Class History*, vol. 96, 2019, pp. 17–37.

Spillers, Hortense. "Mama's Baby, Papa's Maybe: An American Grammar Book." *Diacritics*, vol. 17, no. 2, 1987, pp. 64–81.

Transvaal (Colony). *Report of the Transvaal Labour Commission: Minutes*. Government Printer, 1904.

van der Linden, Marcel. *Workers of the World: Essays Toward a Global Labor History*. Brill, 2008.

Wagner, Bryan. *Disturbing the Peace: Black Culture and the Police Power After Slavery*. Harvard University Press, 2009.

Walker, Kara. "'A Sonorous Subtlety' (Interview with Kara Rooney)." *The Brooklyn Rail*, May 2014, https://brooklynrail.org/2014/05/art/kara-walker-with-kara-rooney.

Wilderson, Frank B. *Red White and Black: Cinema and the Structure of U.S. Antagonisms*. Duke University Press, 2010.

Williams, Evelyn. *Inadmissible Evidence: The Story of the African-American Trial Lawyer Who Defended the Black Liberation Army*. Lawrence Hill Books, 2000.

Willoughby-Herard, Tiffany. *Waste of a White Skin: The Carnegie Corporation and the Racial Logic of White Vulnerability*. University of California Press, 2015.

Wynter, Sylvia. "No Humans Involved: An Open Letter to My Colleagues." *Forum NHI: Knowledge for the 21st Century*, vol. 1, no. 1, 1994, pp. 42–70.

CHAPTER 15

What Else

Gesture and Glitch in "What Is a Better Life"

REBECCA SCHNEIDER

> Books leave gestures in the body; a certain way of moving, of turning, a certain closing of the eyes, a way of leaving, hesitations. Books leave certain sounds, a certain pacing; mostly they leave the elusive, which is all the story. They leave much more than the words. . . . I remember them only in my body.
>
> —Dionne Brand, *A Map to the Door of No Return* (191)

Books leave gestures in the body. And films leave gestures as well. Such gestures might be available to take up again, moving across mediums, across bodies, and back again. Bodies, in turn, leave gestures via books, song, film, dance, and in media among media—often passing hand to hand. Alberta Whittle's 2021 film "What is a better life (exorcised in the middle)" is just such a work, carrying on and carried by the waveform of gesture. In fact, the film itself gestures forth a book as it performs an homage to Brand's *A Map to the Door of No Return,* bringing the book round again in a tidalectic of Black poethical aesthesis.[1]

This essay is about a minor section of a much larger work, and as such it attends to detail—in this case a brief but powerful gesture left in my body as viewer. "What is a better life" is one part of Whittle's 2021–22 installation *Hindsight is a luxury you cannot afford.* The installation is an "evolving multi-part, multi-disciplinary work," and nested within it is a digital film (original shooting format: HD and 2K) that also has a life of its own, circulating beyond

1. With the word "tidalectic" I seek to call not only on Keanu Brathwaite who coined the term (see Mackey), but Caribbean Afro-diasporic thought broadly including Dionne Brand, Édouard Glissant, and Derek Walcott. On the dialectic rendered in tidalectic via dialect see Moten. On the poethical, see Ferreira da Silva; on Black aesthesis, see Bradley, *Anteaesthetics.*

the installation.[2] Like a book, this filmic portion of the installation moves in chapters. Chapter 4, subtitled, "What is a better life (exorcized in the middle)," opens with a cut. In this essay, I will be sitting with this cut at the opening of this filmic chapter, describing it in some detail, even as the cut I describe is itself cut from the digital version of the film circulated by Lux Films. In this way, the minor detail (as well as the work as a whole) might be seen to be full of the poetic force of errantry as conceived by Édouard Glissant in *Poetics of Relation.* The errant moves away from ideas of centers, straight lines, and fixed binaries but also from the 0s and 1s of capture via digital netting. Like a technical glitch, a slipped fish, an embodied twitch, or a sideways gesture, an errant detail deviates from an accepted norm and wanders, continually breaking from totality and other constructs of Knowledge that insist upon immobile absolutes. The errant is strongly articulate of identity in relation—shifting, local, particular. Glitches such as disappearing cuts, titles within subtitles, and multiple changing chapter iterations might confuse the consolidation of such a work into any imperial archive—and in this, among other ways, the work approaches the condition of performance. Rich with details on the move, the project is itself metabolic, posing an (im)possible challenge to any scholar or archivist or eager art patron who would pin it to some finally containable completion or fully isolable, definitive iteration. Like gesture, it migrates, iteration to iteration—body to book to film to body.

Let me narrate what I think I saw. As a chapter within a film within an evolving multipart installation, chapter 4, "What is a better life," opens to a black screen. After a couple of seconds of silence, a pinging sound can be heard, distinctly metallic. I hear it before I see anything, but on the heels of that sound, the image cuts to a close-up sequence that lasts just over a single second before cutting out again suddenly to black.

Ping.

That single second is enough. I have, for a moment, caught the quick pulse of the image—a block of granite close to the ground, an iron ring, a human hand. Lifting the ring fastened tightly to the stone, the hand holds it to drop

2. This description appears on the Modern Institute's website representing Whittle's *Hindsight is a luxury you cannot afford*: https://privateviews.artlogic.net/2/fa744eb6b8b9cd77fb1a73/. Whittle developed the installation along with the film as commissioned for British Art Show 9. The installation evolved over the course of the show, culminating in an exhibition at The Box which included the full film. For a catalog essay that, unlike this essay, addresses the work as a whole, see De Rycker.

it—pinging—back into a hard stone groove the metal has chipped into the rock face. The clip is shorter than a single intake of breath. Before I can assess my body's relation to the scene, it has both entered me and is gone again. Thus, right from the opening, I find I am orienting myself in relationship to an afterimage. What is it that I witnessed? Or truer to experience: What is it that I still seem to see?

I first saw "What is a better life" not within Whittle's installation *Hindsight is a luxury you cannot afford* but screened within the webinar "*A Map to the Door of No Return* at 20: A Gathering." Convened by Andrea Davis and Christina Sharpe in November of 2021, the gathering marked the twentieth anniversary of the publication of Brand's impactful book. After engaging with the chapter in the webinar format, I sought out the full film and accessed it as distributed through Lux Films as *Hindsight is a luxury you cannot afford.* The full work is powerful and moving in each of its four chapters. And yet in it, I came upon a hitch—a moment of refusal interrupting my expectation. As currently circulating with Lux, chapter 4 appears minus the detail of the cut I had fixed to my experience in the webinar showing. In the Lux version, the sudden withdrawal of the image after a single second no longer takes place. This, to me, at first appeared as a "glitch"—in the sense of glitch as error—primarily on my part as a viewer as I looked to secure a definitive version of the artwork to engage. The cut had been cut, apparently. Or perhaps it was a result of an error in streaming on my end or another. But of course, a glitch is not only something that gives pause or marks error. More promisingly, it can interrupt scholarly or authorial intent as well as interrupt technology's smooth functioning—including the ongoing technologies of gender and race that seek to delimit or contain our sensing. Legacy Russell sees the promise of glitch in this regard as enabling us to end "the social practice of the body as we know it" (3). Glitches can suggest an errant materiality on the move in more than human networked agencies. They can underscore for us how differences among iterations (books, films, videos, and other means of "leaving gestures") speak to the changeable, cross-material and fugitive nature of gesture itself, manifesting the instability of the archival bid to imperial containment via scalable, reproducible, pinpoint-able "originals" (Thylstrup et al.; Schneider, *Remains*; Tsing).

In the webinar, Sharpe screens chapter 4 and interviews Whittle. The date is November 4, 2021.[3] But it is possible to think of this event as ongoing given that, even now, chapter 4, "What is a better life," is rolling through the web

3. For the remainder of this essay, I think about the webinar version of chapter 4 presented as *What is a better life (exorcized in the middle).* Other chapters I refer to here are from Whittle's *Hindsight is a luxury you cannot afford* as distributed by Lux.

in recursive waves of animated data encounter. As of this writing in 2024, anyone who pastes the URL into a search engine can partake of "Day 4: What is a better life by Alberta Whittle: Film with introduction and conversation." Media and performance objects like gesture, dance, performance, or any other rewindable, recitable, replayable action or object ensure that any "start" or any individual "showing" cannot be tethered to an overdetermined or definitive "end." Though we rarely approach technological media in this way in scholarship (unless the work is explicitly looped in a museal setting), it is nevertheless often received this way in experience as we dip into media objects again and again. Whittle's film arguably helps us think with recursion given that the waveform is so carefully threaded throughout this film, and the oceanic "(exorcized in the middle)" is a current, theme, site, and method across her work which consistently concerns ongoing afterlives in the wake of the Atlantic flesh trade. As such, the relationship of "opening" to "ending" is neither binary nor predetermined but rather tidal, rolling in and out while overlapping, gathering, pausing, and dispersing to gather, pause, and disperse again. Thus, the film is also, like gesture, migratory or underway *among its iterations* (Ness and Noland; Bradley, "Contagion"). We might think of it this way: A film played in one place is still and also the film played in another place—it is *both* discreet and indiscreet, singular *and* multiple, changing same to use Amiri Baraka's words (180), or, as Karen Barad would say, "cut together-apart." It is ongoing *and* suspended across sometimes errant, entangled iterations. Each iteration includes and perhaps must be considered relative to the interstitial cut, break, hesitation, or spectral overlay among others.

I want to read the minor moment of the cut at the opening to "What is a better life" in its webinar iteration as it flashes up and then withdraws. I would like to consider, too, a few moments later when the withdrawn hand/ring/stone amalgam returns. Please note: There are so many other moments in the film I might have chosen to linger with—scenes of joy, of protest, of beauty, of grief, of dance, of sweat, of song, and many, many scenes of the ocean. These moments are strung together like cowrie shells beaded to a plumbline (such a plumbline actually appears in Whittle's installation *between a whisper and a cry*, ICALA 2023). Each moment could afford a *deep dive (pause) uncoil memory* (the title of Whittle's installation representing Scotland for the Venice Biennale in 2022). But I have chosen to linger with this iron/flesh/stone dance because I am interested in the way Whittle deploys a "double gesture" of refusal and recursion.[4] I am also interested in the explicit, touch-based

4. On "double gesture" and the effort to work both within and against what archives and historical sites of the slave trade have to offer, see Saidiya Hartman ("Venus" 11). See also Snorton 10. The double gesture toward and away might also resonate with before and after, such as before and after the end of the world (Bradley, *Anteaesthetics*; Ferreira da Silva). The double

interinanimation among materialities—stone/flesh/hand.[5] And I am interested that the danger in this scene is the very thing it works to resist: the pornotrope of Black suffering (Spillers, "Mama's Baby").[6]

Ping. Ping.

It is not surprising that a scene of subjection would be instantly accessible at the beat of a glimpse. I notice myself registering, instantly, that the iron hitch fastened to low-lying stone recalls human bondage. Working in multiple media forms, Whittle is a Barbadian-born artist living and working between Barbados and Scotland. The viewer who knows this about the artist might register that the granite block likely sits on the historic site of a sugar plantation. This is all to say that it only takes a flash for the scene to be just as tropic (as in, given to trope) as it is reminding: reminding us of the theft-driven machinery of colonial-capitalism; blackened bodies possessed as the condition for white "self-possession"; foundational antiblackness at the opening scene of liberal human subjecthood.[7] And, what else.

Let's sit here for a moment. Shorter than a single breath. A minor dance in a few motions: a free hand, a riveted ring, a solid block of stone. At speed, "you" catch the scene as if tilted in a common curve toward hindsight. Except, the title under which this fleeting dance is offered has declared that hindsight is "a luxury you cannot afford." Rock, iron, flesh. It's a doubled "too much" because while you cannot look behind you (at what is before you), you also cannot afford to forget. As Whittle has elsewhere said, the "luxury of amnesia"

---

move toward/away is also formally resonant with the oceanic, tidal, or waveform aspect of the film that seems to offer ways to remember that dives both into and out of modernity's ongoing Plantationocene without revalorizing its ways of knowing.

5. On interinanimation see Schneider, "Slough Media" 71–77. To read for interinanimation is to read for a queer intimacy among materialities (Chen 11) and, thus, resist legislating an animacy hierarchy that refuses cross-material entanglements.

6. The pornotrope is the tendency to depict the figure of the suffering Black body in an effort to institute an argument about abolition through so-called empathy and the appeal to so-called humanity, but the effect can be a further erasure of this figure from the political and affective force of critical theorization which is, for Spillers, a critique of gender as well as race. The deployment of this figure risks endlessly replicating Black women as captives and commodities and nothing else.

7. There are by now many volumes on the settler colonial logic of subjecthood that, across modernity, has been predicated on distinguishing subjects from objects, humans from other-than-human in a dialectical drama that has served the social reproduction of bioeconomic man. Bioeconomic man, or *homo economicus*, is a genre of human that extracted (and continues to extract) value from blackened "flesh" for the re-generational wealth of whiteness serviced by the perspectival economic imperialism of white cultural form (Wynter; Weheliye). On reading "blackened" bodies in relation to the hold, see Hartman, "Hold of Slavery."

is also unaffordable, though it is consistently "nurtured by government" and continually peddled by whiteness (Manson).

And so, the image flashes up and just as quickly disappears. In imageless moments of the redacted scene, a five-second blackout follows. Five seconds is not long, but it is five times longer than the scene redacted. In the given loophole of withdrawal, does the title come to mind again? "Hindsight is a luxury you cannot afford." The blackout, as interstice, might be a fecund "space-off" (Spillers, "Interstices"; de Lauretis 25–26; Snorton 11). It might be a means to slow down.

Chapter 3 of the Lux version of *Hindsight* lies before this moment in "What is a better life." It is titled "To dwell in a canefield is to make space for warnings from those that are marked by blood and who can summon what is needed." This chapter also includes a close-up image of touch among materialities—this time human hand and sugar cane. In one sequence, you are given instructions in the form of bright letters forming words that appear across an orange-hued negative-image clip of a hand running along thickly growing cane stalks: "The risk of losing personhood is upon us." Cut. "Try to slow everything down." Cut. "Your heart," "Your breath," "Your labor." "*Slow down!*" The image has cut to a pink-hued slow-motion close-up of Boris Johnson's face. Bright letters: "Every day we are threatened with unbecoming." Whittle has cut to a cane field again, before more letters instruct "We must dream Otherways to refuse and resist" as the negative image of a laborer seems to move through the cane to stare directly into the space between your viewing face and the screen you view.

The instruction to dream, here, might be a refusal of the imperial archive's habit of pinning all modes of waymaking to acquisition, access, preservation, legibility, and the frontierist linear temporality of hindsight. Or perhaps it is an anarchival means to access the archive, or otherwise touch the past that is not past. Sugarcane. Hand. Rock. Iron. Hand. Dream. Across Whittle's work, cross-material tactility is often a pronounced sensibility.[8] Writing of her 2022 film *Lagareh—The Last Born,* Marjorie H. Morgan has written that Whittle's use of hands recurs "as a form of pain, but also as a means of gentle, intimate touch" ("Excavations"). And this is the case in *Hindsight* as well where touch, like shoreline, is emphasized. Hand to hand, hand to stone, iron to hand, water to shore, sound to ear, sugarcane to hand.

8. When asked to identify a primary medium, Whittle has said: "It's really difficult to respond accurately to that. I'm someone who loves working with my hands and, in some ways, being led by materials, images and the different connotations they conjure. I think about my work through the lens of sculpture, thinking about the scale, feelings and textures, and I often have that very immediate, visceral response to materials" (McNay).

If we return to chapter 4 (webinar glitch version) with the impulse to touch, the instruction to dream, and the invitation to slow in mind, we can think again about what it can mean that the image sequence of touch among hand/stone/iron that had been quickly withdrawn, recurs after a five-second blackout. 1—2—3—4—5. When it returns, the scene extends. It lingers—unfolding across a full sixty seconds. Sixty seconds is not a long time, but it is sixty times longer than the initial glimpse *and it takes place in the groove of a gesture of refusal or withdrawal* such that now, when we linger, details amplify. Ping. Ping. Again. The ring, fastened to granite, is lifted and dropped by the hand. The metal dings as it falls back into a granite groove in the shape of itself, chipped down into the rock face over what must have been many, many, many, many years. Generations. A groove possibly as deep and as wide as the middle passage itself. Ping, ping. Hand and ring lift again. Drop. Ping. Lift. Drop. Ping. At one point the hand lingers, its fingery brown flesh touching the rusty surface of the ring gently. I almost lean in as if I might hear the mutual slough of skin across rust, rust across skin.

[. . .]

Moving away from the analytic frame that would obsessively foreground the "lone site of the suffering [Black] body" to situate, instead, "co-relational texts, practices, and narratives that emphasize black life," Katherine McKittrick has written toward the practice of noticing "what else" ("Diachronic"). A deep noticing, a careful noticing, this "what else" is what Tiffany Lethabo King has named, drawing on McKittrick (who draws on Wynter), the "surplus of Black livingness—that exceeds black death, black suffering, and the black body" (King 41; McKittrick, *Dear Science* 182). In the image, the lift and drop begin to slow in speed, feeling increasingly tentative, or careful. Ping . . . Ping. Finally, the hand gently replaces the ring into its groove without letting it fall. Minus the fall, the sound has softened, or the stone has softened, or the metal has softened, or the hand has softened. Then, the hand suddenly lifts away, flying up and off the screen—transversal, birdlike, quickening, beautiful—and we cut to black again. An exhale of breath (my own). Soon will come the sound of waves. And images of Black women side by side, and in each other's arms.

[Hesitate.]

Who is the "you" in the title, *Hindsight is a luxury you cannot afford*?

Like many other Black feminist writers and artists have said (from Toni Morrison to Simone Leigh to Christina Sharpe), Whittle has said that her work is made for (and with) other Black women. Care is required in this case: The surge in white consumption of Black and Indigenous work has compelled many cautionary notes by BIPOC scholars in the humanities (Weheliye 21; King). Care is required of white and nonblack spectators such as myself to abandon the pretension that [our] "perspective" is . . . helpful. Perspective itself, as a geometry borne of a Western lifeway with a European trajectory, must be acknowledged as a technology of imperial colonialism, a means to capture and render a scene *as scene*, available to isolate various (acquisitioning) viewpoints as a means to scalar reproduction. Whittle invites other Black women into congregation with her work not in order to carve out a scalable "sight" or "perspective" but in order to "reword what it means to be human" and build community together.[9] This is a fact borne out across Whittle's works, which very often not only reference but also conjure Black community through song, dance, quietude, or other modes of gathering.[10] And the film's waveform—crest and trough, seen and unseen, gathering and dispersing of chapters, images, and citational texts—works less through linear, dialectical, binary dramas of opposition than through a meditative and rigorously opaque tidalectic. The work seeks out and lingers in shifting interstices that offer something other than resolution, where the sharp ping, ping of technologies of capture (stone/iron/hand) also and im/possibly beckon "what else?"

"What is a better life" is written as a statement not a question.

Sit with it.

Here's another [gesture]:

What else

9. Drawing on Sylvia Wynter, McKittrick writes: "Wynter's insights on creative works are . . . not simply a call to integrate 'race' or 'black art' into the global histories and knowledge systems of the West; rather, she argues that the perspectival economic imperialism of the planet, and attendant racial processes such as plantation slavery, produced the conditions through which the colonized would radically redefine—re*word*, to be specific—the representative terms of the human" ("Rebellion" 80–81).

10. In light of the double gesture, "perspective" is a tired Western geometry because it does not allow for a multiway or reciprocal view where community can be emphasized. Much of Whittle's work against amnesia is about acknowledging entanglements among European, African, and Caribbean places, people, and histories. For an alternative to imperial perspectivalism in Indigenous decolonial methodology, see Kim Tallbear. On Whittle and congregation-building see Anneka French.

Works Cited

Barad, Karen. "Diffracting Diffraction: Cutting Together-Apart." *Parallax*, vol. 20, no. 3, 2014, pp. 169–87.

Baraka, Amiri. *Black Music*. Da Capo Press, 1968.

Bradley, Rizvana. *Anteaesthetics: Black Aesthesis and the Critique of Form*. Stanford University Press, 2023.

Bradley, Rizvana. "Black Cinematic Gesture and the Aesthetics of Contagion." *TDR*, vol. 62, no. 1, 2018, pp. 14–30.

Brand, Dionne. *A Map to the Door of No Return: Notes to Belonging*. Vintage, 2001.

Chen, Mel. *Animacies: Biopolitics, Racial Matterings, and Queer Affect*. Duke University Press, 2012.

de Lauretis, Teresa. *Technologies of Gender: Essays on Theory, Film, and Fiction*. Indiana University Press, 1987.

De Rycker, Sandra. "Alberta Whittle's 'Hindsight Is a Luxury You Cannot Afford.'" *Black Atlantic: Power, People, Resistance*, edited by Victoria Avery and Jake Subryan Richards, Bloomsbury, 2023, pp. 52–55.

Ferreira da Silva, Denise. "Toward a Black Feminist Poethics: The Quest(ion) of Blackness Toward the End of the World." *The Black Scholar*, vol. 44, no. 2, 2014, pp. 81–97.

French, Anneka. "Alberta Whittle: We Gather and Dream New Congregations." *The Burlington Magazine*, 10 Dec. 2022, https://contemporary.burlington.org.uk/reviews/reviews/alberta-whittle-we-gather-and-dream-of-new-congregations.

Glissant, Édouard. *Poetics of Relation*. Translated by Betsy Wing, University of Michigan Press, 1997.

Hartman, Saidiya. "The Hold of Slavery." *The New York Review*, 4 Oct. 2022, https://www.nybooks.com/online/2022/10/24/the-hold-of-slavery-hartman/.

Hartman, Saidiya. "Venus in Two Acts." *Small Axe*, vol. 12, no. 2, 2008, pp. 1–14.

King, Tiffany Lethabo. "Off Littorality, Shoal (1.0): Black Study Off the Shore of 'the Black Body.'" *Propter Nos*, vol. 3, 2019, pp. 40–50.

Mackey, Nathaniel. "An Interview with Keanu Brathwaite." *Hambone*, vol. 9, 1991, pp. 42–59.

Manson, Becky, director. "Alberta Whittle: deep dive (pause) uncoiling memory." Video interview. *Vimeo*, National Galleries, Scotland, 21 July 2022, https://vimeo.com/732156035.

McKittrick, Katherine. *Dear Science and Other Stories*. Duke University Press, 2021.

McKittrick, Katherine. "Diachronic loops/deadweight tonnage/bad made measure." *Cultural Geographies*, vol. 23, no. 1, 2016, pp. 3–18.

McKittrick, Katherine. "Rebellion/Invention/Groove." *Small Axe*, vol. 20, no. 1, 2016, pp. 79–91.

McNay, Anna. "Alberta Whittle—Interview: 'No one can find Barbados on a map, whereas everyone can find the UK. That level of inattention galvanises so much of my work.'" *Studio International*, 9 May 2020, https://www.studiointernational.com/alberta-whittle-interview-no-one-can-find-barbados-on-the-map-that-level-of-inattention-galvanises-so-much-of-my-work.

Morgan, Marjorie H. "Alberta Whittle's Excavations into History: A Call to Change." *Art UK*, 3 Oct. 2022, https://artuk.org/discover/stories/alberta-whittles-excavations-into-history-a-call-to-change.

Moten, Fred. "Not in Between Lyric Painting, Visual History, and the Postcolonial Future." *TDR: The Drama Review*, vol. 47, no. 1, 2003, pp. 127–48.

Ness, Sally Ann, and Carrie Noland. Introduction. *Migrations of Gesture,* edited by Sally Ann Ness and Carrie Noland, University of Minnesota Press, 2008.

Russell, Legacy. *Glitch Feminism: A Manifesto.* Verso, 2020.

Schneider, Rebecca. *Performing Remains: Art and War in Times of Theatrical Reenactment.* Routledge, 2011.

Schneider, Rebecca. "Slough Media." *Remain,* by Ioana B. Jucan et al., University of Minnesota Press, 2018, pp. 49–107.

Snorton, C. Riley. *Black on Both Sides: A Racial History of Trans Identity.* University of Minnesota Press, 2017.

Spillers, Hortense. "Interstices: A Small Drama of Words." *Pleasure and Danger: Exploring Female Sexuality,* edited by Carol Vance, Routledge, 1984, pp. 73–101.

Spillers, Hortense. "Mama's Baby, Papa's Maybe: An American Grammar Book." *Diacritics,* vol. 17, no. 2, 1987, pp. 64–81.

Tallbear, Kim. "Standing with and Speaking as Faith: A Feminist-Indigenous Approach to Inquiry." *Journal of Research Practice,* vol. 10, no. 2, 2014.

Thylstrup, Nana Bonde, et al., editors. *Uncertain Archives: Critical Keywords for Big Data.* MIT Press, 2021.

Tsing, Anna Lowenhaupt. "On Nonscalability: The Living World Is Not Amenable to Precision-Nested Scales." *Common Knowledge,* vol. 18, no. 3, 2012, pp. 505–24.

Weheliye, Alexander. *Habeas Viscus: Racializing Assemblages, Biopolitics, and Black Feminist Theories of the Human.* Duke University Press, 2014.

Whittle, Alberta. "Day 4: What is a better life: Film with Introduction and Conversation." With Christina Sharpe. *YouTube,* uploaded by A Map to the Door, 6 Nov. 2021, https://www.youtube.com/watch?v=DuanoGoE67k.

Wynter, Sylvia. *On Being Human as Praxis.* Edited by Katherine McKittrick, Duke University Press, 2015.

CHAPTER 16

Slow Scrape Event Scores

TANYA LUKIN LINKLATER

PRELUDE BY KELLY KIVLAND

A Prelude

Tanya Lukin Linklater's series of Event Scores serve as dynamic frameworks for evoking what she terms "felt structures"—embodied practices embedded in Indigenous knowledge (173). Her Event Scores do not frame actions; instead, they open relations—with materials, people, land, and histories, as well as the invisible and unspoken.

Lukin Linklater's perception of time and place comes across in her sculpture, installation, rehearsals, video, works on paper, and writing. Citing Indigenous art lineages, her practice embraces ancestral belongings and evokes how weather organizes communities as well as our environment. She explains that she is inspired by her upbringing in the Kodiak archipelago of Alaska: "I look to my Alutiiq/Sugpiaq knowledges in relation to our homelands, waterways, atmospheres and our minds" ("Tanya Lukin Linklater").

Central to Lukin Linklater's approach is what is shared and withheld, refusing the containment of Indigenous knowledge. Her works incorporate silence, improvisation, and open-ended processes. The Event Scores in this volume exemplify this ethos, serving as invitations to observe, listen, move, speak, and touch. By evoking the names of Indigenous figures (Eber Hampton, Helen Simeonoff, Maria Tallchief, and Eve Tuck, among others), the Event Scores also remind us that history is not static. They instead call for a refusal against erasure, proposing an affective reckoning that leaves space for the emergent. In their simplicity and rigor, they insist that Indigenous belongings, knowledge, and memory are active, relational, and alive.

Through her Event Scores, Lukin Linklater proposes a continuous process of restoration, repair, and imagining that is both deeply grounded in ancestral relations and expansive in its capacity to dream futures yet to come.

The exhibition *Tanya Lukin Linklater: Inner blades of grass (soft) inner blades of grass (cured) inner blades of grass (bruised by the weather)* was organized at the Wexner Center for the Arts in 2024 by Kelly Kivland, former head of exhibitions.

Works Cited

Lukin Linklater, Tanya. "On Felt Structures." *Arctic/Amazon Networks of Global Indigeneity*, edited by Gerald McMaster and Nina Vincent, The Power Plant, 2022, pp. 172–75.

"Tanya Lukin Linklater: *Inner Blades of Grass (Soft) Inner Blades of Grass (Cured) Inner Blades of Grass (Bruised by the Weather).*" *Wexner Center for the Arts*, 2024, https://wexarts.org/exhibitions/tanya-lukin-linklater-inner-blades-grass-soft-inner-blades-grass-cured-inner-blades.

Slow Scrape Event Scores[1]

Tanya Lukin Linklater

1. Reproduced by permission of the publisher from *Slow Scrape* © 2022 Tanya Lukin Linklater, Talonbooks.

Suk

A human being. Afognak dialect: the S is pronounced SH. It sounds like shook but with a shorter o. Perhaps we shake. Or past tense, we shook. When are we shaken?

An Event Score for Indigenous Epistemologies (Eber Hampton)

A person enters and reads

The audience listens but does not look

Then

The audience looks only to follow with its body

Then

The audience's body turns to the east

Then

The audience holds its heart

Then

The audience listens but does not look

An Event Score for Haunting (Eve Tuck)

A person enters and reads

The audience remembers relentlessly

Then

The audience feels no ease

Then

What can decolonization mean other than the return of stolen land?

Then

What must it feel like to be haunted

An Event Score for Maria Tallchief, Dylan Robinson, and Helen Simeonoff

A person enters and says

The museum or gallery exerts a force in its looking.

Then

The look of a choreographer is like an everyday structure that exerts a force on the body of a dancer.

Then

Our bodies exert a force.

Then

Our objects exert a force.

Then

When do our bodies' force exceed the look of a choreographer?

Then

When do our objects' force exceed the look of the museum or gallery?

An Event Score for Kodiak Alutiit 1 (Helen Simeonoff)

An Alutiiq person enters and says

This event score is longer than most. My job is to tell. Your job is to listen. Listen to the quiet around the words. Listen for the sparse and melancholic.

Then

Alphonse Pinart collected Alutiiq masks on our island in 1872 and took them to France.

Then

Over a century later Helen Simeonoff, our relative, travelled from Kodiak Island to the masks held in a collection in France. She was the first.

Then

Many Alutiit travelled from Kodiak Island to the masks held in a collection in France. They tell us that when they touched the masks they wept.

Then

The Alutiiq masks eventually travelled back to Kodiak Island but only because we had an Alutiiq Museum to exhibit them and only if we promised to never repatriate the masks.

Then

The promise was made and vitrines were built.

Then

We looked at the masks behind glass. Some masks we quickly looked away from. Which masks were we supposed to see? Mostly we looked at the texts alongside the masks that attempted to tell us what the masks meant.

Then

We felt the masks when we looked at them.

Then

We felt the masks when we touched them.

Then

We think about the text remnants (behind glass, placed next to the masks) left by Alphonse Pinart and all that was held in our people before he ever travelled to our island to collect.

Then

We exceed the text remnants in Pinart's translations of our songs and dances from Alutiiq to Russian to English to French and back again.

Then

We exceed the Alphonse Pinart collection of Alutiiq masks.

An Event Score for Kodiak Alutiit 2 (To Aleš Hrdlička)

An Alutiiq person enters and says

We exceed the archaeological site.

Then

We exceed the discipline formation of Anthropology.

Then

We exceed the structures imposed on us.

An Event Score for the Epistemic Violence of Translation (Edgar Heap of Birds)

1. A person enters and speaks in Alutiiq

2. A person enters and speaks in Alutiiq

The audience listens

Event Scores for Afognak Alutiit 1–3 (Abridged)

An Alutiiq person enters and says

Our memory marks Afognak.

Afognak marks us.

What are we tethered to?   What holds us together?

When I am home on our island I sense that the land exudes grief.

This feeling.

Many of us have left the land of our ancestors

perhaps because the grief becomes   unbearable.

An Event Score for Afognak Alutiit 4

An Alutiiq person enters and tells a story about Afognak.

The audience listens

Then

Someone tells a related story.

And so on. And so on. And so on. And so

Suk

A human being. Afognak dialect: the S is pronounced SH. It sounds like shook but with a shorter o. Perhaps we shake. Or past tense, we shook. When are we shaken?

CHAPTER 17

mookii, agaasaa

poems

JOHANNAH BIRD

Introduction: Ethical Adjacency and Responding to Art

How we respond to the archive is not unrelated to how we respond to art. While "art" and "archive" do retain their own distinguishing features, practices, histories, they draw attention to the networks of signification and meaning-making involving not only creators but also recipients of the work, in whatever form. Whether through individual works or objects, or in larger bodies or collections, art and archive incite response, affective, intellectual, political, or otherwise, even though the processes of how and why can differ. In cases where art deals in archives and archives deal in art, such questions become even more pronounced, as in the work of many Indigenous writers, artists, and scholars whose creative and critical practices investigate the relationship between archives of various kinds and the work creative expression can do to open them up, call attention to them, interpret them in new ways, and expand their registers.

When I was invited to write in relation to Tanya Lukin Linklater's exhibition *Inner blades of grass (soft) inner blades of grass (cured) inner blades of grass (bruised by weather)* in 2024, the process of being with her work brought up questions for me that echoed similar ones from my work in archival research. I asked how I could write in respectful relation to Tanya's work and honor its subjectivity without claiming comprehensive knowledge of it. Tanya's exhibition featured work emerging from her artistic practice of considering how she can be in relation to unrepatriated cultural belongings—a particular kind of archive—and responding in a range of media that relocates cultural belongings, such as a gutskin parka, in relation to Sugpiaq knowledge and methods of making. However, the specificity with which Tanya works reminds us that the particularities of history and personal experience must be respected, even as they connected to broader Indigenous histories, shared experiences across Indigenous communities. How could I also claim space for myself to respond from my bodies of knowledge and realms of experience, honoring those things brought up for me in her work without imposing them on it, thinking about correspondences without falling into conflation? Indeed, Tanya's artistic practice also provokes such questions in its consideration of how to be in relation to different kinds of archives: Indigenous land knowledge, aesthetics and practices of making, narrative traditions, spatial and place-based relationships, unrepatriated cultural belongings, embodied knowledge.

My approach to Tanya's work began reflecting my own creative-critical research and writing practice in which I respond to moments of provocation in the archive, of difficult feeling or sense of connection, by considering what produces them, what other histories, knowledges, narratives link with them, and by creating work—poetry or creative nonfiction that weaves these threads of knowledge, feeling, and experience together. However, in narrating connections grounded in a sense of interrelation, I also negotiate, as I did with Tanya's work, how to be in relation with work without claiming ownership of it or its meaning.

What emerged in the process of responding to Tanya's work, and in conversation with Tanya herself, was a response-practice of "ethical adjacency," an approach and way of thinking about how to frame response alongside work but explicitly against totalizing claims of knowing or comprehension. My approach of "writing adjacently" finds correspondence in Dylan Robinson's "apposite methodology," in which forms of writing "share space alongside or move in relationship with another subjectivity," as expressed in creative works, through a process of "writing with," side by side or alongside, rather than always "writing about" (81). What my approach of adjacency adds is a more intentional consideration of positionality and how it comes to bear on the practice of response. I came to understand ethical adjacency as an intentional process of mutual respect and care by which I could write direct response and description, narrate my sense of signification in Tanya's work, and respond with my own stories that her work brought up for me without claiming they demonstrated what her work was "about." This approach became a way for me to be in relation with her work without claiming a different ownership of it. An approach of ethical adjacency works against open-ended, abstracting responses that negate the histories, places, and sets of relation that ground *her* work as well as *mine* and do so differently.

Furthermore, this process of engagement emerged from our prior relationship. It mattered that she and I are both Indigenous people, Sugpiaq and Anishinaabe respectively, with our own respective practices of creative and critical attention working from related, but also varied, spheres of attention to Indigenous and settler colonial histories and our ongoing contention with them. Tanya and I are both drawn to archives and responding to them in creative work as means of possible repair. We share a practice of needing to *respond* to the trouble, beautiful, challenge, grief. The following poems in many ways arise from this shared practice as much as from the challenge of interpreting and relating to one another's work ethically as we continue the work of repair.

1.

ancestors, it would seem, loved drama

totem pole extension

apasoy diagonal ascendancy

wiingashk smoke rise

drum beats climbing

Indigenous geometries, aesthetics

gesture to *migizi* as

they do *miskwaadesi*

reach out to *nigig* in kayaks made to fit

spread the kitchen table

outstretched hides for home

2.

here is a sacred gift:

when water bends wood

when hands form clay

when shell edge gives

when	peel	scrape	write
	stitch	smoke	carve
	weave	slice	shake
	paint	steam	burn
	mark	cut	smear

when Ayeetapepetung, covered in white earth, waved *migizi*'s wing at treaty 1

and said:

> *When you came here you thought you would have this land some day or other; I understood you are going to buy the land from me. Well, gizhe-manidoo made me out of this very clay that is besmeared on my body.*
>
> *This is what you say you are going to buy from me.*

3.

make a procession

born of rehearsal

this is how to be with land

this is how to be with water

mino-bimaadiziwin comes not only by mind, that tender flesh,

but by breath song curve drift press

I could mark the moment with an etch

This time, I dip *niinizisan* in *ode'imin* *miskomin* and *miin*

and play my colours back to the land

casting about its pleasure

I press *niinizisan* in *zhizhoobii'igan*

and play them in the water

strand song and story

whorl tide and strong

4.

gathering labour

harvest of spirit and prayer

collect us and spread

in shimmering pools

nestled—tucked

                remainders

careful tumbling

ease of work, patience, and learning

how to gather

how to harvest

Grandpa's fish cleaning spot glittered with

heads, eyes, scales, fins, bones

dropped-down mounds

                        of brightness

gathered on a grey plywood board

under a hatched stump

Notes to the Poems

Each of the preceding poems responds to one or more works from Tanya Lukin Linklater's 2024 exhibition *Inner blades of grass (soft) inner blades of grass (cured) inner blades of grass (bruised by weather)* at the Wexner Center in Columbus, Ohio. From August 13 to 17, I wrote in relation with works in the exhibition and during open rehearsals with dance artists of *Scrape soak steam pour crack sew bend brace.* The poems emerged from this week of engagement and response, drawing from language used in rehearsals, the works, and from my notes. The poems were presented at the gathering to celebrate the exhibition on August 19, 2024. Below, I list works each poem is more closely in relation to, but each poem also responds to or draws upon other works which I do not name. *Mookii* is an Anishinaabemowin, or Ojibwe, term meaning "she emerges, surfaces, comes out of somewhere"; *agaasaa* means "it is small."

1. "ancestors, it would seem, loved drama"

This poem draws upon the following works by Tanya Lukin Linklater: *Held in the air I never fell (spring lightning sweetgrass song)*, 2022; *A continuous narrow mark or band; a length of material serving a particular purpose; a procession.*, 2024; and with Tiffany Shaw, *Indigenous geometries*, 2019. *Apasoy* is Nêhiyawêwin, or Plains Cree, meaning lodgepole or tipi pole. This poem also uses the following Anishinaabemowin words: *wiingashk* (sweetgrass), *migizi* (bald eagle), *miskwaadesi* (painted turtle), *nigig* (river otter). Anishinaabemowin does not have extensive terminology for oceanic geographies and beings, so I use the word *nigig*, applying it to sea otter, as way of misnaming in order to name.

2. "here is a sacred gift"

This poem responds to *. . . the ongoing storms of colonialism, weather patterns that weather us.*, 2024 by Tanya Lukin Linklater. The Anishinaabemowin term *gizhe-manidoo* is variously translated as the great spirit, divine being, creator, god. Ayeetapepetung was an *ogimaa*, leader or chief, of the Portage la Prairie band of Anishinaabeg who participated in the 1871 councils for Treaty 1 in Manitoba, Canada. His speeches are recorded in news coverage of the negotiations.

3. "make a procession"

The Anishinaabemowin term *mino-bimaadiziwin* means the good life or good way of living. The poem also uses the following Anishinaabemowin terms: *niinizisan* (my [strands of] hair), *ode'imin* (strawberry), *miskomin* (raspberry), *miin* (blueberry), and *zhizhoobii'igan* (paint). Three of Tanya's works incited this poem: *Hair Prints 1, 2, 3, 4, 5, 7, 8, 9, 10,* and *12*, 2022; *Hair Prints 16–25*, 2024; and *This moment an endurance to the end forever*, 2020.

4. "gathering labour"

This poem is a response to *I am turning toward tides, winds, clouds, rainfall.*, 2024.

Works Cited

The Ojibwe People's Dictionary. Edited by Nora Livesay and John D. Nichols, University of Minnesota, 2012–21, https://ojibwe.lib.umn.edu.

Robinson, Dylan. *Hungry Listening: Resonant Theory for Indigenous Sound Studies.* University of Minnesota Press, 2020.

Wolvengrey, Arok, editor. *Cree: Words.* University of Regina Press, 2011. Quoted in *itwêwina: Plains Cree Dictionary,* Alberta Language Technology Lab, University of Alberta, Edmonton, https://itwewina.altlab.app.

CONCLUSION

Entanglements in Expanding Archival Contexts

PUJA BATRA-WELLS AND HARMONY BENCH

This book maps evolving trajectories in archival work—shaped by critical, community-based, and interdisciplinary engagements. Across the chapters, contributors demonstrate a methodological capaciousness that takes multiple forms—ranging from the speculative to the situated, from the reparative to the embodied, and from the collaborative to the experimental. Openness in this form reflects an acknowledgment that our methods must be responsive to context. In resonance with critical turns in archival studies, particularly those influenced by feminist and decolonial interventions, this elasticity makes room for ambiguity and incommensurability, while staying accountable to the people, places, and temporalities entangled with archival materials. It means confronting extractive tendencies and cultivating approaches grounded in interdependence, co-constitution, and mutual affective responsibility, not only in theory but also in practice (Caswell and Cifor 24). This orientation underscores the processual dimensions of knowledge-making, highlighting its emergence through praxis. It invites experimentation with form—moving beyond conventional genres toward modes that can better engage with care and humility as well as ambiguity and incompleteness.

Archival Entanglements takes shape through the counterhistorical imaginaries of speculative writing; the sensorial, affective, and performative dimensions of embodied engagement; the immersive and participatory assemblages that enable environmental witnessing and urgent communal response; and attention to hidden traces in data that invite new forms of interpretation. Expanding the archive and archiving also unsettles assumptions about how time is organized and made legible. It brings into view temporalities that do not align with institutionalized periodization, attending to histories that unfold unevenly or recursively stretching across generations. Such materials don't just expand historical narratives; they reframe sequence and causality and require methodologies that accommodate nonlinearity, interruption, and repetition.

It is not only a matter of reimagining what a collection is or how an archive functions but of returning to the question of archive as a field of possibility. To take possibility seriously in this moment is also to recognize the role that archival practice can play amid overlapping crises—ecological, political, epistemological, technological. The so-called meta-crisis we face is not just a convergence of systemic failures but also a crisis of imagination—of how to embrace complexity, sustain collective memory, and dream of a future without falling into despair. When approached as flexible and responsive, archives offer more than historical insight—they are spaces in which to reconsider what and how we carry forward as resources for the futures we are collectively creating.

Archival Entanglements grounds itself in archival pluralism—assembling diverse approaches and epistemologies to show how multiple ways of knowing coexist without collapsing difference into reductive universality. Archival pluralism moves beyond merely acknowledging diversity; it requires a critical engagement with those differences to actively challenge and disrupt the dominant frameworks that have historically shaped what counts as knowledge. This approach relies on sustained reflection and dialogue, an acute awareness of power relations embedded in archival practices, and a willingness to be unsettled by alternative traditions and perspectives (Caswell 285–87). Such multiplicity reframes archival practice as a site of negotiation and stewardship where conflicting narratives and values must be navigated rather than erased, and open dialogue pursued over consensus.

Finally, if the archive is a space of possibility, so too is the record. Across this book, the record is treated as generative, as something dynamically situated within ongoing processes and open to reinterpretation. Some contributions draw on Indigenous and land-based epistemologies, where record-making emerges through relation rather than inscription. Others explore disruption, viewing the glitch as a meaningful interruption that exposes the limits of archival form and infrastructure. While the approaches vary, they share a commitment to engaging what the record might become across contexts. Yet there are significant ethical concerns that must be foregrounded. Archival records function as critical forms of evidence, anchoring collective memory, enabling claims to justice, and holding institutional power to account.

Approaching records as open to reinterpretation requires balancing conceptual flexibility with respect for the integrity of materials, especially those tied to communities whose histories have been marginalized or erased. Relational and non-Western epistemologies offer valuable models but also raise critical questions about authority, custody, and consent: Who can reinterpret the record, and under what conditions? Recognizing the record's fluidity does not absolve us of responsibility; instead, it calls for rigorous methodologies of care that acknowledge the political and ethical stakes that are entangled with preserving and accessing the past, and in turn, the possible futures we can imagine.

Works Cited

Caswell, Michelle. "Constructing Archival Pluralism: Lessons from Religious Studies." *Archival Science,* vol. 13, nos. 3–4, 2013, pp. 273–92.

Caswell, Michelle, and Marika Cifor. "From Human Rights to Feminist Ethics: Radical Empathy in the Archives." *Archivaria,* vol. 81, spring 2016, pp. 23–43.

ACKNOWLEDGMENTS

Archival Entanglements is the result of many gatherings, conversations, and workshops grounded in reconsidering how archival logics and inheritances operate in the arts and humanities. We thank all the contributors for their sustained interest in this project and their critical engagement with contemporary archival studies and practice across many fields. This volume took shape in relation to a specific constellation of events at The Ohio State University unfolding since 2016, during which an interdisciplinary turn across the university led to investment in the Global Arts + Humanities. This university-wide initiative foregrounds the role of the arts and humanities in fostering integrated, cross-disciplinary collaborations.

Developed through a collaboration between Global Arts + Humanities and the Wexner Center for the Arts, this book is the second installment in the series On Possibility: Social Change and the Arts + Humanities. Each book in the series aligns with the annual theme of the Global Arts + Humanities' signature Society of Fellows Program, which brings scholars, artists, and activists together to share scholarly and creative research. The 2022–23 program convened a robust interdisciplinary cohort to produce and share research on issues related to the theme "Archival Imaginations." As a collective, we endeavored to engage in dialogue about decolonizing public history; multivoiced and community collections; the politics of memorialization, erasure, and recovery; the ethics of representation; digital archives and access; and governmentality and surveillance in documentation. We are grateful to all the participants in the Society of Fellows program at The Ohio State University, many of whom are represented in these pages: Franco Barchiesi, Harmony Bench, Melissa Anne-Marie Curley, Alcira Dueñas, Molly Farrell, Brian Harnetty, Wendy Hesford, Julia Keblinska, Crystal Michelle Perkins, Martin Joseph Ponce, Mytheli Sreenivas, and Michelle Wibbelsman.

We further extend our gratitude to the 2022–23 "Archival Imaginations" graduate fellows: Andrea Armijos Echeverria, Noah Bukowski, Lorna Closeil, Emily Kaniuka, Ishmael Konney, Mariah Marsden, Camille Snyder, and faculty mentors Harmony Bench and Leigh Bonds, and to the undergraduate student apprentices: Angela Ciarochi, Lauren Dahler, Emily Lay, Cameron Logar, Rheanna Velasquez, and faculty mentor Michelle Wibbelsman, for the thoughtfulness of the research they developed and shared throughout the year. Special thanks go to Global Arts + Humanities designer extraordinaire Breanne LeJeune, who extensively supported the student groups and influenced all our thinking about what archives have been and what they could be.

We also thank those who shared their practices and perspectives in the Digital Dialogue series: "Archival Violence and Justice": Sine Hwang Jensen, Tara Hart, Jennifer R. O'Neal; "Queer Archives: Let the Record Show": Sarah Schulman, Amy Fairchild; "Performing Archives: Bodies, Histories, Memory": Brian Harnetty, Crystal Michelle Perkins, Michelle Wibbelsman; "Archives as Pedagogical Practice": Leigh Bonds, Nick Breyfogle, Mytheli Sreenivas. Special thanks to our workshop leaders: Michelle Caswell for her workshop on Urgent Archives; Alexander Sasha Kondakov for his workshop on Queer Archives; Jamie A. Lee for their workshop on the Archival Body; and Adela C. Licona and Susana Sepulveda (aka Susy Riot) for their workshop on Zine-Making for Social Justice and Comunidad. Thanks also to Jolie Braun for hosting an open house of the Rare Books and Manuscripts Library's zine collection.

We appreciate all those who have supported us throughout the process of writing and editing this book, especially Global Arts + Humanities Faculty Director Wendy S. Hesford, whose insights and guidance have been invaluable. We are sincerely grateful to former Head of Exhibitions at the Wexner Center for the Arts, Kelly Kivland, whose early contributions to this project gave shape to the artistic interventions and voices in these pages. Many thanks to Taralee Cyphers and the production team at OSU Press for making the process so smooth. We would also like to thank our anonymous reviewers for their feedback, Carly Dearborn for her clear-eyed reading, Cameron Bench and Allison Hargett for their assistance in manuscript preparation, and Breanne LeJeune for thinking visually alongside us.

In addition, Harmony offers thanks to Debra Burrington for making the work possible, Puja Batra-Wells for her amazing collaboration, Hannah

Kosstrin for her relentless enthusiasm, Susan Manning and all the new writing friends at Seminary Hill, and the Faculty Professional Leave program at Ohio State that created the additional time and space needed to complete this volume.

Likewise, Puja would like to express gratitude to her family, whose constancy grounds her; to the Global Arts + Humanities, for convening the space in which this endeavor could take form; and to Harmony Bench, whose collaboration, rigor, and generosity rendered the process not merely possible, but truly joyful.

We are grateful to be able to include previously published work with permission.

CONTRIBUTORS

ANURIMA BANERJI is associate professor in the Department of World Arts and Cultures/Dance at UCLA. She is the author of the monograph *Dancing Odissi: Paratopic Performances of Gender and State* (Seagull Books / University of Chicago Press, 2019), which received the 2020 de la Torre Bueno Prize from the Dance Studies Association. With Violaine Roussel, she co-edited the volume *How to Do Politics with Art* (Routledge Press, 2017). Currently she is working on a new book, *The Impossibility of Indian Classical Dance,* as well as co-editing the forthcoming *Oxford Handbook of Indian Dance* with Prarthana Purkayastha.

FRANCO BARCHIESI is associate professor in the Departments of Comparative Studies & African and African American Studies at The Ohio State University. Barchiesi's research interests include critical theory and race, political theory, and global and comparative labor studies. His book, *Precarious Liberation: Workers, the State, and Contested Social Citizenship in Postapartheid South Africa* (State University of New York Press, 2011), won the CLR James Award of the Working Class Studies Association for best Published Book for Academic or General Audiences in working-class studies.

PUJA BATRA-WELLS is associate director for the Global Arts + Humanities | Cross-Disciplinary Research Exchange at The Ohio State University, where her work centers on fostering a culture of collaborative practice. She is a scholar of material cultures and folklore with a particular interest in modes of cultural presentation and display. She is co-editor of *The Folklorist in the Marketplace* (Utah State University, 2019), a volume examining the intersections of folklore and economics, and holds a PhD in comparative studies.

HARMONY BENCH is an interdisciplinary scholar based in dance and performance studies whose research cuts across technology, media, and society. She is associate professor in the Department of Dance at The Ohio State University, where her work examines research practices, performances, and circulations of dance in digital, screen, and computational contexts. She is author of *Perpetual Motion: Dance, Digital Cultures, and the Common* (University of Minnesota Press, 2020). With longtime collaborator Kate Elswit, she brings techniques of computational analysis and data visualization to dance history.

JOHANNAH BIRD is a postdoctoral fellow at the University of Manitoba working on a research-creation project that employs poetry as a mode of inquiry for Indigenous archives. Her research considers late nineteenth- and early twentieth-century discourse by Cree and Anishinaabe people and expressions of relational thought. Her interests include archives, affect, life writing, poetry, and poetics.

LEIGH BONDS holds a PhD in English from Texas Tech University with specializations in the long nineteenth century and book history. She co-edited *The Routledge Companion to Romantic Women Writers* (2023), to which she contributed the "Mary Robinson" entry that provides an overview of biographical resources, works, editions, archival holdings, and critical reception from the eighteenth century to present. As the digital humanities librarian, Bonds supports Ohio State's digital humanities practitioners, consulting on research and curricula, collaborating on projects, and coordinating learning opportunities.

IÑAKI BONILLAS (b. 1981, lives and works in Mexico City) is a conceptual artist whose work traces family and social histories through photography, video, installation, site-specific works, and artist books. In his deeply researched exhibition projects, from interventions inside Casa Luis Barragán to collaborations with photographers and printers, he pushes beyond the two-dimensional to plumb private and collective memory. His work integrates photography in a creative process wherein reality, fiction, and the fluctuating worlds of word and image all coexist. Bonillas's work has been exhibited at major institutions in Mexico, the United States, and Europe.

MELISSA ANNE-MARIE CURLEY is associate professor in the Department of Comparative Studies at The Ohio State University. She studies modern Buddhism and Japanese philosophy and is interested in how twentieth-century intellectuals, artists, and reformers borrow elements from the popular Buddhist imagination in articulating what the future of Japan (and the world) should look like. Her first book, *Pure Land / Real World: Modern Buddhism, Japanese Leftists, and the Utopian Imagination* (University of Hawaiʻi Press, 2017), examines leftist interpretations of Buddhist images of paradise and exile in the context of the Fifteen Years' War (1931–45). She is currently working on a study of Buddhism and the culture of self-help in East Asia and North America.

ERIC GONZABA is a historian of race and sexuality in the United States and an associate professor of American Studies at Cal State Fullerton. His research examines the politics of pleasure and leisure in modern America, especially in nightlife. He is currently completing a book on the history and culture of gay male nightlife since 1970. His work has been supported by the Point Foundation, the University of Pennsylvania, Cornell University, and the Elton John AIDS Foundation.

BRIAN HARNETTY is an interdisciplinary sound artist, composer, and author. He is known for his recording projects with archives, socially engaged works, sound and video installations, live performances, and writings. His approach has been compared to "working like a novelist . . . breathing new life into old chunks of sound by radically recontextualizing them" (Clive Bell, *The Wire*). Harnetty describes this process in his first book—*Noisy Memory: Recording Sound, Performing Archives*—published with the University of North Carolina Press in 2025.

BRIAN EUGENIO HERRERA is a writer, teacher, and scholar—presently based in New Jersey, but forever rooted in New Mexico. Brian's work, whether academic or artistic, examines the history of gender, sexuality, and race within and through US popular performance. He is author of *The Latina/o Theatre Commons 2013 National Convening: A Narrative Report* (Howl Round, 2015) and *Latin Numbers: Playing Latino in Twentieth-Century U.S. Popular Performance* (University of Michigan Press, 2015), which was recognized with the George Jean Nathan Award for Dramatic Criticism. With Anne García-Romero, he co-edited *María Irene Fornés in Context* (Cambridge University Press, 2025).

KELLY KIVLAND is an interdisciplinary curator and creative producer. Her collaborative approach explores intersections of new media, ecologies, performance, and technology. In her current role at Michigan Central Art, she is developing a diverse program that explores creativity, technology, and society, while deepening partnerships within Detroit and beyond. Across projects, Kivland expands the reception of contemporary creative practices, supports diverse interests, and encourages new models of production. She began her career commissioning and producing performances in New York City before turning to curating.

TANYA LUKIN LINKLATER thinks with weather, embodiment, and beingness in her practice. Sensation, scores, orality, poetics, embodied inquiry, and being in relation to ancestral belongings structure her work. Her recent exhibitions and performances have shown at Dia Chelsea, New York; Camden Art Centre, London; Wexner Center for the Arts, Ohio; and Tate Modern, London. She completed her PhD in Cultural Studies at Queen's University in 2023, and she is a faculty mentor for the Institute of American Indian Arts' MFA in Studio Arts. She is Sugpiaq from the Kodiak archipelago of Alaska.

MARIAH E. MARSDEN is a writer and folklorist from the Missouri Ozarks. She received her PhD in English and Folklore Studies from The Ohio State University and her MFA in Creative Writing & Media Arts from the University of Missouri–Kansas City. She is the co-author of three graphic novel adaptations, *Anne of Green Gables: A Graphic Novel* (2017), *The Secret Garden: A Graphic Novel* (2021), and *Heidi: A Graphic Novel* (2025), with plans for more collaborations on the way. Mariah now works in the Arts & Humanities Grant Studio at the University of North Carolina at Chapel Hill.

MIMI ỌNỤỌHA is a Nigerian American artist whose work questions and exposes the contradictory logics of technological progress. Through print, code, data, video, installation, and archival media, Ọnụọha offers new orientations for making sense of the seeming absences that define systems of labor, ecology, and relations.

MARTIN JOSEPH PONCE is associate professor of English at The Ohio State University. He is the author of *Beyond the Nation: Diasporic Filipino Literature and Queer Reading* (2012) and co-editor of *Samuel Steward and the Pursuit of the Erotic: Sexuality, Literature, Archives* (2017). His current projects include a queer examination of contemporary Asian American literature's retrospective critiques of the Asian American movement and a queer diasporic analysis of Asian American literature's critical reckonings with Japanese imperialism and US exceptionalism.

REBECCA SCHNEIDER is professor of Modern Culture and Media at Brown University in Providence, Rhode Island. She is the author of *Performing Remains: Art and War in Times of Theatrical Reenactment* (2011) and *The Explicit Body in Performance* (1997), among other books. She has published well over fifty essays, including "That the Past May Yet Have Another Future: Gesture in the Times of Hands Up" (2018); "Slough Media" in *Remain* (2019); and "This Shoal Which Is Not One" in *Island Studies* (2020). She has been supported by the Mellon Foundation and received a Guggenheim fellowship in 2021.

AMY SHUMAN is emeritus Ohio State University professor and a Guggenheim Fellow. She is the author of articles on conversational narrative, literacy, political asylum, and disability and of *Storytelling Rights: The Uses of Oral and Written Texts by Urban Adolescents*; *Other People's Stories: Entitlement Claims and the Critique of Empathy*; *Rejecting Refugees: Political Asylum in the 21st Century* (with Carol Bohmer); and *Political Asylum Deceptions: The Culture of Deception*. She is a recipient of the OSU College of Humanities Exemplary Faculty Award; the OSU Distinguished Scholar Award, 2015; the OSU Distinguished Teaching Award; and the American Folklore Society Lifetime Achievement Award.

MICHELLE WIBBELSMAN is associate professor of Latin American Indigenous Cultures, Ethnographic Studies and Ethnomusicology in the Department of Spanish and Portuguese at The Ohio State University. Originally from Ecuador, Wibbelsman specializes in the expressive culture of Indigenous peoples of the Andean highlands and Amazonia. Her work has focused on symbolic and semiotic analytical approaches to Indigenous performance, art, music, ritual practices, and politics. She is the author of *Ritual Encounters: Otavalan Modern and Mythic Community* (2009) and director of the *Kawsay Ukhunchay Andean and Amazonian Indigenous Art and Cultural Artifacts Research Collection* at Ohio State.

NICOLE WOOD is a doctoral candidate in Information Studies at the University of California, Los Angeles, and a librarian at California State University, Dominguez Hills. Her research explores the intersection of archival theory, environmental history, and data infrastructure. Her dissertation, "Documentary Climate Data and Counter-Narratives: Rainfall in California, 1769–1900," examines how archives function as latent sources of environmental data and as infrastructures that shape what becomes measurable and remembered about climate change.

INDEX

ON POSSIBILITY: SOCIAL CHANGE AND THE ARTS + HUMANITIES

Wendy S. Hesford, Puja Batra-Wells, and Dionne Custer Edwards, Series Editors

Archival Entanglements
Edited by Puja Batra-Wells and Harmony Bench

Human Rights on the Move
Edited by Wendy S. Hesford, Momar K. Ndiaye, and Amy Shuman